The Product Manager's Toolkit

Gabriel Steinhardt

The Product Manager's Toolkit

Methodologies, Processes and Tasks in High-Tech Product Management

 Springer

ISBN 978-3-642-04507-3   e-ISBN 978-3-642-04508-0
DOI 10.1007/978-3-642-04508-0
Springer Heidelberg Dordrecht London New York

Library of Congress Control Number: 2009941529

Cover design: WMXDesign GmbH, Heidelberg, Germany

Printed on acid-free paper

Springer is part of Springer Science+Business Media (www.springer.com)

Foreword

Product management in the high-tech industry has always experienced varied interpretation as to its character and internal structure. Often product management is performed informally or in a non-standardized form, and organized differently in each company – commonly located in the marketing department or sometimes in the engineering department. In addition, although the product management profession has existed for many years, there has not been a product management best-practice or standard that has been globally adopted. This book offers a holistic methodology as a solution to these concerns.

Product management is a discipline responsible for product planning (articulating the market problem) and product marketing (generating awareness, differentiation, and demand). Companies have come to appreciate the organizational value of other well-defined professional disciplines, such as project management, quality management, and business analysis as well as the results achieved by the orderly implementation of these disciplines. Accordingly, standardized product management done consistently well can greatly increase the probability of product success and profitability.

Product management practitioners frequently perform a broad spectrum of roles with varying responsibilities and skill sets, and communicate with both internal and external stakeholders like sales, marketing communications, engineering, customer support, customers, partners, and suppliers. Identifying the various roles and responsibilities in the product management domain is imperative to understand what needs to be accomplished in order to deliver a successful product. Product management is not a role performed in the interest of one or more product lines; it is a distributed set of roles and related responsibilities covering definitive aspects of the product delivery process.

Defining roles and responsibilities in product management is a very preliminary step. One also needs to understand how to do what needs to be done – creating deliverables that can be successfully used in the delivery of a product. In addition, a repeatable process that creates successful products needs to be documented, followed, audited, and improved upon. The product management models and templates in this book are intended to help facilitate the implementation of that process.

For over seven years I have assisted Gabriel Steinhardt in his development of the Blackblot product management body of knowledge, including the "Blackblot Product Manager's Toolkit™" (PMTK). I have met few people as dedicated to defining and standardizing the product management profession as Gabriel Steinhardt, who has made it his professional goal. The primary purpose of the PMTK methodology is to help companies and their product management teams become more successful in their product delivery efforts. With the release of this book it is hoped that product management will mature further and be viewed as a structured and well-defined critical business function.

This book will help students of product management, product management practitioners, product management organizations, and corporations understand the value of product management and the distinct roles and responsibilities in product management. It will aid in the efforts to clarify role definitions, identify responsibilities, define processes and deliverables, and improve the ability to communicate with stakeholders.

Daniel Stadler
Business Consultant, MBA/Technology Management

About the Author

Gabriel Steinhardt is Blackblot's Managing Director, a recognized international high-tech product management expert, author, lecturer, and developer of practical tools and methodologies that increase product managers' productivity.

A marketing and information systems MBA with over a decade of experience in product management in the computer software and hardware industry, Gabriel has assumed diverse leadership roles with major corporations and start-ups in marketing, product management, and technical undertakings.

Gabriel created the highly successful "Blackblot Product Manager's Toolkit™" (PMTK) professional template collection, designed Blackblot's entire product management training program, and wrote the "Blackblot Product Management Professional™" (BPMP) certification program.

Acknowledgments

I have been developing the Blackblot product management body of knowledge, including the "Blackblot Product Manager's Toolkit™" (PMTK) professional template collection, for over fifteen years. Without the help and support of some very special people, my work and this book would have never become a reality.

Daniel Stadler, a product management expert and technology business advisor, has been providing me with insight, suggestions, critical review, commentary, advice, guidance, and support for several years during the development of PMTK and Blackblot's product management training and certification programs. A special note of gratitude is extended to him for his invaluable contribution.

My sincere thanks go to all my business partners, fellow instructors, and students worldwide whose feedback and creativity has challenged me. They had candidly shared their thoughts and I have gained much from each of them. I am grateful for their continued support.

I am also thankful to the ever-professional editorial staff at Springer Science+Business Media publishing and their partners who had contributed to this literary project. This book was made possible by the diligent work of Dr. Birgit Leick, Dr. Martina Bihn, Christian Rauscher, Renate Muenzenmayer, Gabriele Fischer, Gurupatham Jayalakshmi, and Manfred Bender.

Finally, I thank Prof. Yael Hanein for her help, commitment, patience, perseverance, faith, support, and love in the life journey she has accompanied me so far. Without her I would not be where I am today.

Gabriel Steinhardt

Introduction

Product management is an occupational domain which holds two professional disciplines: product planning and product marketing. This is because product functionality is built for the user via product planning and the product's value is presented to the buyer via product marketing. A somewhat more expanded interpretation would be to view product management as an occupational domain that is based on general management techniques which are focused on product planning and product marketing topics.

A high-tech company is a business entity that either develops technology that is incorporated in a product or is used in the assembly or manufacturing of a product, or manufactures a product that contains technology and that same product relies on that technology to perform its core function. In reality, most high-tech companies view product management as a collective term which describes the broad sum of diverse product related activities, excluding sales and development activities, which are performed in the interest of delivering a particular product to market. With such a vague and misleading definition it is possible to fit most anything (even product testing) into the realm of product management.

This commonly used vague definition of product management misleads and allows many people to place their own personal interpretation on the role of product management, and that accounts for the multitude of diverse definitions in the high-tech industry. Every company is different and handles product management differently – meaning that the product management discipline is not standardized as much as it could be across the high-tech industry. Further complicating the situation is that in each company there are individual stakeholders who often view and interpret product management very differently from each other.

For companies to be recurrently successful, other than just being lucky, a consistent understanding of product management must be present in the company and all aspects of product management must be fully addressed and handled efficiently. However, the contributing factors to both failure and success can be extremely complex to analyze. One can attempt to investigate why certain companies and products have failed, only to quickly realize that the cause is multifaceted and that many factors need to be considered.

Product management is comprised of activities that profoundly impact a product's chances of success. For example, providing incorrect market requirements, erroneous pricing, or an inaccurate profiling of the target market can all be detrimental and critical. If just one of these aspects of product management is amiss, then the product's chances of success are greatly diminished. Therefore, in order to succeed a company must execute all fundamental tasks and follow all key processes in product management. Even though there is still a chance of failure, the probability of success is increased if a company implements and consistently follows a complete product management methodology.

Companies with formal and well-defined product management practices are companies which realize that product management is a core strategic function to the organization. These companies also realize that there is greater importance in making sure that management processes are sound, properly staffed, and implemented.

Some products are successful because of external factors, timing, or merely good fortune. Not all successful products have had great product management behind them, but it is clear that many product failures have had poor or no guidance from product management. Companies will be more successful for each dollar they invest in product development if they improve in the area of product management. The obvious conclusion is that combining a definitive product management methodology with disciplined technology development practices is the key to commercial success in the high-tech world.

The product management profession and the related body of knowledge have reached a greater level of maturity and acceptance in the high-tech industry. However, across the high-tech industry drastically different duties and responsibilities are attributed to product management professionals. Diverse interpretations regarding the role of product management practitioners have only confused and stifled the ability to develop clear and consistent product management methodologies. This book provides a consistent and holistic managerial approach to product management and is based on Blackblot's applicable work models and practical methodology that covers nearly all aspects of product management.

This book, a companion to Blackblot's comprehensive product management training and certification programs, includes the "Blackblot Product Manager's Toolkit™" (PMTK) professional template collection and offers companies and product management professionals with a practical primer for implementing an efficient product management practice in order to increase the practitioner's workplace productivity and improve a product's chances for commercial success.

Contents

Part I
Product Management Concepts

Chapter 1
Who's Driving Your Company?

Examination of Common Product Delivery Strategies

1.1 Introduction

Every company claims it wants to deliver value to its customers, be profitable, and establish leadership in its core markets. Such assertions seem only natural and one would expect to be presented with a corresponding corporate strategy that supports such goals. However, closer inspection reveals that many companies often employ product delivery strategies that lead these companies far away from their business objectives.

Delivering products is a process that begins with a combination of innovation, technology, and market sensing. Each of these driving elements contribute to the initial product concept and its development, but over time and depending on the company, some driving elements will demonstrate a stronger and more lasting impact on the product concept and its roadmap. This is not necessarily due to merit or market forces, but more commonly is an outcome of the corporate culture and business perspectives which dominate the company.

Certain corporate functions that embody the aforementioned driving elements take charge of directing the company's overall product delivery strategy. For example, in one U.S. software firm, a business unit manager noted: *"Marketing has had a relatively limited role in the past; technology is what has driven this company. We're a technology-oriented firm."* In contrast, in a U.S. packaged-goods firm, a marketing manager said: *"Engineering has absolutely no sense of the consumer. They're a group of educated technology scientists who can do amazing things, but they need focus."*

Corporate business goals and wants are relatively similar across diverse industries, but the methods they use to reach their goals vary greatly. This chapter explores these different approaches to product delivery strategies, known as technology-driven, sales-driven, and market-driven.

G. Steinhardt, *The Product Manager's Toolkit*,
DOI 10.1007/978-3-642-04508-0_1, © Springer-Verlag Berlin Heidelberg 2010

1.2   Technology-Driven: Take My Road

Some companies believe they know what is best for the customer. They operate under the notion that they can develop technology, design products based on that technology, and have entire markets buy their products because they are *technologically superior*. These technology-driven companies, whose product delivery strategy is determined by their engineering departments, often create products without thoroughly researching the market and without fully understanding the prevailing market requirements.

This sounds somewhat detached from end-user needs, and may very well be so, but a technology-driven approach has its advantages. It enables a company to rapidly deliver products to market since it skims and skips lengthy traditional market research, and consequently bases product design decisions on internal company expertise.

An example of a company who chose to strive forward with a plan to launch a new product in the market without having conducted market-research first is that of Sir Clive Sinclair, a British entrepreneur who was also a brilliant engineer and consummate salesman. Sinclair trusted his intuition for all his product decisions. At the time, he believed that the moment had arrived where the general public was sufficiently interested in electronic wizardry to provide for a completely new market of inexpensive and relatively simple-to-use computers. Without conducting any market research whatsoever, in 1980 he ordered 100,000 sets of parts so he could launch at high-volume his new ZX80 computer. By 1982, Sinclair's company revenue was £30 million, compared with £4.65 million the previous year.

Sinclair and his engineers had intuitively succeeded in assessing the combined potential of technological developments and changing consumer needs, as opposed to researching the market potential for an innovative product. Sinclair's business decisions proved enormously successful, yet very fortuitous.

Technology-driven products are often advanced and therefore appeal to early adopters and niche markets who seek the latest technological developments. Additionally, technology-driven products may also become a high-risk/high-reward venue to be favored by speculative investors. Such products await a triggering event that causes a dramatic surge in demand. Those events may range from the hypothetical (for example, future governmental legislation that would promote vehicles with fuel cell engines) to the actual sales of survival gear when people were confronted with the spectra of Y2K (year 2000 computer bug) or the tremendous demand for security equipment post 9/11 [September 11, 2001]. Nevertheless this is the problem with being technology-driven; it is a risky approach to delivering products. Adopting a technology-driven posture has, over time, proven low growth potential due to the failure to implement proper marketing activities and because of the isolated manner in which products are managed. Many technology-driven products are characterized by having complex features or unnecessary features, and some technology-driven products are realistically unneeded.

At the 2004 Consumer Electronics Show (CES) in Las Vegas, Nevada, Gerard Kleisterlee, the CEO of Philips, quoted data from a Yankee Group survey:

"Thirty percent of all recently introduced home networking products sold today were returned to the store because the consumer could not get them to work, and forty eight percent of potential digital camera owners were delaying their purchase because they perceived the products to be too complicated."

The conclusion is quite obvious. Although some may succeed with a technology-driven approach to product management and development, there is a bigger chance that driving the best technology to customers will not yield a prosperous outcome. This is simply because the company and its product are focused on providing better technology and not focused on closely matching customer needs and abilities with that technology.

1.3 Sales-Driven: A Cruising Taxi

A technology-driven company is focused on its technology and a sales-driven company is focused on maximizing short-term return on investment. Accordingly, the prime responsibility of most corporate departments in a sales-driven company is to help the sales channels with knowledge, ways to sell, and sales support.

Like a taxi driver cruising city streets looking for passengers who are heading to different locations, sales-driven companies cruise their markets seeking deals with customers who very often have different needs. Such as with the proverbial taxi driver who will deviate out of his way to accommodate the passenger going in the opposite direction, so will these companies alter their product's feature set in order to accommodate the particular wishes of a specific customer.

There is nothing fundamentally wrong with being sales-driven and providing custom work. Generations of tailors have sewn fitted clothes to people of different shapes and sizes, and scores of taxi drivers worldwide transport passengers to their varied destinations.

The advantage of being sales-driven is less risk because there are always unique business opportunities and individual needs to satisfy. A sales-driven product strategy can be a lifesaver and used as a survival mode tactic if market segments start deteriorating or are in a chaotic phase which precludes targeted marketing programs. The downside is that a sales-driven product strategy is a short-term approach that does not build highly-sustainable product lines. Without those sustainable product lines it is very hard to build market leadership and promote company growth.

The eventual outcome of a sales-driven approach in high-tech companies is a plethora of product variants (produced via modification of core products) which are sold to different customers. These product variants are full of highly-individualized custom features that are developed, tested, documented, and supported. This situation invariably leads to resource duplication, wasted effort, loss of distinctive competence, and great difficulty in implementing product roadmaps.

Due to market dynamics, the majority of sales-driven companies struggle in the long run because there is nothing much to differentiate them from the competition, other than price which becomes their primary marketing tool.

1.4 Market-Driven: Driven to Success

To gain a status of being market-driven, a company has to engage its customers and listen to their needs. It is all a matter of timing since asking customers what they want during the sales process is not considered actually listening to the market. Being market-driven requires a proactive product management process; engaging customers before the product is planned, defined, designed and developed.

Only by taking a long hard look at end-markets and paying attention to customers' demands, before proceeding to develop a technology platform or products, can a company be regarded as one that employs a market-driven approach to product management and development.

A case of sales-driven culture posing as market-driven happened to Big Blue. IBM$^®$ was the dominant force in the technology industry and synonymous with innovation and cutting-edge technology. IBM achieved its leadership position through a market-driven approach by using its massive sales force to determine customer needs. However, the company ran into trouble when it stopped listening for needs and began telling customers about its latest new product or technology.

Applying a market-driven approach demands commitment and discipline as it is a very procedural approach. Companies with an informal work culture and loose organizational structures fail at applying this methodology and so do companies eager to rush into the market because of the lengthy time involved in executing all phases of the market-driven process. But when a market-driven approach is properly applied, the result is a product that will solve a pervasive market problem in an established market segment, and for which customers are willing to pay. Experience has shown that rewards do come for those who patiently follow the course.

Market-driven companies produce sustainable products with visibly notable targeted value. The biggest reward is that a market-driven product helps establish market leadership and revenue-growth potential.

1.5 Summary

A study conducted several years ago by querying top marketing executives working at one-hundred leading U.S. technology companies, showed that despite all the talk about being market-driven and customer-focused, 54% of respondents viewed their company as actually being technology-driven. Companies do understand which approach they should follow and publicly declare it, but indeed it is hard to mend ways and transition because becoming market-driven will demand a painful shift in corporate culture and business practices.

For those who take the path, success is lasting. In the high-tech world (e.g. Microsoft$^®$) and consumer goods industry (e.g. Procter & Gamble), a leadership position can be established and maintained by being a very effective market-driven organization that has superior skills in understanding, attracting, and keeping valuable customers with products that deliver real value. This is not just a cliché but a formula for success.

What ultimately prevails in companies is the understanding that product value is always determined by the customer, not by the company or its technology. This understanding in turn leads to the realization that developing technology that solves known market problems is better and more profitable than trying to discover markets that could possibly use an existing and newly developed technology.

Chapter 2
Product Management Team

Formalizing and Structuring the Responsibilities and Makeup of the Product Management Team

2.1 Introduction

The role of a product manager is challenging, complex, and often misunderstood. Across the high-tech industry, the product manager title is used in many ways to describe drastically different duties and responsibilities. Diverse interpretations regarding the role of the product manager have created for some an untenable situation where they struggle to define their own role.

Properly defining and structuring the roles and responsibilities of the product management team will enable the team members to be more efficient and productive; leading to better revenues and higher-quality products that meet customer needs.

This chapter explores the challenges faced by modern high-tech product managers and proposes a solution to formalize and structure the responsibilities and makeup of the product management team.

2.2 Your Role

Job titles are important and the role one plays in an organization is often identified by one's job title. In most cases, job titles allow an observer to construe the role and scope of responsibilities associated with a specific job title, but often this is not the case when it comes to the world of product management. The myriad of interpretations and diversity that surround product management job titles, especially the product manager title, make it very difficult to ascertain which roles and responsibilities are associated with a specific product management job title.

Ask several product managers what their responsibilities are and you will get a variety of answers and descriptions. This situation can reach a point where several product managers working at the same company and department provide very different perspectives on their position.

G. Steinhardt, *The Product Manager's Toolkit*,
DOI 10.1007/978-3-642-04508-0_2, © Springer-Verlag Berlin Heidelberg 2010

Many people mistakenly accept a definition that presumes that product management is a collective term used to describe the broad sum of diverse activities performed in the interest of delivering a particular product to market. Such a broad definition, used by many companies today, is the root cause of much grief and problems because it lacks the professional focus needed to be successful, and allows virtually any product-related task to be assigned to the product manager.

2.3 Jack of All Roles, Master of None

It is challenging for humans to multitask activities, and that is why people prefer to focus on a sole task or sequentially perform a few select tasks. The inherent difficulty of multitasking hinges principally on humans' limited ability to maintain a high level of cerebral focus when confronted with a multitude of dynamically changing issues. To a lesser degree, fatigue and lack of resources (primarily time) are also contributing factors to multitasking hardships.

According to the prevailing (yet erroneous) definition of product management as outlined earlier, it is clear that the nature of performing product management activities is the epitome of multitasking diverse tasks. Multitasking product management assignments is particularly challenging because it requires a multitude of complimentary or differential skills. In addition, the multitasking of these assignments becomes profoundly more complex when product managers have several products to manage.

Such a broad colloquial definition of the product management profession is the result of individual and industry interpretations. These free interpretations invariably led to the ever-familiar challenges that the majority of product managers encounter daily. These challenges can be caused by a combination of the following: ambiguous role definition, imbalanced relationships with other departments, overlapping responsibilities, an overwhelming volume of activities, a lack of processes, poorly defined processes, no definitive methodology, and a shortage of uniform work tools in the profession.

The overall perceived obstacle the typical product manager encounters is the permeating lack of professional focus. One can be adequate at many things but it is difficult to excel at many. This is the reason many product managers view themselves as trapped in a never-ending juggling routine. Having too many tasks to juggle eventually leads to tasks being dropped and the outcome is poor overall performance by the product manager, which is not beneficial for the company.

Ostensibly, the title of product manager has proven itself more harmful than helpful. Other official and unofficial product management title variations, such as product CEO or product champion or product executive, have failed because they are often accompanied by a blurred and wide-scoped job description that describes or implies the product manager being the owner and as a result, responsible for the commercial success of the product. Being labeled or treated as a product CEO can be a daunting situation, since it nearly always means operating without the authority and resources available to a corporate CEO.

When a job title has an overly broad set of diverse activities (roles and responsibilities) associated with it, there is a high probability that performing to the expectations of that job title will result in failure. Obviously a semantic change is needed and this change is based on the well-known fact that being professional means being focused on a particular domain or discipline.

2.4 Breaking It Down

The two main disciplines that reside in the product management domain are product planning and product marketing. Product planning and product marketing are very different but due to the collaborative nature of these two disciplines, some companies erroneously perceive them as being one discipline, which they call product management. Done carefully, it is very possible to functionally divide the majority of activities within the product management domain into two distinct disciplines (functions), product planning and product marketing, and yet retain the required synergy between those two disciplines.

Accordingly, product management is correctly defined as an occupational domain which contains two professional disciplines: product planning and product marketing. A slightly more expanded definition is that product management is an occupational domain that is based on general management techniques that are focused on product planning and product marketing activities. The product planning and product marketing disciplines focus on the users' and buyers' needs. Therefore, the product management domain resides solely in the "Problem Space", and the engineering domain resides in the "Solution Space".

Product planning is the ongoing process of identifying and articulating market requirements that define a product's feature set. Product marketing is an outbound activity aimed at generating product awareness, differentiation, and demand. Product planning and product marketing are different and distinct professional disciplines because they foster different roles and different quality goals.

With these understandings in mind, it is easy to address the respective tasks of product planning and product marketing as belonging to the roles of a product planner and a product marketer. Whether these two roles are handled by two individuals or performed by one person is irrelevant. Indeed there are cases where one person, or two people sitting in one room, or different departments that collaborate; assume both disciplines. The point is that there is now a clear and unambiguous link between the job title and the job responsibilities.

It should also be clear that the disciplines of product planning and product marketing are inextricably linked because companies design product functionality for the user and market the product's value to the buyer. To clarify this point, an intuitive example of this supposition is a child's toy. The parent is the buyer and is interested that the toy is safe to use, will help the child grow smarter, keep the child occupied, and be reasonably priced. Product value is therefore marketed to the buyer, the parent. The child only cares about product functionality such as: is the toy fun and engaging, visually pleasing, and will it do what he/she wants. The toy's functionality is designed for the user, the child, and not for the buyer. The same approach is taken with high-tech products where buyers are often not the users, and this approach means distinct product management roles that separately analyze and address buyer and user needs.

The recent fast-paced growth of high-tech industries and shifting interpretations of product management have created skewed responsibility sets for product managers. The already problematic broad definition of product management was further complicated when tactical activities were added to a product manager's job definition.

Tactical activities are assignments, usually self-contained and specific, that fulfill short-term business needs, such as delivering a presentation, writing collateral material, or assisting a salesperson. Such assignments are time consuming and demand a disproportionate allocation of individual resources (mental focus, time and physical effort), relative to their overall importance. By monopolizing the scope of work, tactical activities detract from product managers' ability to fulfill their assigned strategic responsibilities.

A strategic mission is one that aims to establish and plan the overall and long-term course of action a company should engage in to achieve corporate objectives. The strategic mission for the product marketer would primarily involve evaluating market opportunities and writing market plans that address these market opportunities. For the product planner, it is identifying market needs to deliver winning products that help a company become a market leader, market follower, or an innovator.

2.5   Roles and Goals

Executive managers have very clear work goals that primarily center on achieving corporate profitability. Software developers, for example, also know what they aim for, and that usually is generating a lean and efficient programming code.

However, many product managers provide widely different answers when asked to convey the goal(s) of their job. They often find it quite difficult to provide a definitive answer, with this situation obviously stemming from an overly broad and task-oriented (not goal-oriented) job description. By breaking down the product management domain to its disciplines, it becomes feasible to clearly define the roles and goals of each discipline.

The product planner determines and defines product functionality by virtue of writing the market requirements, and therefore the prime goal is to have product buyers and users who are satisfied with the product. This satisfaction level means contentment with the product's ability to solve business or consumer problems and satisfy needs, and being satisfied with the non-tangible aspects of product ownership such as service, price, warranty, status, or prestige.

The product marketer's goal is to have a satisfied sales force. This goal is somewhat indirect to the marketing actions being performed, but is an excellent predictor of how effective the product marketer's actions are in generating awareness, differentiation, and demand for the product. Salespeople have a relatively easy job when product marketers perform their roles well. The market environment, created by the actions of the product marketer, leads to a very favorable situation where the market buys the product as opposed to the salespeople actively selling the product.

Salespeople are very happy when *the product sells itself*, which really means that the sales cycle is minimal or reduced because of quality marketing actions initiated by product marketers. In short, product planning's quality goal is satisfied customers; product marketing's quality goal is a satisfied sales force.

After defining the strategic roles of the key disciplines within the product management domain, there is a need for a cooperative scheme, a team concept, to maximize the effectiveness of these strategic roles through collaboration, and complement them with outbound tactical support functions. Product management is not accomplished successfully by one person, but by a product management team who fulfill various roles and functions.

2.6 Blackblot Product Management Team Model

The product management team is a task group, comprised of four distinct roles, which organizationally reside in the product management department. The four roles in the "Blackblot Product Management Team Model" are the product planner, product marketer, sales engineer, and marketing communications (MarCom) manager. These four roles are the basic providers of the planning, deliverables, and actions that guide the inbound oriented product definition and the outbound marketing efforts (Fig. 2.1).

Sales Engineer
Advocacy Expert

MarCom Manager
Media Expert

Product Planner
Market Expert

Product Marketer
Marketing Expert

Fig. 2.1 Blackblot Product Management Team Model

The primary responsibility of the product planner is to constantly research the market and identify market needs, which are later translated into market requirements that in turn will foster new products or new features to existing products. The product planner prepares the documents that profoundly impact the product's success. These documents include the "Market Requirements Document" (MRD), product use cases, product roadmap, and the pricing model.

The primary responsibility of the product marketer is to analyze product oriented business opportunities, formulate plans that evaluate those business opportunities, and plan and guide the subsequent marketing efforts. For example, the product marketer prepares the product business case and following approval, writes the market plan.

The sales engineer is primarily responsible for outbound product-centric activities, such as pre-sale support and product demonstrations. Sales engineers, relying on their technical skills, help customers understand how the product delivers the necessary value and functionality that address the customers' business or consumer problem.

The sales engineer's other objective is to provide critical input to product planners on customer needs and problems. Sales engineers often operate under titles such as product evangelist, technical evangelist, technical sales support, pre-sale engineer, outbound product manager, or technical product manager; yet regardless of the title they all perform a relatively similar set of tasks.

The MarCom manager is primarily responsible for creating interest and memorable presence through the conception and copywriting of all collateral material, advertising, direct response mail, web, and other types of communications media. This person is also tasked with maintaining a consistent image and positioning in the target market, according to messages and directives provided by the product marketer.

The product management team is managed by the director of products or vice president of product management who provides overall product vision, product and market strategies, and team leadership. Other titles are sometimes used to designate this leadership position, such as director of product management or Chief Products Officer (CPO), in order to indicate the encompassing nature of this role. This position is responsible for balancing corporate goals with long-term market trends and opportunities, and for directing, establishing, maintaining, and planning the overall policies and strategies for the product management department. The director of products role creates and manages the overall product management process and oversees its effective execution (Table 2.1).

2.7   Odd Couple(s)

In startup companies it is common to see one individual assume all four roles listed in the "Blackblot Product Management Team Model". That person will do market planning, deliver product demonstrations, formulate market requirements, and write collateral material.

Table 2.1 Blackblot Product Management Team Model (Summary Table)

Role	Responsibility	Goal	Expertise
Product planner (strategic role)	Identify and articulate market requirements	Satisfied product buyers and users	Market expert
Product marketer (strategic role)	Generate awareness, differentiation and demand	Satisfied sales force	Marketing expert
Sales engineer (tactical role)	Outbound product-centric activities, i.e., pre-sale support and product demos	Customer knowledge of product value and functionality	Advocacy expert
MarCom manager (tactical role)	Conception and copywriting of all collateral material	Consistent image and positioning in the target market	Media expert
Director of products (strategic role)	Balancing corporate goals with long-term market trends and opportunities	Successful formulation and execution of the product and market strategies	Strategy and process expert

It is obvious that product manager is a title assigned to a person who performs a single role or a combination of the four roles listed in the "Blackblot Product Management Team Model". At some point in time, usually as the company grows, the roles are delegated to other individuals who specialize in the role assigned to them. However, for a wide variety of reasons and reasoning, it is quite common to see two roles coupled together in order to define a position that is entrusted to one person.

Frequently the product planner and sales engineer roles are combined into one position in which the person is charged with doing product demonstrations and providing pre-sale support because he/she is also defining the product, and thus has more expertise and in-depth product knowledge than the average salesperson.

Another possibility is the product marketer and MarCom manager combination, where this individual does all tasks that upper management may perceive to be *marketing*. This usually consists of actual market planning, writing copyright, and managing advertising.

A very prevalent situation in high-tech industries, such as the software development industry, is the combining of the product marketer and product planner roles. Corporate job descriptions for open positions that prefer candidates with a technical undergraduate degree and an MBA with an emphasis in marketing are a clear indication that the company views the position as a combination of the two roles.

It does make sense to a certain level to have the product marketer and product planner roles cooperate with each other. Product success hinges on understanding customer behavior and the business aspects of the industry in order to build value into a product. Complementing that ability is in-depth product knowledge, which is used to plan marketing actions that deliver meaningful messages about the product. The problem is that both of these roles (or capabilities) are strategic and demand expertise that can only be achieved by professional focus.

In addition, people come from different educational or professional backgrounds and therefore naturally gravitate toward their comfort zone; eventually causing one of two roles to receive more attention than the other. Under performing, or in the worst case scenario not performing some of the product management team roles, may dramatically impede the product's chances of marketplace success.

2.8 Roles and Activities

Any of the various couplings of roles, as previously outlined, can create workflow obstacles for the following conceptual reasons. Having one person simultaneously perform both strategic and tactical roles and activities, such as with the product marketer and MarCom manager combination, is very inefficient because tactical activities will always monopolize the person's time and demand increasingly more effort. On the other hand, having one individual perform two strategic roles, as with the product marketer and product planner combination, can be equally debilitating since each role demands an acute learning curve and full devotion.

It is acknowledged that the joining of roles is justifiable under a variety of circumstances; such as budget limitations, personnel quotas, company or department formulation, and product complexity. However, role coupling should always be regarded as a temporary or evolutionary measure – not as a permanent arrangement.

2.9 Solution

Product management is an encompassing domain of disciplines. Acknowledging that fact leads to the realization that it is extremely hard and often impossible to specialize and excel at performing all product management tasks. This is because being multi-faceted and multi-disciplined often results in lack of professional focus.

Adding to the situational difficulty is the expansive view of a product manager's job description that leads to product managers being assigned tactical activities, most of which result because others simply do not want to do them. Tactical activities significantly impair the product manager's ability to perform crucial strategic tasks.

In some companies, the product marketing manager and product manager are interchangeable titles as they both relate to the same function and individual. This inconsistency further causes functional problems within companies and across industries.

This problematic reality is not planned and is seldom the result of malicious intent. It is just that some companies believe in the laissez-faire approach where internal politics and forces shape corporate processes, responsibilities, and even the organizational structure. There is some advantage to having role ambiguity because it allows individuals to be proactive and define their role as they want it to be.

People can work within the ambiguity and chart their way to a desired job description. Unfortunately, more often than not, the fast-paced structured world of high-tech is not supportive of this approach because there is just too much inherent ambiguity or variance associated with the title of product manager. Therefore, the solution is to abolish the title product manager from the corporate lexicon and use the clearer, more understandable and uniform titles of product planner and product marketer.

As a result of such action, a different organizational approach is required. Under the charge of the vice president or director of product management, is the corporate product management department that holds product management teams. Each team, whether real or virtual, holds four roles (as described in the "Blackblot Product Management Team Model") with the intent of having these roles eventually assigned to four separate individuals.

Tactical activities and logistics formerly imposed on the product manager will now go to the program manager or release manager, thus relieving those in product management from the tactical overload they routinely experience. The program manager, a role outside product management, is essentially the project manager for the entire product delivery project, and is tasked with applying a suitable product delivery process that ensures deliverables from all contributing corporate functions. The release manager, also a role outside product management, is responsible for handling all logistical and operational matters that pertain to the delivery of the product.

Properly defining and structuring the roles and responsibilities of the product management team will enable the team members to be more efficient and productive. This most likely will lead to better products, better marketing and higher revenues.

2.10 Summary

Product management is a domain, not a role, which changes and evolves with the organization. It is a multi-faceted and multi-disciplined domain and there will always be a certain level of ambiguity involved with product management, but applying a proper product management team concept and structure, with well-defined roles and responsibilities, can significantly mitigate that ambiguity. This act is crucial whether the company is building or rebuilding the corporate product management function.

As a result of the team restructuring and the redefinition of roles, the newly attained occupational focus helps build professional expertise. The product planner can now devote time and effort to excel as a market expert and problem-teller, whose role is to perform customer advocacy better than everyone else in the company, while backing assertions with quantitative market/customer data. The product marketer is now focused on becoming a marketing expert, perfecting corporate competency in using tools and executing techniques, processes and tasks that promote winning products in the target market. All this decreases departmental rivalry and allows the engineers to develop their professional expertise as technology experts and problem-solvers.

Doing the right things and doing things right, especially in the early stages of company inception, will help those in product management to professionally grow and contribute fully according to their potential. Undoubtedly, companies will also benefit because now members of the product management team will be able to generate long-term value for their company by focusing more on strategy formulation.

The final deduction is that those involved in product management must be provided with clear job descriptions (roles, responsibilities and goals) as well as focused goals and objectives. All talk and effort can prove quite futile without this basic premise.

Chapter 3
Product Definition Team

Establishing a Market-Driven Product Definition Process and Team to Match

3.1 Introduction

Product planning and product definition are critical starting points for the delivery of any new product. In many companies, there are recognized product development teams and product development processes, but often absent is a clear concept of a product definition team and a product planning process. This is the result of companies employing different strategies to plan, define and develop products. Each strategy demands different areas of expertise and generates different dynamics, responsibility sets and internal processes.

The common technology-driven approach to product delivery fosters a technology-focused product definition process, which primarily requires a deep understanding of technology and heavily relies on the competencies of development personnel. Conversely, the market-driven approach to product delivery promotes a market-focused product planning process, which primarily requires a deep understanding of buyer/user needs, and hinges on the leadership and competencies of product management personnel. Both these approaches must be considered in the formation of the product definition team, so that a successful product is delivered.

The absence of clear guidelines for defining and structuring individual roles on a cross-departmental product definition team, coupled with the lack of a structured and documented market-driven product planning process, results in an inefficient product definition process. The risk to organizations is that of misconceived products, poor market acceptance, and subsequently wasted financial and resource investment. This inefficiency can be successfully countered with the concept of a well-defined team of individuals (belonging to both the product management and engineering departments) that have different roles and different domains of expertise, and that follow structured and repeatable product planning and product definition processes.

This chapter describes a market-focused product planning process for high-tech companies, and presents a solution to formalize and structure the responsibilities and makeup of the product definition team to ultimately help products reach marketplace success.

G. Steinhardt, *The Product Manager's Toolkit*,
DOI 10.1007/978-3-642-04508-0_3, © Springer-Verlag Berlin Heidelberg 2010

3.2   Key Concepts

A business customer's or a private consumer's "Problems" are past, present, or future difficulties – situations that require change, and "Products" are essentially the solution – something that removes or controls that difficulty. The existence of a problem creates a "Need" – a state of felt deprivation, essentially a condition or motivation in which something is sought after to affect a change. Therefore, products solve a business customer's or a private consumer's problems and satisfy needs.

The "Need" itself creates a "Want" – the request for specific objects that might satisfy the need, which in turn brings about "Demand" – a want for specific products coupled by an ability to pay for them. For example, hunger is a "Need" that creates a "Want" for nourishment or appetite suppressing medication or anything else that removes hunger.

A "Want" for nourishment often generates "Demand" in the market for affordable foods that can be obtained quickly; such as fast-foods. Obviously, the same need can produce different wants and demands.

Subject to the market-driven approach, products are built to solve "Market Problems" – situations where the group or groups of customers, selected by a company to sell to, have unmet needs. Customers are domains that hold buyers and users, and customers are the virtual entities that take financial responsibility for purchasing a product. For example, the buyer of a network router is the company's "Chief Technology Officer" (CTO), the user is the network administrator, and the company itself is the customer since it pays for the purchase.

The existence of a "Market Problem" does not necessarily mean there is a "Market Opportunity" – a lucrative, lasting and sizable market problem. Ascertaining the existence of a market opportunity, and consequently the worthiness of developing a product, is company specific and done via a series of evaluator steps. These evaluator steps, with respect to the market, include: verifying that the market is big enough, that the market need is strong enough, the market need is recognized by potential customers, and the projected business is sustainable over time.

In addition and with respect to the company, the following are verified:

- Competitive advantage is attainable.
- The business model has to be clear and understandable.
- The company possesses the required resources or competencies, or can readily acquire them to make the product successful.

Deficiencies in even one of the market opportunity evaluator steps mean that there is no market opportunity for that particular company. As a result, the existence of a market opportunity is always tested in relevance to a specific company or companies. It is common that the existence of a market problem will mean a significant market opportunity for some companies, but none for others.

We want to verify the existence of a "Market Opportunity" so we can potentially generate monetary profit, then fully understand the "Market Problem" in order to build a product that will be its solution, and lastly, understand the "Need" in order to market that solution.

It should be noted that there is no economic reason to build certain products if they do not solve a business or consumer problem. However, there might be marketing reasons that would justify their creation, for example to demonstrate a particular technology. Thus it may be reasonable to build certain products although there is no market opportunity, given special company motivations.

3.3 Market Requirements

Market problems can be simple or complex. Most market problems have many facets, meaning they embody and represent multiple customer needs. In order to understand how to solve a market problem, the problem must be thoroughly described. Problem definition is obtained by listing all the users' and buyers' different needs, relevant to that market problem. These needs are referred to as *requirements*. Since both users and buyers belong to customer domains, which in turn constitute a market, we refer to the users' and buyers' requirements for a particular solution to a particular market problem as "Market Requirements".

A "Market Requirement" is properly defined as an aggregate unit of information which represents with sufficient detail the functionality that is sought to address a specific facet of a particular market problem. This is the full and comprehensive definition.

The product delivery process is mostly sequential and begins with identifying and articulating market requirements. Ambiguous market requirements will lead to flawed products and dissatisfied customers, but well-defined market requirements are the basis for a smooth development process and marketplace success.

Market requirements describe what the user needs to do, while product requirements detail the functionality that the product provides, and enables the user to do what is needed. Virtually all market requirements begin with the phrase: *"The user shall be able to. . .",* and matched with one or more product requirements that begin with the phrase: *"The product shall provide. . .".*

For example, a market requirement such as, *"The user shall be able to operate the product in Europe and North America"*, could foster the following product requirement: *"The product shall provide the ability to work with 220 volt and 110 volt electrical power grids"*. Clearly other product requirements can be provided to answer the market requirement, such as those that detail the product relying on commercially available portable battery power.

Again, it is evident that the same market requirement can be satisfied in different ways. That is why it is so crucial to properly identify and define market requirements because they are the basis that dictates the outcome of the innovation and development effort. Therefore, there is an imperative need for practices that aid in clearly identifying and articulating market requirements, and that creates a strong framework for defining the product. The absence of these practices has the affect of compromising product success.

3.4   Blackblot Product Frames Model

This chapter introduces the "Blackblot Product Frames Model" and the concept of "Product Frames", which are the conceptual building blocks that amount to the product's overall functionality.

Product planning is the ongoing process of identifying and articulating market requirements from which the product's feature set is ultimately defined. The "Blackblot Product Frames Model" is a descriptive model that demonstrates how product functionality is built and how, in total, the product solves the market problem. This model serves several objectives: to validate the product's functional completeness with respect to the market problem, to synchronize user/buyer needs with product features, and to provide a backbone for a product delivery process.

The inner workings of a single product frame show how a certain product feature addresses a particular facet of the market problem. The sum of all of the product frames defines a product that has the overall functionality that solves the entire scope of issues presented by a market problem.

A product frame is comprised of four elements: market requirements, product features, product attributes, and technical specifications. These elements are interconnected in the following manner:

1. Market requirements describe a user/buyer need.
2. Market requirements foster "Product Features" – a product capability that satisfies a specific user/buyer need.
3. Product features generate "Product Attributes" – a real characteristic or property of the product.
4. Product attributes are built via a "Technical Specification" – a precise description of an attribute's implementation details.

Table 3.1 lists the product frame elements and their descriptions.

For example, people are confronted with hindered mobility in their homes when immediate darkness sets in following an electrical power outage. This is a very simple market problem that can be solved with a flashlight. Listed in Table 3.2 is an example of a product frame that represents a solution to this common market problem.

Again, similar to a need being satisfied with different want/demand sets, it is clear a market requirement can be satisfied with different feature/attribute/specification combinations. This is a crucial concept that must be fully understood.

Table 3.1 Product Frame – Elements and Description (Summary Table)

Product Frame Element	Description
Market requirement	A user/buyer need
Product feature	Something the product does or has
Product attribute	An actual trait of the product
Technical specification	The attribute's implementation

Table 3.2 Product Frame – Flashlight (Summary Table)

Product Frame Element	Description
Market requirement	*"The user shall be able to...find his/her way in dark"*
Product feature	*"The product is capable of...emitting light"*
Product attribute	*"The product physically has a...light bulb"*
Technical specification	*"The attribute is implemented via...2w 1.5v DIN 7.1"*

For example, the market problem represented by the market requirement: *"The user shall be able to find way in the dark"*, can be solved by products that emit light in various ways: chemical, combustion, electrical; or by products that enhance the ability to see in the night, such as infra-red night vision goggles. The product attributes and technical specifications would change based on the selected technology; but market requirements remain the same and independent from the solution or technology.

Direct linkage exists between product frame elements. This means that for every market requirement, there are at least one or more product features (via product requirements) that are linked to it. The ability to verify this linkage is referred to as "Traceability" and is confirmed by establishing a literal association between market requirements and product requirements.

Assuming due process, lack of downward traceability exists when there are no product requirements assigned to an existing market requirement, and this means that the functional solution is not whole and does not completely address the market problem.

The lack of upward traceability, being no market requirement that is linked to an existing product requirement, means that superfluous functionality is being built into the product for which the customer has no need.

3.5 Product Definition Foundation Documents

Several key foundation documents are prepared in the product planning process. These documents are the "Market Requirements Document" (MRD), which contains a description of the market opportunity, market problem and the resulting set of market requirements. The MRD defines product objectives in terms of user needs and from the user's perspective. This is the *user view* of the solution.

Derived from the MRD is the "Product Requirements Document" (PRD) that provides a high level description of the solution, intended use, and the set of features it provides. The PRD offers a solution that addresses the market problem and satisfies needs. The PRD defines product functionality and features from the solution's perspective. This is the *product view* of the solution.

The "Technical Specification" (Tech. Spec.) is a highly detailed description of the solution's design, attributes and standards, and is a guidebook on how to build the solution.

Table 3.3 Product Definition Documents and Product Frame Elements (Correlation Table)

Document	Product Frame Element
MRD	Market requirements
PRD	Product features
Tech. Spec.	Product attributes + Product technical specification

The foundation documents correspond, and are mapped to, the product frame. The MRD outlines the market requirements. The PRD describes the product and its features. Lastly, the Tech. Spec. document contains the product attributes and detailed technical specification information required to build the product.

Table 3.3 correlates the product definition documents with product frame elements.

It is very important to distribute the information used to define the product among several documents, especially for complex systems, and be explicit about what is and what is not accurate at each level. This is because the product delivery process is phase-based, and aggregating information from different classes into one document will blur the document's and the writer's focus.

In product planning, this intermixing of information occurs when the MRD becomes an aggregate of business, market, and product information. The writer often finds it easier to specify a solution than to identify the underlying market need, and the common outcome is a document that is laden with product requirements that are likely to be detached from market needs.

Finally, it is important for each document to be clearly written in explicit terms and form because it becomes the input to the next phase of the product delivery process.

3.6 Blackblot Product Definition Team Model

Different roles are required to create a product. These roles require different skills sets, and in some cases, even a different psychological make up to successfully plan, define and build a product that meets customers' expectations.

Extreme due diligence needs to be performed during the product planning and product definition processes to properly and accurately define a product. This requires people that possess different skills, abilities, backgrounds, experience, education, personalities, and other qualities or characteristics. Professional and distinct roles are needed to create the foundation documents required to accurately define the product. Hence, in order to be successful, a team approach is implemented, bringing together a cohesive set of individuals that have unique qualities to perform all that is needed to define a successful product.

As previously eluded to, there are three key roles that all product definition teams must have:

1. "Product Planner" – a market expert who is able to articulate the market problem and needs.

2. "Product Architect" – a product expert who is able to create a high-level design for the solution.
3. "Lead Developer" – a technology expert who is able to describe how to build and implement the solution's design.

These three roles make the "Blackblot Product Definition Team Model", depicted in Fig. 3.1. The structure implies peer collaboration without any organizational hierarchy.

The product planner researches the market, identifies the market opportunity, and articulates user and buyer needs in the form of market requirement statements. The product planner's job is to do all the above and produce a deliverable which is a complete, and accurate "Market Requirements Document" (MRD).

The product architect understands the market opportunity, interprets market requirements, and knows technology and development processes. The product architect's job is to devise a functional solution to the market problem according to the market requirements that are outlined in the MRD. The product architect's deliverable is the "Product Requirements Document" (PRD). The product architect creates a PRD that it is useable by the lead developer.

The lead developer understands products and is an expert in technology. The lead developer's job is to design the product's implementation guidelines, subject to the prescribed set of measurable product features. The resulting deliverable is the technical specification.

Table 3.4 summarizes the roles of product definition team members.

Members of the product definition team need to be able to collaborate with each other. They not only lead the development of each of their foundation documents, but also act as a reviewer of each of the other foundation documents in order to ensure that product definition continues to be consistent and clear, avoiding requirement dilution or scope creep.

"Scope Creep" is a situation where uncontrolled modifications, mostly additions, are made to the product's feature set. Scope creep occurs when the product's feature set is not fully defined or not fully documented, or not properly controlled.

Members of the product definition team work together with one goal in mind; to define a product in a viable way that actually solves the market problem, and

Fig. 3.1 Blackblot Product Definition Team Model

Table 3.4 Product Definition Team Members Roles (Summary Table)

Role	Responsibility	Product Frame	Deliverable	Expertise
Product planner (strategic role)	Articulate market problem	Market requirements	MRD (*"What to solve?"*)	Market expert
Product architect (tactical role)	Devise functional solution	Product features (via Product Requirements)	PRD (*"How to solve?"*)	Product expert
Lead developer (technical role)	Design product implementation	Product attributes and specifications	Tech. Spec. (*"How to build?"*)	Technology expert

satisfies needs. This is done via a process that fosters an environment that is free of egos, free from political agendas, and free of personal goals and objectives. The focus is on the user/buyer and their needs, and to properly convey those needs to the development team.

3.7   Product Delivery Process

The product definition team works together to create a solution that solves the market problem. Each member performs a role that is focused on a particular aspect of the product delivery process.

Each individual provides data that inspires his/her peer's deliverable, and is an integral part of the discussion around feature set definition/tradeoffs, scheduling and budgets. Each role has clear ownership of decisions that pertain to the specified deliverables for which the role is responsible.

The product delivery process consists of phases in which participating individuals are responsible for a specific product frame work document. The team members have shared responsibilities, as well as individual responsibilities. Each team member takes a leadership role during the product delivery process, and contributes where and when needed to deliverables owned by other team members.

For clarification, the "Product Delivery Process" is a company-wide project aimed at ensuring deliverables from all contributing corporate functions, in the interest of bringing a product to market. The product delivery process, often called a product program and managed by a program manager, is an umbrella term that contains many corporate sub-processes, among them three key sub-processes which are the product planning process, the product definition process and the product development process.

At an abstract level, Table 3.5 presents the typical product delivery process.

The entire product delivery process is comprised of stages one through nine. Stages one and two constitute the product planning process, which is owned by the product planner. Stages three through six constitute the product definition process,

Table 3.5 Product Delivery Process and Sub-Processes

Task	Task Owner	Sub-process
1. Uncover unsatisfied market needs	Product planner	Product planning process
2. Define market requirements		(Stages 1-2)
3. Identify product concept	Product architect	Product definition process
4. Define product requirements		(Stages 3-6)
5. Design product	Lead developer	
6. Define product specification		
7. Implement the design	Product developer	Product development process
8. Test the product		(Stages 7-9)
9. Manufacture the product		

which is owned by the product architect. The remaining stages, seven through nine, form the product development process, are owned by the lead developer and are executed by the product development team. The first six steps of the product delivery process, being the product planning and the product definition processes, are the main focus of this chapter and critical to the success of the eventual product development effort.

Many companies, especially those who are technology-driven, go directly to stage three ("*Identify product concept*"), skipping the first two stages, meaning they do not actually perform product planning and they do not create a true MRD. Instead, their primary focus is on executing autonomous product definition.

The product delivery process inspires constant feedback and interface between the product management department and the engineering department, and effectively coordinates market analysis and technical design efforts that eventually allow for building a successful product.

Regarding organizational placement, the product planner position belongs in the product management department, while the product architect and lead developer usually reside within the engineering department. However, with the right individuals and corporate mindset, it is also possible to have the product architect position placed in the product management department.

Through the actions and deliverables of the product definition team, and via execution of the product definition process, market requirements are translated into product requirements, which themselves are translated into engineering design requirements and specifications, to be used by the product developers.

It is imperative that roles and responsibilities of the product definition team members are profoundly clear and known to everyone in the company, and are consistently communicated and interpreted in the same manner by anyone that is involved in the product delivery process. There must be corporate acceptance that the product management department owns and controls the product's market requirements, while the engineering department owns the solution and the product development project schedule. This is a critical factor for the successful execution of the product planning and product definition processes.

3.8 Conclusion

In many instances, product definition teams base design direction on documentation that contains product features rather than specific market requirements. The disconnect with market needs is further amplified as companies often frame their market worldview and define products in terms of what the company has to offer rather than what the customer actually wants. Countering this phenomenon should be and is the realization that product planners outline what customers want, and that the engineers respond with what they can build and how long it will take to bring the product to market.

There are many possible partitions and terminologies surrounding the product planning and product definition processes. Indeed, the details of the product delivery process vary from company to company, but the fundamentals are the same and revolve around clear market and product requirements, and a well-understood methodology.

The way to produce successful market-driven products is by properly structuring a product definition team and governing its actions with well-defined product planning and product definition processes, within the context of a product delivery process. The key to making this happen is the notion that product planners are problem-tellers and market experts, while engineers are problem-solvers and technology experts.

Chapter 4
Crafting Market Requirements

Methodology to Identify and Articulate Market Requirements

4.1 Introduction

Crafting market requirements is arguably the most important step of the product planning process, after uncovering the market problem. Identifying and articulating market requirements is a task owned by the product planner, who records them in a document aptly named the "Market Requirements Document" (also known as the MRD).

Writing market requirements is in part an art form, and this chapter focuses on demystifying the task of crafting quality market requirements using a comprehensive and structured methodology, called the "Blackblot Procedural Requirements Management Model".

This chapter builds on the concepts and terminology previously introduced in the "Blackblot Product Definition Team" chapter.

4.2 Voice of the Customer

"Voice of the Customer" (VOC) is a process for eliciting needs from customers. It embodies a market-driven approach that involves spending time with current and future customers to determine past, present and future market problems that customers need to solve in order to meet their business goals and objectives.

The VOC process is based on in-depth interviews that lead interviewees through a series of situations in which they have experienced, and perhaps found, solutions to the market problem being investigated.

Executing the VOC process are members of the product definition team which is comprised of individuals with different roles and responsibilities. Product definition team members, primarily the product planner and product architect, respectively contribute to this process which should ultimately yield a product that meets customer needs and expectations.

G. Steinhardt, *The Product Manager's Toolkit,*
DOI 10.1007/978-3-642-04508-0_4, © Springer-Verlag Berlin Heidelberg 2010

After the VOC process is complete, the next step is to build the "Market Requirements Document", which serves as the blueprint for driving the product concept and its functionality.

4.3   Market Requirements Document

The product planner is the in-house market expert, and has a deep understanding of the most acute market problems that are dealt with by the company. With the support of the product management team and paired with the help of outside research and consulting talent, the product planner produces one of the key product management reference documents – the "Market Requirements Document".

The MRD is a written representation of the overall functionality that users seek in order to address a particular market problem. Therefore, the MRD represents or describes the *user view* of a solution to the market problem.

Since the market constantly changes and evolves, so does the product planner's understanding of the market problems that exist. As such, the MRD becomes a living document that reflects market change via the revised functionality the solution must hold.

The MRD only describes desired functionality. It does not describe the specific features and attributes that the solution should have to solve a particular market problem. The solution to the problem and its features are documented in a subsequent document called the "Product Requirements Document" (also known as the PRD).

The MRD is intended for all those in the company or outside of it, who contribute to the product delivery program, including executive management, usability specialists, product marketers, documentation writers, engineers, and testers.

The MRD captures the essential information that is required as input to devise a functional solution to a specific market problem. In general, the goal when writing an MRD is to present as much information as clearly and concisely as possible within a consistently organized format so that engineers can first determine if a product concept can be developed, and then describe a suggested solution (product) and its features.

4.4   Blackblot Procedural Requirements Management Model

This chapter introduces the "Blackblot Procedural Requirements Management Model" (also known as the "Blackblot PRM Model") – a methodology to create market requirements. This model serves several objectives: provide a structured approach to crafting market requirements, establish a market requirement's internal structure, and validate a market requirement's integrity.

A market requirement is an aggregate unit of information which represents with sufficient detail the functionality sought by users to address a specific facet of a particular market problem. This is the full and comprehensive definition of a market requirement. Unlike product requirements, market requirements are lasting and do not expire when technology or the solution evolve.

The sum of all market requirements collected describes the total functionality needed to address the whole market problem. By understanding the overall functionally that is described by the sum of market requirements, it is possible to construe the scope of the market problem. Essentially, the market problem is described by the sum of market requirements, and the market problem scope is described by the overall functionality that is in the market requirements.

Market requirements are built using four components: directive, constraints, rationales and sources. The essential component of a market requirement, that must be present in any market requirement, is the directive. Constraints, rationales and sources are considered vital components, and their presence is strongly desired in any market requirement.

The four market requirement components are defined as follows:

- "Directive" – instruction that guides what is to be accomplished.
- "Constraints" – limitations imposed on the solution.
- "Rationales" – reasoning that support a claim.
- "Sources" – information that validate a claim.

Each market requirement is composed of a "directive", which is further defined by "constraints" and "rationales", which are further supported by "sources". Ideally, all rationales should be accompanied by the source from which they came, thus providing credence to the assertion made by the rationale.

Rationale and source sets can be attributed to either directives or constraints, since directives and constraints can both be viewed as claims. Therefore, the market requirement would optimally have rationale and source combinations assigned to the directive and to each constraint.

The relationship between the market requirement's components is depicted by the market requirement's internal structure, as mandated by the "Blackblot PRM Model" (Fig. 4.1).

The relationship between the components is one-to-many throughout the internal structure, when viewed top-down. The directive can have several rationales supporting it; the directive can have many constraints assigned to it; a rationale

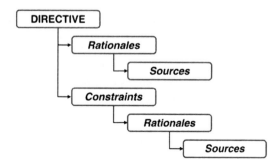

Fig. 4.1 Market Requirement's Components and Internal Structure

can have many sources validating it; a constraint can have several rationales supporting it.

Defined in this manner, the directive is a compulsory (essential) component, while the others are considered discretionary (vital) components in support of the directive, as well as each other.

4.5 Directive

As previously described, the essential component of the market requirement is the "directive". It is a statement which is phrased as an instruction that guides and directs the functionality being sought by the user. The directive explains what is to be accomplished.

The directive is the most important part of the market requirement, and the way it is crafted and supported with data will profoundly impact the market requirement's quality. It will also determine the quality and form of the proposed solution.

Market requirements detail functionality – essentially the solution a user seeks to a defined market problem. At the basic level, all market requirement directives relate to the user, and are consistently phrased in the same manner. For example:

"User [persona] <shall/should> be able to <functionality>".

The special conventions used in the directive statement are:

- Square brackets "[ ]" denote optional arguments
- Pointed brackets "<>" denote mandatory arguments
- Slash symbol "/" denote the "OR" logical operator

Special note is made to the matter of directive conditioning, which defines the market requirement's relative priority.

All crucial market requirement directives must include the verb "shall" for consistency. Functionality that has the "shall" directive conditioning, is obligatory and must be present in the solution. Market requirements that have the "shall" directive conditioning signify the product's core functionality – the product's functionality backbone. There is no prioritization required with the "shall" directive conditioning, as that functionality is inherently considered most essential.

All desirable market requirement directives (i.e. beneficial but not critical to the core product), must include the verb "should" for appropriate prioritization. The functionality represented in market requirements that have "should" directive conditioning is optional, yet worth having in addition to the core functionality. Prioritization levels are used with the "should" directive conditioning because that functionality is considered worthwhile yet supplementary to the core functionality.

Prioritization of "should" directive conditioning is done with sub-qualifiers:

- Should (high) – include if at all possible.
- Should (medium) – desirable feature.
- Should (low) – include only if resources permit.

As such, the expanded and more advanced syntax of a market requirement's directive is:

"User [persona] <shall/should[(high/medium/low)]> be able to <functionality>".

The directive is the most important component of the market requirement. Directives themselves have their own foundation elements and structure. All directive elements must exist within each directive so that the directive itself is valid.

Directive elements are:

- "Event" – trigger that initiates requirement.
- "Entity" – persona to which it applies.
- "Action" – strong verb (shall/should).
- "Criteria" – pass/fail metric(s).

For example, parsing the directive *"User Bob shall be able to find a dropped flashlight"*, confirms this directive holds all required elements. The event is the "dropped flashlight", the entity/persona is "User Bob", the action is "shall", and the criteria is "find".

Ultimately, the structure of a useful market requirement allows it to be easily modified and understood by non-technical and technical persons who will be acting on it in the future. This is important because there will be times when the people who originally wrote the market requirement are not available to continue work on the MRD. Such a scenario makes a strong case for why market requirements need to stand on their own and be self-sufficient for future use.

Incidentally, people often view the market requirement directive as being synonymous with the entire market requirement unit of information. This happens because the directive is the most dominant component of a market requirement, but clearly the two are not the same.

4.6 Constraints

The market requirement's directive provides the gist of the functionality that is being sought by the user to address a particular facet of a market problem. The true underlying market need embodied in a directive will be lost if the directive is ambiguously worded, or if the directive is expressed with broad or subjective terms, such as "easy" or "fast" or "friendly". Such expressions and wordings will lead to very different personal interpretations of the directive. Accordingly, the proposed solution and its scope will vary considerably.

This inevitably will lead to a disconnect between the desired functionality the market requirement attempted to convey, and the actual functionality that will be proposed.

For example, the directive: *"User shall be able to find a dropped flashlight"* allows considerable interpretative leeway to any reader even though it is the essence of the functionality being sought. In order to guide the reader to better understand the environment to which the directive relates, "Constraints" must be introduced. Constraints are limitations imposed on the solution, and are another component of the market requirement.

In the following example, the directive previously used in the example is revised and interjected with constraints: "*User shall be able to quickly find a dropped flashlight, while dark*". However, the directive remains flawed in several respects.

From the outset, the directive did not detail the terrain where the flashlight was dropped, which could be snow, mud, sand, water, grass, concrete, etc.; any of which would profoundly impact the type of solution needed to provide the required functionality. The same would apply to the added constraints, which are the subjective terms of "quickly" and "dark".

Rectifying ambiguity is accomplished by quantifying the directive, as in: "*User shall be able within ten seconds to find in one foot deep snow a dropped flashlight, while dark*".

Additional information can be introduced to define the meaning of "dark", the height from which the flashlight was dropped, and more.

It is immediately apparent that the directive must be qualified using constraints, and that the constraints must be quantified. Directives will present different implications and different optimal solutions when they are differently qualified and quantified. This means that market requirement constraints must be as scalable and measurable as possible, because what is not measured cannot be controlled.

The objective in writing high-quality market requirements that are properly constrained is to provide anyone reading the directive, particularly the product architect, with enough information to propose a way to accurately and efficiently provide the needed functionality. There is a balance however, as too many details and constraints will impede creativity and innovation.

4.7 Rationales and Sources

The product delivery process is lengthy, and the product planner is often challenged by others involved in the process to explain why a particular directive or a specific constraint was introduced. Additionally, when dealing with complex products with long development cycles, it helps to document the reasons why certain functionality was requested. When adequately captured, the reasons can be used during reevaluation and for marketing purposes.

"Rationales" and "Sources" support the directive. The rationale represents the logic and justification of a directive or constraint, while the source provides the rationale with credibility based on data or respected opinions.

Constraints are meant to intentionally limit the options open to the architects of the solution. Because of their impact, each constraint should be accompanied by a rationale and a source. The sources may come from a variety of origins: customers, customer support, development, research, sales channels, research papers, or consulting firms.

Rationales are used to document the reason for a given market requirement, and allow future readers of the MRD, especially the product architect and product developers, to be able to completely understand the market requirement in the absence of further explanation.

Readers need to know the reason for which a particular directive or constraint was introduced, and rationales are the given explanation. Rationales provide the justification and backup for a directive or constraint, allowing readers to gain a better insight as to the merit of that component.

Sources are very important and they allow any rationale or constraint to be validated by documentation, surveys, statistics, or views of market analysts. Sources complement the rationales, and prove that the rationales are not mere opinions of the writers, but actual justifications supported by facts.

The rationales and sources provide more helpful information to those faced with writing the PRD – the next important document in the product development cycle. In general, it is optimal when rationales and their related sources are assigned to all directives and constraints within all market requirements.

4.8   Presentment Modes

A well-defined and valid market requirement will include all four of the components previously covered. Once defined, there are two ways to present a market requirement – "Story" mode and "Data" mode.

With the story mode, all components are interwoven into the directive and the result is a long sentence or paragraph that holds the entire market requirement's required information. Story mode is helpful when dealing with simple products without too many constraints, or when the developers prefer the narrative, flowing form of knowledge transfer.

An example of story mode representation would be:

"User shall be able within ten seconds to find in one foot deep snow a dropped flashlight, while dark".

With data mode, a less verbose directive is presented and supplemented with data in the form of bullet points which hold the other market requirement components. Data mode is helpful when the product is complex, subjected to many constraints, and is of a deep technical nature. The data mode approach is more suited for high-tech products, while the story mode is favored by those who deal with consumer goods.

An example of data mode representation would be:

Directive: "User shall be able to find dropped flashlight".
Constraints:
- *Terrain: Snow (< one foot deep)*
- *Recovery Time: Quickly (< ten seconds)*
- *Visibility: Darkness (< five candela)*

An example of a more complete market requirement with samples of constraints, rationales and sources might be (using fictitious data and sources):

1. Directive: "User shall be able to find dropped flashlight".

1.1. Rationales:

1.1.1. Loss of flashlight impairs critical navigational abilities and limits spotting by rescue force in 75% of rescue cases.

1.1.1.1. Source: 2001 Red Cross report.

1.2. Constraints:

1.2.1. Terrain: Snow (< one foot deep)

1.2.1.1. Rationales: Over 20% of hikers have lost flashlight in snow.

1.2.1.1.1. Source: 2001 USFS Survey.

1.2.2. Recovery Time: Quickly (< ten seconds)

1.2.3. Visibility: Darkness (< five candela)

Another type of naming convention that can be used to document a complex market requirement is through the use of notation identifiers (versus outline numbers). For a market requirement, the identifier convention is the letters MR proceeded by product initials followed by a tracking number. For example, a market requirement for a product named MGL would be MGL.MR200, the market requirement's rational would be MGL.MR200.R10, the market requirement's constraint would be MGL.MR200.C10, the constraint's rational would MGL.MR200.C10. R10; and so forth.

Gaps should be introduced into the identifiers, so future components can be inserted without the need for renumbering. The key with any notation or numbering system is that it allows to reference components in a clear and consistent manner.

4.9   Whole Picture

Table 4.1 describes the complete structure of a market requirement record.

4.10   Verifying Wholeness

Each market requirement needs to be tested for wholeness to ensure that it is viable and useable in the next step of the development process. To help verify the wholeness of each market requirement, there are six qualifiers called "The Six C's of a Market Requirement".[1] They are as follows:

- "Complete" – all four directive components and key information are present.
- "Consistent" – requirements do not conflict.

---

[1]Larry L. Wear, Ph.D., Writing Requirements, 2002.

Table 4.1 Complete Structure of a Market Requirement Record

Field	Description
MR Identifier	A unique identifier using a consistent name convention
MR Name	A short name for easy reference to the market requirement
Directive	An instruction that guides and directs functionality being sought by the user. Each directive addresses a facet of the market problem. The directive format is:
	"User [persona] <shall/should[(high/medium/low)]> be able to <functionality>"
Priority	"Shall" directive conditioning – critical functionality
	"Should" directive conditioning – desirable functionality (high, medium, low)
• Rationales	A list of all possible rationales; the reasons that support the introduction of this market requirement
o Sources	Each rationale must be supported by a source. Sources are a list of references and information origins that validate the market requirement
Constraints	A list of all possible constraints; the limitations imposed on the solution relevant to this particular market requirement. Each constraint should be supported by its own rational and source
• Rationales	A list of all possible rationales; the reasons that support the introduction of this constraint
o Sources	Each rationale must be supported by a source. Sources are a list of references and information origins that validate the market requirement
Persona	Names of all personas applicable to this market requirement
Use Case	A use case statement or use case identifiers applicable to this market requirement. Entry of use case information is applicable only if a product or product concept actually exists
Buying Criterion	A Boolean indicator that this market requirement will foster a product feature used as a buying criterion
Differentiator	A Boolean indicator whether this market requirement will foster a product feature that is a key differentiator, relative to competing products

- "Correct" – accurate description of user needs.
- "Clear" – only one semantic interpretation.
- "Criterial" – verified using a pass/fail metric.
- "Concise" – complexity and clutter have been eliminated to enhance universal understanding.

Once a market requirement or set of market requirements have passed the wholeness test, they are then ready to be placed into the MRD.

4.11 Market Requirements and Engineering

The MRD is a critical part of the development process. After one is developed and finalized, it will get used by someone else in the product process. As a result, the MRD has to be a standalone document that can be used successfully by the next person in the development process to develop the right product for the intended customer.

The MRD and its market requirements become input to the PRD. When the product planner completes and finalizes the MRD, it is passed on to the product architect who is responsible for creating the PRD. The PRD should not be started until the MRD has been finalized.

4.12   Market Requirements Database

There are several ways to create and store market requirements. Typically the MRD is stored as a textual document and the most common way of doing so is with MS-Office tools, as many product managers are familiar with Microsoft Word or Excel. While word processors are good at producing textual documents, they have deficiencies that significantly decrease their ability to provide a suitable platform for creating market requirements. Word processors and spreadsheets are not good at querying information, sorting and baselining data, maintaining relationships between statements, and linking information internally and across documents. They are however inexpensive and easy to learn and use.

There are other more effective and efficient methods and means for building market requirements and an MRD. An example of an alternate method is using a database to store and create all market requirements. For some products, a market requirements database can be more useful than a document for accessing and utilizing the various directive components, arguments, operators, metrics, and supporting material.

The database method utilizes a computerized database and application software that aid in the generation of market requirements and an MRD. Implementing market requirements in an electronic medium can facilitate the crafting of market requirements such that they are particularly useful further down the product delivery process.

Every market requirement can be presented to the reader via a table of data; essentially a database record with data fields. In addition, the volume of market requirements can be organized in database form and formatted in structural representations that can be managed relatively easily using a computer.

A database is also helpful when there is a new product launch and decisions need to be made with regard to first release functionality. Customer critical items that are universally acceptable form the bulk of the initial release. However, requirements that did not make the first release, but are relevant to the product roadmap, can be considered for the next development cycle.

Once complete, the MRD is used to create the PRD which will contain the descriptions of all of the functionality that will go into a product. The PRD represents or describes the *product view* of a solution to the market problem.

The matter of traceability – the linkage between market requirements and product requirements – is of great importance to product planners so they can verify the product is not lacking needed functionality, or conversely, has superfluous features that should be eliminated. Databases are a clear choice to monitor traceability between market requirements and product requirements.

There are several software applications on the market that were built for managing requirements of all kinds (market, product, technical). These applications are very much the same in principal – essentially database systems with configurable or fixed data entry screens and query mechanisms. However, these applications are designed to handle data, not enforce processes, and thus, to a large extent, the majority of them do not guide the product planner through a built-in methodology. Consequently, the methodology used with any general requirements management software application tool is the product planner's actions as applied to that application.

4.13   Summary

This chapter introduced a structured way of capturing user needs and presented a set of concepts to better articulate them. Because market requirements are crucial to the product definition process, their quality immensely impacts the development process and the product's level of suitability to customer needs. With so many potential interpretations to the nature of a market requirement, the definitions and components presented in this chapter help demystify the inherent ambiguity in the industry surrounding what a market requirement is and its purpose.

Each market requirement must be tested and verified against consistent guidelines so that it is valid for use in the product definition process. Once all market requirements are complete, they form a "Market Requirements Document" (MRD), which represents a true commitment to customers by addressing their problem.

Once the MRD is complete, it is used as input to generate the "Product Requirements Document" (PRD). Software applications that use databases as an alternative to textual documents improve the management of the entire product delivery process, and ensure the much needed traceability between market requirements and product requirements.

Writing quality market requirements demands a very special skill set of product planners. They must possess superb linguistics skills, a profound comprehension of the market's and customers' needs, a deep understanding of the product delivery process, mastery of the market requirement's structure, and competency crafting market requirements. While familiarity with markets is crucial, the key to developing quality market requirements is often determined by understanding the mechanics and methodologies for creating them.

The aim is that by understanding the concepts introduced in this chapter, the product planner will have a framework for producing complete, clear and concise market requirements. These will serve as the key to reducing risk of product failure and increasing the chance for product success in the marketplace.

Chapter 5
Concept of Marketing

Insight into the Concept, Structure and Elements of the Marketing Domain

5.1 Introduction

Marketing is an instructive business domain that serves to inform and educate target markets about the value and competitive advantage of a company and its products. The goal of marketing is to build and maintain a preference for a company and its products within the target markets.

Volumes have been written about the marketing domain and what it entails, but little has been noted about how it is ordered and organized. In order to clarify the essence of the marketing domain, Blackblot introduces the "Blackblot Marketing Model". This model maps the marketing activities within the marketing domain, presents the division and location of departments identified with the marketing domain in the corporate organizational hierarchy, and describes the types of strategies and plans related to the marketing domain.

This chapter provides insight into the concept, structure and elements of the marketing domain from the Blackblot perspective.

5.2 Business Domains

A "Domain" is a sphere of knowledge. In the context of doing business, a "Business Domain" is considered to be a fundamental corporate activity and essential to the company's ability to function or exist.

Business domains include business related functions such as business management, operations, engineering, manufacturing, product management, and marketing. Business domains themselves are vast, layered, and made of different elements. All the business domain elements are based on a common collection of knowledge areas and processes.

G. Steinhardt, *The Product Manager's Toolkit*,
DOI 10.1007/978-3-642-04508-0_5, © Springer-Verlag Berlin Heidelberg 2010

Table 5.1 Blackblot Marketing Model – Business Domain Concept Definitions (Summary Table)

Business domain	Fundamental corporate activity that is based on a sphere of knowledge
Discipline	Knowledge area or activity that is governed by processes
Method	Plan or course of action
Mode	Particular form or way of achieving goals
Technique	Procedure used to accomplish a specific activity or task

A business domain is comprised of a specific set of "Disciplines", which are knowledge areas or activities that are governed by processes. Each discipline is accomplished using "Methods", which are a set of plans and organized actions that are achieved via the execution of modes. A "Mode" is a particular way that the method gets applied or acted on, via the use of techniques. A "Technique" is a procedure that is used to accomplish a specific activity or task.

The layers of a business domain are organized and sequenced in the following hierarchical manner:

Business Domain > Disciplines > Methods > Modes > Techniques

Table 5.1 summarizes the business domain concept definitions.

Most companies implement the elements in the business domain by using a conjoint approach. Without attesting to its merit, a characterization of this very commonplace implementation is as follows:

1. Within a particular domain, the majority or virtually all disciplines are constantly being executed.
2. Within each discipline, several methods are used concurrently with one particular method being the dominant one.
3. Within each method, several modes are used alternately.
4. Within each mode, a multitude of techniques are used concurrently or alternately.

By using the business domain concept it is possible to explain the internal structure and relationships of the marketing domain.

5.3   Marketing Domain

Marketing is an instructive business domain that serves to inform and educate target markets about the value and competitive advantage of a company and its products. "Value" is worth derived by the customer from owning and using the product. "Competitive Advantage" is a depiction that the company or its products are each doing something better than their competition in a way that could benefit the customer (Fig. 5.1).

Marketing is focused on the task of conveying pertinent company and product related information to specific customers, and there are a multitude of decisions

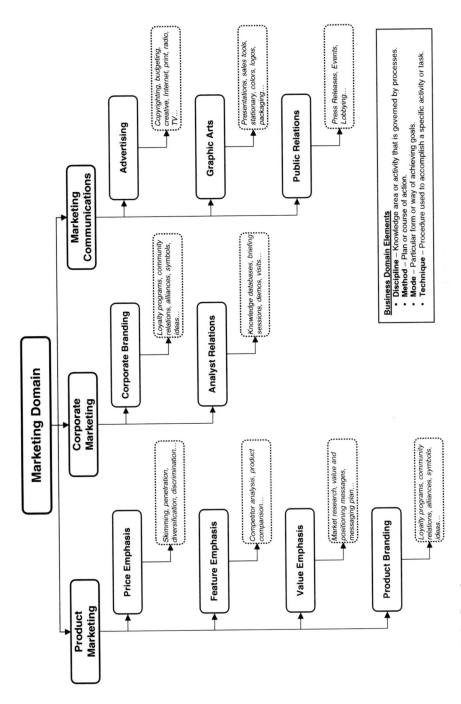

Fig. 5.1 Marketing Domain

(strategies) to be made within the marketing domain, regarding what information to deliver, how much information to deliver, to whom to deliver, how to deliver, when to deliver, and where to deliver. Once the decisions are made, there are numerous ways (tactics) and processes that could be employed in support of the selected strategies.

The goal of marketing is to build and maintain a preference for a company and its products within the target markets. The goal of any business is to build mutually profitable and sustainable relationships with its customers. While all business domains are responsible for accomplishing this goal, the marketing domain bears a significant share of the responsibility.

Within the larger scope of its definition, marketing is performed through the actions of three coordinated disciplines named: "Product Marketing", "Corporate Marketing", and "Marketing Communications".

5.4 Marketing Domain Disciplines

The "Product Marketing" discipline is an outbound activity aimed at generating product awareness, differentiation, and demand. The "Corporate Marketing" discipline is an outbound activity aimed at generating awareness and differentiation to the company. The "Marketing Communications" discipline is the employment of a mix of media vehicles that support marketing objectives.

Table 5.2 summarizes the marketing domain concept definitions.

Table 5.2 Blackblot Marketing Model – Marketing Domain Concept Definitions (Summary Table)

(Marketing Domain) Definition	Instructive business domain that serves to inform and educate target markets about the value and competitive advantage of a company and its products
(Marketing Domain) Task	Convey pertinent company and product related information to specific customers
(Marketing Domain) Goal	Build and maintain a preference for a company and its products within the target markets
(Marketing Domain) Disciplines	Product Marketing, Corporate Marketing, and Marketing Communications
Value	Worth derived by the customer from owning and using the product
Competitive advantage	Depiction that the company or its products are each doing something better than their competition in a way that could benefit the customer
Product marketing	Outbound activity aimed at generating product awareness, differentiation, and demand
Corporate marketing	Outbound activity aimed at generating awareness and differentiation to the company
Marketing communications	Employment of a mix of media vehicles that support marketing objectives

5.5 Blackblot Marketing Model

This chapter introduces the "Blackblot Marketing Model" which includes three components:

1. Structured representation and mapping of the marketing activities within the marketing domain (marketing activities is everything that is being done in the marketing domain).
2. Structured representation of the division and location of marketing related departments in the corporate organizational hierarchy.
3. Description of the types of strategies and plans in the marketing domain.

Based on the layered manner of description and by a graphic and tabular presentation, the "Blackblot Marketing Model" serves several objectives:

- Foster clearer understanding in the application of marketing activities.
- Provide a structured approach to mapping the elements of the marketing domain.
- Aid in building efficient corporate departments and structures that perform marketing activities.

Table 5.3 summarizes the marketing domain elements.

Table 5.3 Blackblot Marketing Model – Marketing Domain Elements (Tabular Form)

Marketing Disciplines	Marketing Methods	Marketing Modes	Marketing Techniques
Product marketing	Value emphasis	Messaging model	Market research, value and positioning messages, messaging plan...
	Feature emphasis	Feature comparison	Competitor analysis, product comparison...
	Price emphasis	Cost-plus, going-rate	Skimming, penetration, diversification, discrimination...
	Product branding	Uniqueness, labeling	Loyalty programs, community relations, alliances, symbols, ideas...
Corporate marketing	Corporate branding	Personification	Loyalty programs, community relations, alliances, symbols, ideas...
	Analyst relations	Engagements, resources	Knowledge databases, briefing sessions, demos, visits...
Marketing communications	Advertising	Entertainment, information	Copyrighting, budgeting, creative, Internet, print, radio, TV...
	Graphic arts	Signals, imagery, perception	Presentations, sales tools, stationary, colors, logos, packaging...
	Public relations	Relationship, media coverage	Press Releases, events, lobbying...

*Additional elements can be added to this component of the "Blackblot Marketing Model"; however, the current mapping is relatively whole and effectively encompasses the essence of the marketing domain. See Fig. 5.1 for a graphical presentation of the marketing domain component of the "Blackblot Marketing Model"

5.6   Product Marketing Methods

The goal of the "Product Marketing" discipline is to generate product awareness, differentiation, and demand. There are three principal methods to achieving this goal.

Each of these principal methods concentrates on one of the various aspects of the product: price, features, or value. The price emphasis method is called "Price Competition". The features emphasis method is called "Comparative Marketing". The value emphasis method is called "Value Marketing".

In the price emphasis method, the goal of product marketing is reached by emphasizing and communicating to the market the price of the product as a marketing signal. For example, touting the product's high price may signify a premium product and attempt to positively affect a perception of quality via inference. The goal of the price emphasis method is to create a situation where the customers primarily consider the product's price as the main buying decision factor.

In the feature emphasis method, the goal of product marketing is reached by emphasizing and communicating to the market the existence or merit of the product's features in comparison to the features of other competing products. The goal of the feature emphasis method is to create a situation where the customers primarily consider the product's feature set as the main buying decision factor.

In the value emphasis method, the goal of product marketing is reached by emphasizing and communicating to the market the value the product holds relative to the customer and comparatively to the value offered by other competing products. The goal of the value emphasis method is to create superior perceived value and prove superior actual value. "Superior Perceived Value" is a state where customers perceive the product (bought from a particular company) gives a net value more positive than its alternatives, and "Superior Actual Value" is a state where the product factually gives customers a net value more positive than its alternatives. The result of these states would be a situation where the customers primarily consider the product's value as the main buying decision factor.

The price emphasis and feature emphasis methods (price competition and comparative marketing) are considered significantly easier to implement than the value emphasis method (value marketing). This is because the price emphasis and feature emphasis methods convey simple quantitative concepts that are easy to understand and require minimal interpretation by the customers. Conversely, the value emphasis method relays abstract and qualitative concepts which project conjecture and argumentation, and thus are more challenging to grasp.

Another method in the product marketing discipline is product branding. "Product Branding" is the process of building and maintaining a brand at the product level. "Brand" is an identity, made of symbols and ideas, which portray a specific offering from a known source. Product branding is executed concurrently with one or more of the principal methods in product marketing.

The process of product branding and the derived brand is often the result of a deliberate and conscious effort by the company, but can also be an unintentional by-product resulting from the execution of any of the three principal methods of product marketing. Product branding is therefore not considered a principal method on its own since the formation of a brand can be the outcome of applying any of the three principal methods in product marketing.

5.7   Corporate Marketing Methods

The corporate marketing discipline objectives are supported by two principal methods: corporate branding and analyst relations.

"Corporate Branding" is the process of building and maintaining a brand at the institutional level. Corporate branding aims to create a favorable image and a positive identity relative to the company, with customers (existing and potential) in the target market. The goal of corporate branding is to leverage corporate brand equity in support of product brand equity.

"Analyst Relations" is a bi-directional information exchange with financial analysts and industry analysts to inform and favorably influence them. Financial analysts are individuals often employed by investment banks, who provide private and institutional investors with valuable perspectives on the market in support of investment decisions. Industry analysts are individuals often employed by research firms, who present companies with knowledge and perspectives on a select industry in support of business decision making. Analyst relations attempts to indirectly influence customers via the analysts. The goal of analyst relations is to sway analysts so they in turn positively affect potential investors and customers with their recommendations.

5.8   Marketing Communications Methods

From a domain perspective, the marketing communications discipline is viewed as an implementation function to the product marketing and corporate marketing disciplines. Marketing communications manages and employs different media vehicles in order to communicate information about the company and its products to the target audience.

The information that is conveyed is provided to marketing communications by product marketing and corporate marketing, and is designed to serve these disciplines' respective interests. The core and most crucial form of information provided to marketing communications is referred to as "Messages", which are ideas about the company and its products that will be communicated to the target markets.

The marketing communications discipline objectives are supported by three principal methods: advertising, graphic arts, and public relations.

The "Advertising" method, which is non-personal communication from an identified sponsor using mass media, is used to convey messages about the company and its products to the target audience.

The "Graphic Arts" method, which is the conception and copywriting of all collateral material, is responsible for maintaining a consistent image and visual positioning in the target market.

The "Public Relations" method, which are actions that promote and distribute information for a company, is focused on encouraging media coverage of the company and its products and building a virtual relationship between the company and its target audience.

5.9   Corporate Organizational Structures

The various disciplines of the marketing domain are usually assigned to corporate departments of similar names which own these disciplines. These departments guide and/or execute multiple and specific discipline related methods, modes, and techniques to enable the discipline to fulfill its business goal (Fig. 5.2).

Because of the different interpretations and views of the marketing domain and of the marketing disciplines, there is neither a consistent place nor uniform allocation of the relevant corporate departments in the organizational corporate structure. The corporate departments which represent the three marketing disciplines are occasionally aggregated to one corporate division called Marketing, sometimes grouped along with disciplines from other domains, and sometimes scattered among different corporate divisions.

The "Blackblot Marketing Model" also includes a structured representation of the corporate organizational structures and shows the division and location of marketing related departments in the corporate organizational hierarchy. As with the representation of the marketing domain, the model uses a layered manner of description and a graphic and tabular presentation.

Table 5.4 summarizes the corporate organizational structure.

Some disciplines from other business domains are occasionally grouped with the marketing disciplines and placed within the Marketing corporate division. Commonly interjected in to the Marketing corporate division are the sales and business development disciplines which actually belong to the operations domain.

The "Sales" discipline is centered on the act of personally interacting with and persuading potential customers to buy the product. The "Business Development" discipline encompasses the actions that improve the performance of the enterprise, its access to markets, and its ability to compete, by creating strategic relationships with logistical, content and technological partners. Both the sales and business development disciplines are actually part of the supportive operations business domain and therefore do not belong in the marketing domain.

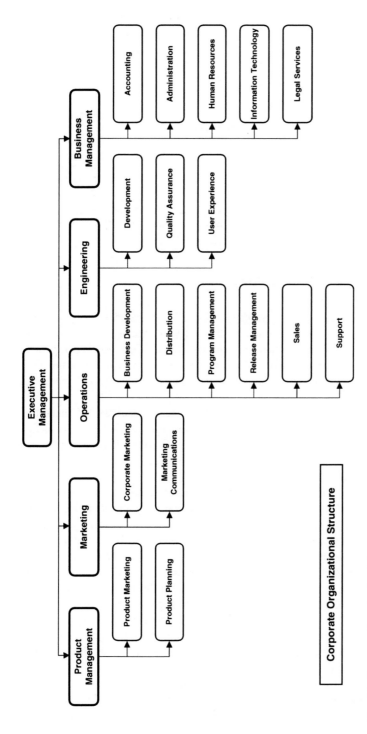

Fig. 5.2 Corporate Organizational Structure

Table 5.4 Blackblot Marketing Model – Corporate Organizational Structure (Tabular Form)

Product Management	Marketing	Operations	Engineering	Business Management
"Product Marketing"	"Corporate Marketing"	Business development	Development	Accounting
Product Planning	"Marketing Communications"	Distribution	Quality assurance	Administration
		Program management	User experience	Executive management
		Release management		Human resources
		Sales		Information technology
		Support		Legal services

*Framed in quotes are the three marketing domain disciplines. See Fig. 5.2 for a graphical presentation of the corporate organizational structure component of the "Blackblot Marketing Model"

5.10 Marketing and Strategies

In the generic business sense, "Strategy" is the coordinated set of long-term decisions that help achieve corporate objectives. Every strategy has two goals: to provide more value than the competition, and help build a sustainable competitive advantage. Inside the marketing domain there are two key decisions making areas that form the two marketing related strategies: market strategy and marketing strategy.

The "Market Strategy" is decisions that define target markets, set marketing objectives, and outline how to build a corporate competitive advantage. The market strategy is determined by roles in both the product marketing and product planning departments with contributions from other corporate departments, notably the executive management department.

The "Marketing Strategy" is decisions that determine how to achieve marketing's goal (build and maintain a preference for a company and its products) in a particular target market, through the selection and application of marketing mixes. The "Marketing Mix", originally known as "The Four Ps", is a combination of product, price, place [distribution], and promotion activities that are applied to a particular target market. The general idea is to combine (mix) the variables to generate an optimal, positive, and desired response in the target market. Diverse and numerous combinations of marketing methods, modes, and techniques can be selected and applied to create a marketing mix. The marketing strategy is mostly determined by roles (who focus on the promotion element of the marketing mix) in the marketing communications department with contributions from other corporate departments, notably the product marketing department.

Although extraneous to the marketing domain, an influential strategy on marketing activities is the "Product Strategy", which is decisions that build and enhance products to fit market needs and outline how to build a product competitive

Table 5.5 Blackblot Marketing Model – Marketing Domain Strategies (Summary Table)

Strategy	Coordinated set of long-term decisions that help achieve corporate objectives.
Market strategy	Decisions that define target markets, set marketing objectives, and outline how to build a corporate competitive advantage.
Marketing strategy	Decisions that determine how to achieve marketing's goal in a particular target market, through the selection and application of marketing mixes.
Product strategy	Decisions that build and enhance products to fit market needs, and outline how to build a product competitive advantage (Product strategy belongs to the product management business domain).

advantage. The product strategy belongs to the product management business domain and is determined by roles in the product planning department.

Table 5.5 summarizes the marketing domain strategies.

5.11 Marketing and Plans

The decisions that are made at the strategy level are documented and used as directives in the formulation of plans which guide marketing activities. Inside the marketing domain there are two plan types: market plan and marketing plan.

The "Market Plan" is a description of the long-term goals and messages delivered to the target market relative to a particular company or product. The market plan documents the market strategy, but when prepared in support of the product marketing discipline it also documents certain elements of the product strategy, which pertain to building a product competitive advantage. Market plans are created by roles in the product marketing department (relative to the product) and in the corporate marketing department (relative to the company).

The "Marketing Plan" hinges upon the guidelines set forth in the market plan and is a description of the selection and application of marketing mixes in the target market. The marketing plan contains the marketing strategy and is created by roles in the marketing communications department, with contributions from the corporate marketing department, but primarily from the product marketing department.

The marketing strategy is permeated on an ongoing basis by various marketing activities, but is also expressed by very specific and focused measures taken in the market. Such measures are planned and noted in the "Marketing Program", which is a description of the short-term marketplace effort designed to obtain a specific marketing goal. Examples of marketing programs include events (conventions or conferences), advertising campaigns, and limited-time discounting promotions.

Table 5.6 summarizes the marketing domain plans.

Table 5.7 summarizes the marketing domain plan/strategy/department mapping.

It is noted that support strategies and plans, which are more operational and tactical in nature, are derived from the market plan and the marketing plan. These include strategies and plans for advertising, analyst relations, and public relations.

Table 5.6 Blackblot Marketing Model – Marketing Domain Plans (Summary Table)

Market plan	Description of the long-term goals and messages delivered to the target market relative to a particular company or product.
Marketing plan	Description of the selection and application of marketing mixes in the target market.
Marketing program	Description of the short-term marketplace effort designed to obtain a specific marketing goal.

Table 5.7 Blackblot Marketing Model – Marketing Domain Plan/Strategy/Department Mapping (Summary Table)

Plan Type	Market Plan	Marketing Plan
Strategy type	"Market strategy" and elements of the "Product Strategy"	Marketing strategy
Corporate department	• Product marketing (relative to the product) • Corporate marketing (relative to the company)	Marketing communications

5.12 Summary

This chapter focused on clarifying the marketing domain and introduced the "Blackblot Marketing Model" that strives to create a complete and consistent view of the elements, structure, corporate departments, strategies, and plans that belong to the marketing domain.

The basic underlying premise of the "Blackblot Marketing Model" is that the essence of marketing is about communicating information to customers. Marketing's main task is to convey pertinent company and product related information to specific customers, in support of marketing's goal which is to build and maintain a preference for a company and its products within the target markets.

Many definitions abound as to what marketing is and its purpose. Some definitions are very expansive and some more focused. At the heart of these diverse definitions are different perceptions which view marketing mainly as a process, an activity, or a corporate department, or all of them combined. Consequently, the abundance of interpretations that proliferate in the industry creates different corporate structures and role definitions to support them. Some even view the term marketing as loosely synonymous with the terms sales or advertising.

By understanding the concepts, definitions and structures introduced in this chapter, those responsible for marketing now have a complete and clear framework for executing marketing activities and assigning them to the appropriate corporate departments. This will serve as a key to more efficient use and management of the company's marketing function with the aim of increasing the chance of product success in the marketplace.

Chapter 6
Value-Marketing Model

Presenting the Value Marketing Method and Marketing Messages Model

6.1 Introduction

Marketing is an instructive business domain that serves to inform and educate target markets about the value and competitive advantage of a company and its products. Within the larger scope of its definition, marketing is performed through the actions of three coordinated disciplines named: product marketing, corporate marketing, and marketing communications.

The goal of the product marketing discipline is to generate product awareness, differentiation, and demand. Three principal methods used to achieve this goal and each of them emphasizes one of the various aspects of the product: price, features, or value. The price emphasis method is called price competition. The features emphasis method is called comparative marketing. The value emphasis method is called value marketing.

This chapter describes the underlying concepts of the value marketing method and how to perform value marketing. In support of this task, Blackblot introduces the "Blackblot Value-Marketing Model", a collective name for several work models and their supporting definitions. This model's components present, map and structure the process and different activities necessary to execute the value marketing method.

This chapter also builds on the concepts and terminology previously introduced in the "Who's Driving Your Company?", "Blackblot Product Management Team", and "Blackblot Concept of Marketing" chapters.

6.2 Value Concept

From a marketing perspective, "Value" is defined as the worth derived by the customer from owning and using the product. Attribution of value to a product is the outcome of a dynamic human reasoning process which infers from subjective interpretation the gap between the customer's perception of the product's quality, and the expenses incurred by the customer from buying and using the product.

G. Steinhardt, *The Product Manager's Toolkit*,
DOI 10.1007/978-3-642-04508-0_6, © Springer-Verlag Berlin Heidelberg 2010

Several different formulas were introduced over the years in an effort to explain and represent value. Some formulas are rudimentary and simple, and some are complex and may include cultural, emotional, social, mental and psychological coefficients to indicate the highly perceptive nature of value. In all cases, the value formulas are intuitive and/or mathematical expressions, and are sometimes erroneously called cost/benefit ratio, which is actually a financial term (financial return for each dollar invested).

The most basic value formula is **Value = Benefits − Costs[customer]**, where "Benefits" are product features that are desirable to the customer, and "Costs [customer]" are the aggregate expenses incurred by the customer from buying and using the product (essentially "Total Cost of Ownership" or TCO).

(Note: "Costs[customer]" are different than "Costs[manufacturer]", which are the aggregate expenses incurred by the manufacturer in the process of manufacturing, selling, and supporting the product.)

In a sales-driven company, the sales people wish to increase the product's value by lowering the price of the product, which is part of the costs[customer]. In a technology-driven company, the engineers wish to increase the product's value by inflating the product's feature set (benefits). In a market-driven company, the product's value is proactively determined by the product planner according to market needs.

Depending on how the value formula is applied, the outcome of the application can be either "Perceived Value", which is an unsubstantiated estimation of worth that the customer obtains or could potentially obtain from owning and using the product, or "Actual Value", which is the measured and validated worth that the customer or similar customers factually obtain from owning and using the product.

Customers will always prefer to base their decisions and opinions on actual value rather than perceived value, because actual value is inherently more realistic and somewhat more objective. Actual value is always based on actual components (actual benefits and actual costs[customer]). However, perceived value can either be based solely on perceived components, or on perceived and actual components. To create perceived value it is enough that one variable in the value formula is of the perceived type.

Ultimately, positive value (either actual or perceived) derived from owning and using a product is what customers seek and will pay for.

Table 6.1 summarizes the value concept definitions.

6.3   Value Formula Scale

The value formula holds three components (value, benefits, and costs), each of which is expressed on a different scale, yet can be intuitively compared via normalizing the scales.

Costs are predominantly defined in monetary terms, but can also be expressed in non-monetary terms. Benefits are amorphously defined as the usefulness or utility the product's features can provide. Accordingly, value can be expressed either on a monetary or utility (non-monetary) scale, or ostensibly both.

Table 6.1 Blackblot Value-Marketing Model – Value Concept Definitions (Summary Table)

Value formula	Value = Benefits − Costs[customer]
Value	Worth derived by the customer from owning and using the product
Benefits	Product features that are desirable to the customer
Costs[customer]	Aggregate expenses incurred by the customer from buying and using the product (essentially "Total Cost of Ownership" or TCO)
Perceived value	Unsubstantiated estimation of worth that the customer obtains or could potentially obtain from owning and using the product
Actual value	Measured and validated worth that the customer or similar customers factually obtain from owning and using the product
Product quality	Market's perception of the degree at which the product can consistently meet or exceed customers' expectations
Customers' expectations	Hopes for deriving benefits from the product and establishing a rewarding relationship with the vendor

Comparing variables of different scales is done by the customer via a very unscientific, intuitive process of converting one measurement scale to the measurement units of another scale. In practicality, this is done by either monetizing the product's utility (usefulness) units, or transforming an amount of money to utility units. Both transformations are based on the known utility that other alternative products can provide for that amount of money.

Depending on the given situation, value could therefore be expressed as a combination of monetary and/or non-monetary units of value, all of which could be completely subjective. Monetary units are considered intuitively easier to measure and justify than non-monetary units of value. Overall, value can be actual or perceived, tangible or intangible, and can be monetary, non-monetary, or a combination of both.

In a "Business to Consumer" (B2C – transaction of goods or services between businesses and private individuals) scenario, when dealing with consumer products which are used for personal gain, the more logical use of the value formula is by converting the costs element to utility units that can be compared to the value formula's benefits utility units. The resulting value is therefore subjectively and wholly expressed in utility units.

In a "Business to Business" (B2B – transaction of goods or services between businesses) scenario, when dealing with products which are used to perform business tasks to help make money, the more logical use of the value formula is by converting the value formula's benefits element to monetary units and comparing them directly with the costs element. The resulting value is subjectively expressed in monetary units.

Many products will hold both utility and monetary value, and both these forms of value scales will influence the customer to buy and continue using the product. However, it is cognitively difficult to jointly consider these two very different scales of value. Thus, the customer often focuses on one value scale as the key factor to consider, while the other value scale is regarded as an advantageous or positive (compelling) attribute. Again, value is something customers want and will pay for, no matter how it is expressed.

6.4   Value Concept Application

In most cases it is difficult for customers to calculate a monetary or non-monetary value amount. Customers will often rely on their intuition in an attempt to understand and realize the level of value the product holds for them.

Customers therefore first intuitively attribute a level of value to a product, relative to the degree in which the product solves the customers' market problem. The customers try to determine the degree of the product's "Resultant Value Proposition", which is an implicit promise a product holds for customers to deliver a fixed combination of gains in time, cost, and status. This proposition reflects the product's main and relevant benefit, in absolute terms, to the customer and is what primarily is needed of the product.

Common business oriented resultant value propositions, which are based on the benefits derived from features include: cost savings, improved usability, streamlined business processes, ability to perform entirely new tasks, automation of previously manual tasks, improved productivity, reduced rework, or conformance to standards or regulations.

Companies try to communicate the resultant value proposition to the customers and demonstrate that their products hold "Actual Resultant Value", which is a fixed combination of gains in time, cost, and status the product factually delivers to customers. Customers try to determine the type, relevancy, and magnitude of the resultant value proposition the product holds for them, and corroborate that with available information (public knowledge or own experience) about the actual value proposition.

After customers ascertain the type, relevancy, and magnitude of the resultant value proposition the product holds, they need to comprehend and compare to other products the value received in relative terms, proportionate to the costs. The "Relative Value Proposition" is an implicit promise a product holds for customers to deliver a desired ratio of benefits and costs[customer]. It is a notion that the customers use to differentiate products of seemingly similar value, although their respective absolute benefits and costs may be different.

Common relative value propositions, which are based on the ratio between benefits (features) and costs (TCO), include:

- Much more features for more TCO.
- More features for the same TCO.
- More features for less TCO.
- Same features for less TCO.
- Less features for much less TCO.

[Note: The term features is loosely interchangeable with benefits, and is used here for convenience only].

Companies try to communicate to customers the relative value proposition of their products and demonstrate that their products hold "Actual Relative Value", which is a ratio of benefits and costs[customer] the product factually delivers to customers. Customers try to determine whether the type of relative value proposition the product holds corresponds to their perception of quality, and corroborate the relative value proposition with the actual relative value.

Table 6.2 Blackblot Value-Marketing Model – Value Concept Application Definitions (Summary Table)

Resultant value proposition	Implicit promise a product holds for customers to deliver a fixed combination of gains in time, cost and status
Actual resultant value	Fixed combination of gains in time, cost and status the product factually delivers to customers
Relative value proposition	Implicit promise a product holds for customers to deliver a desired ratio of benefits and costs[customer]
Actual relative value	Ratio of benefits and costs[customer] the product factually delivers to customers
Perceived value formula	Perceived value = Resultant value proposition + Relative value proposition
Actual value formula	Actual value = Actual resultant value + Actual relative value

It is not exactly known which factors affect the psychological approach customers take to select the relative value proposition that they will wish for in the product, although financial viability is clearly an overriding factor. Companies may attempt to influence and shape the customers' desired relative value proposition, but it is ultimately the customer who decides which relative value proposition best fits them. However, if a company knows that its target market is comprised of customers with a definitive affinity to a particular relative value proposition, then that company can choose to offer a product with an actual value proposition that matches the particular relative value proposition being sought.

Traditionally, it has been considered that the relative value proposition of European products made by highly developed countries such as Switzerland or Germany is "much more features for more TCO". Goods from various developing Asian countries were often considered to have a relative value proposition of "less features for much less TCO", although this proposition is changing as these countries develop.

Perceived value is therefore the summation of the resultant value proposition and the relative value proposition. Accordingly, actual value is the summation of the actual resultant value and the actual relative value. These formulas can be expressed as:

Perceived Value = Resultant Value Proposition + Relative Value Proposition

Actual Value = Actual Resultant Value + Actual Relative Value

Table 6.2 summarizes the value concept application definitions.

6.5 Internal Value Marketing Dynamics

The ultimate goal of the value marketing method is to achieve "Superior Perceived Value", a state where customers perceive the product gives a net value more positive than its alternatives. Superior perceived value is essentially the manifestation of the

Table 6.3 Blackblot Value-Marketing Model – Value-Marketing Dynamics Definitions (Summary Table)

Superior perceived value	State where customers perceive the product gives a net value more positive than its alternatives
Superior actual value	State where the product factually gives customers a net value more positive than its alternatives

customer's belief in a powerful resultant value proposition coupled with an assumption that the product's relative value proposition level is what is being sought.

Companies try to create superior perceived value and prove "Superior Actual Value", a state where the product factually gives customers a net value more positive than its alternatives. In a market-driven company, the "Product Planner" in effect defines the product's value and the "Product Marketer" is tasked with presenting that value to the market in order to achieve superior perceived value.

From a more holistic perspective, companies go through a sequential process where they first attempt to uncover the existence of a market problem. The companies then verify the availability of a market opportunity, continue to build a product that will solve the market problem (essentially performing product planning, product definition, and product development), then create superior perceived value, and finally prove superior actual value. The latter part of the process is essentially executing value marketing activities to perform product marketing. If this process is done properly then the company would be able to realize the financial potential in the market opportunity.

Summarily, the value marketing method of product marketing tries to create superior perceived value and prove superior actual value.

Table 6.3 summarizes the value marketing dynamics definitions.

6.6 External Value Marketing Dynamics

In the customer's value estimation process, the value formula is initially used to ascertain if the product's perceived value is a positive figure (meaning the product has some explicit worth to the customer). At this point the customer also surmises the tangible and intangible facets of the purported value, such as cost-savings (tangible), morale, reputation, image or status improvement (intangible). This part of the process is completely intuitive.

After the customer has established that the product has some positive perceived value, the customer then attempts to realize and validate the type, relevancy, and magnitude of the product's resultant value proposition, and conjointly comprehend the product's relative value proposition.

The next step the customer takes is to try to factually quantify and qualify the specific type of value that the product actually holds. The customer now attempts to obtain information that would attest to the product's actual value. With the

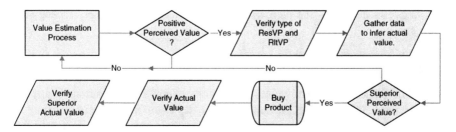

Fig. 6.1 External Value Marketing Dynamics

collected information the customer is able, with some degree of confidence, to infer the product's actual value.

The customer surveys the industry for competing products, and through information gleaned from the market, possibly concludes that the product has superior perceived value. The resulting action would be to purchase the product.

If the customer concludes that the product does not have superior perceived value, then the product would be deemed as unsuitable, and the customer's value estimation process will revert to the original starting point. The value estimation process would then restart and apply to a different product that potentially has superior perceived value.

After purchasing the product, through use and ongoing tracking, the customer can independently and empirically measure the product's actual value (actual resultant value and actual relative value).

Based on all this experience with the product and other market data about the experience others had with the product, the customer can realize whether the product indeed does or does not hold superior actual value.

The flowchart in Fig. 6.1 summarizes the external value marketing dynamics.

[Note: In the flowchart the term ResVP means resultant value proposition, and the term RltVP means relative value proposition.]

6.7 Creating Superior Perceived Value

The goal of the product marketing discipline is to generate product awareness, differentiation, and demand. The value emphasis method (value marketing) supports achieving that goal by creating superior perceived value, since superior perceived value is a major determining factor in the customer's buying decision. The following is a top-down explanation of the logics and process of creating superior perceived value.

Every method in product marketing is guided by strategies, which are documented in different plans within the marketing domain (see the "Blackblot Concept of Marketing" chapter). In the generic business sense, "Strategy" is the coordinated set of long-term decisions that help achieve corporate objectives. Every strategy has two goals:

1. Provide more value than the competition.
2. Help build a sustainable competitive advantage.

While value is a relatively complex concept, competitive advantage is a rather simple idea. "Competitive Advantage" is a depiction that the company or its products are each doing something better than their competition in a way that could benefit the customer.

Relative to value marketing, the most important plan which guides the course of marketing activities to follow is the market plan. "Market Plan" is a description of the long-term goals and messages delivered to the target market relative to a particular company or product. The market plan documents the market strategy, but when prepared in support of the product marketing discipline it also documents certain elements of the product strategy, which pertain to building a product competitive advantage.

The "Market Strategy" is decisions that define target markets, set marketing objectives, and outline how to build a corporate competitive advantage. The "Product Strategy", which is decisions that build and enhance products to fit market needs, and outline how to build a product competitive advantage.

In accordance with the goals of the contained market and product strategies, the market plan outlines marketing messages about the value and competitive advantage of the product, while simultaneously being synchronized with the corporate competitive advantage. Building a competitive advantage at either the corporate or product level is accomplished through devotion to quality.

As mentioned previously and from a marketing perspective, "Quality" is the market's perception of the degree at which the company or product can consistently meet or exceed customers' expectations. "Customers' Expectations" are the hopes for deriving benefits from the product and establishing a rewarding relationship with the vendor.

Therefore, exceeding the hopes of the customers in deriving benefits from the product will yield a product competitive advantage, and exceeding the hopes of the customers in establishing a rewarding relationship with the vendor will yield a corporate competitive advantage. Customer expectations management is really about a promise a company makes to its customers. *A promise of quality.*

The promise of corporate quality, and the origin of a corporate competitive advantage, is when the company delivers a relationship more rewarding than the customers had expected to receive. This promise is conveyed to the customers primarily via corporate marketing activities.

The promise of product quality, and the origin of a corporate competitive advantage, is when the product delivers more benefits than the customers had expected to get. This promise is conveyed to the customers primarily via product marketing activities.

The embedded conclusion is that market strategy also states the reward which customers get from establishing a relationship with the company; and that the product strategy also depicts specific benefits, perceived as quality, which customers get by owning and using the product.

Competitive advantage is based on quality, and so it can be deduced that an overall competitive advantage the market perceives will hinge upon both corporate quality and product quality. Accordingly, the (overall) competitive advantage formula can be represented as the summation of quality values:

$$\text{Competitive Advantage} = \text{Corporate Quality} + \text{Product Quality}$$

If the product holds positive value (perceived or actual) and the company has an overall competitive advantage, then the market could perceive that the value provided by the company and its product is more than the value provided by the competitors. This state is called superior perceived value and it can be presented as an intuitive formula:

$$\text{Superior Perceived Value} = \text{Competitive Advantage} + \text{Value}$$

Superior perceived value is the condition which value marketing strives to achieve. This condition is attained by distilling information and data about the overall competitive advantage and product value in to messages that are communicated to the target market. The messages attempt to influence customers to form an opinion that the product gives a net value more positive than its alternatives. Superior perceived value is thus achieved once that opinion is formed.

Table 6.4 summarizes the definitions related to the logics and process of creating superior perceived value.

Table 6.4 Blackblot Value-Marketing Model – Creating Superior Perceived Value (Summary Table)

Strategy	Coordinated set of long-term decisions that help achieve corporate objectives. Every strategy has two goals: 1. Provide more value than the competition 2. Help build a sustainable competitive advantage
Competitive advantage	Depiction that the company or its products are each doing something better than their competition in a way that could benefit the customer
Market plan	Description of the long-term goals and messages delivered to the target market relative to a particular company or product
Market strategy	Decisions that define target markets, set marketing objectives, and outline how to build a corporate competitive advantage
Product strategy	Decisions that build and enhance products to fit market needs and outline how to build a product competitive advantage
Quality	Market's perception of the degree at which the company or product can consistently meet or exceed customers' expectations
Customers' expectations	Hopes for deriving benefits from the product and establishing a rewarding relationship with the vendor
Competitive advantage formula	Competitive Advantage = Corporate Quality + Product Quality
Superior perceived value formula	Superior Perceived Value = Competitive Advantage + Value

Fig. 6.2 Schematic Presentation and Relationships of the Entities That Help Build Superior Perceived Value

The diagram in Fig. 6.2 schematically presents the relationship between the entities that help build superior perceived value.

6.8   Product Marketing Messages

Product marketing is aimed at generating product awareness, differentiation and demand for a particular product.

Creating differentiation is accomplished via the communication of positioning messages which attempt to affect the customer's perception of a product or service as compared to its competition. "Positioning" is the customer's unique psychological placement of the relative qualities of a product or company with respect to its competitors.

Stimulating demand is influenced via the communication of value messages that convey to the customer the product's value propositions – the worth derived from owning and using the product. Establishing product awareness is a by-product of issuing the positioning messages and the value messages.

Messages are ideas to be communicated, often corroborated by facts, yet foundational knowledge is required in order to formulate messages. Foundational knowledge for preparing positioning messages is primarily the positioning statement that was crafted for the product and the product's sales axioms (see the product positioning and sales axioms templates in the "Blackblot Product Manager's Toolkit™" (PMTK)). The foundational knowledge required for preparing value messages is more elaborate.

6.9   Value Messages' Foundational Knowledge

The foundational knowledge to build value messages is based on the product's different value propositions, quality factors, and the product's unique selling proposition.

The "Unique Selling Proposition" (USP) is a key statement that describes the distinct and compelling value of the product, which sets the product apart from other competing products. The USP concept relates to the product's unique value asset, as it is both a competitive differentiator and a source of worth to the customer. The USP concept is therefore loosely related to the value concept. The same notion can be applied to a company and that is referred to as distinctive competency or "Core Competency", which is a company's unique ability to deliver value while differentiating itself from the competition.

Regarding quality factors, customers often consider the following elements as a signal that depicts **corporate quality**:

- Honesty – fair pricing.
- Facilitation – attention to convenience.
- Assistance – dedication to customer service.
- Caring – dedication to customer satisfaction.

Customers often consider the following elements as a signal that depicts **product quality**:

- Usability – ease of operation.
- Productivity – scope of useful features.
- Longevity – how long a product lasts.
- Reliability – how long before breakdowns.
- Durability – how long without degradation.

Customers often consider the following elements as a signal that depicts **service quality**:

- Tangibles – equipment, facilities, and people.
- Responsiveness – promptness in helping.
- Reliability – promising and delivering.
- Assurance and empathy – caring attitude.

Based on the above, the following are the six "Value and Quality Factors" which build superior perceived value and which will be used as foundational knowledge to create value messages:

1. Promise of Corporate Quality.
2. Promise of Product Quality.
3. Company Core Competency.
4. Resultant Value Proposition.
5. Relative Value Proposition.
6. Unique Selling Proposition.

Table 6.5 presents hypothetical examples of the value and quality factors for different types of companies.

Logically, the "Promise of Corporate Quality" and the "Company Core Competency" factors are foundational knowledge elements that are used for corporate branding via corporate marketing activities. These corporate-related value and

Table 6.5 Examples of the Value and Quality Factors for Different Types of Companies

Company Type	Large Software Company	Large Consultancy Firm
Promise of corporate quality	Fair pricing	Responsiveness
Promise of product quality	Functionality	Comprehensiveness
Company core competency	Distribution	Business knowledge
Resultant value proposition	Increased productivity	Efficiency
Relative value proposition	Same features for less TCO	More features for same TCO
Unique selling proposition	Usability (Better UI)	Pragmatism

quality factors are listed so they can be referenced, and care taken to ensure they are synchronized (and do not contradict) with the other product-related value and quality factors.

The foundational knowledge, once established, will be used to aid creating marketing messages. These messages will be communicated to the target market via a messaging model and plan.

6.10   PMTK Market Messaging Model

The "PMTK Market Messaging Model" is a collective name for three sub-model components:

1. PMTK Product Positioning Messages Model.
2. PMTK Product Value Messages Model.
3. PMTK Marketing Messages Model and Plan.

The product positioning messages must reflect a product feature or capability and the derived benefit to the customer, relative to the market problem. Building product positioning messages is done by first establishing a product positioning statement (such as Regis McKenna's two-sentence positioning statement), defining three to four key marketing messages that reinforce the product positioning statement, and providing two to three data points that validate each key marketing message. Each data point must be based on measurable, objective, factual, provable information, and each message must be supported with data points the customer can actually verify.

The diagram in Fig. 6.3 schematically presents the product positioning messages model.

The product value messages must reflect a perceived monetary or material or psycho-social worth that the customers shall gain from owning and using the product. Building product value messages is done by first establishing the product's six value and quality factors, defining three to four key marketing messages that convey the product's value and quality factors, and providing two to three data points that validate each key marketing message. The diagram in Fig. 6.4 schematically presents the product value messages model.

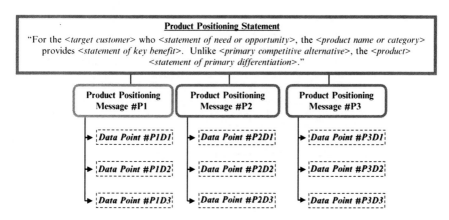

Fig. 6.3 Product Positioning Messages Model

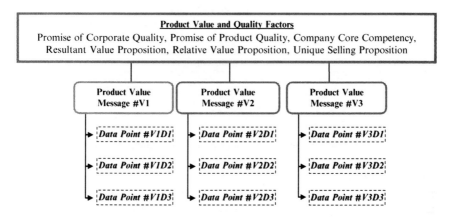

Fig. 6.4 Product Value Messages Model

6.11 PMTK Marketing Messages Model and Plan

The PMTK marketing messages model and plan provide guidance for the manner of which the marketing messages will be introduced to the target market.

Table 6.6 describes the elements of the PMTK marketing messages model.

Once determined, the elements of PMTK marketing messages model form a plan that guides the marketing activities. Table 6.7 presents an example of a PMTK marketing messages plan.

The PMTK marketing messages plan is the last step in implementing the value marketing method. It contains all the high-level content that is necessary to perform any type of promotional activities on behalf of the product.

The marketing messages plan is provided to all relevant internal departments and external partners who will operationally communicate the marketing messages to the

Table 6.6 Blackblot Value-Marketing Model – PMTK Marketing Messages Model

Messages	Ideas to be communicated
Media	Selection of media vehicles that will be employed to communicate the messages, including: public relations, advertising, sales, electronic marketing, direct marketing, telemarketing, (key selection factors: reach, frequency, and impact)
Schedule	The marketing messages frequency of appearance along a timeline. Common schedules include: continuous (ongoing and uninterrupted marketing messages exposures), intervals (periods of marketing messages exposures that are regularly interspaced), and blink (very brief marketing messages exposures that are irregularly interspaced)
Sequencing	Order and pattern of presenting the marketing messages
Proof support	Rotation of data point inclusion

Table 6.7 Blackblot Value-Marketing Model – PMTK Marketing Messages Plan (Example)

Messages	Message_A, Message_B, Message_C
Media	Print advertising and telemarketing
Schedule	Continuous/60days, intervals (on/12day-off/7days)
Sequencing	Order (Message_C, Message_A, Message_B)
	Pattern (2* Message_C, 1* Message_A, 3* Message_B)
Proof support	Rotate data point every third exposure

target market. These partners specifically include: marketing communications, corporate marketing, analyst relations, investor relations, public relations and advertising firms.

The messages in the PMTK marketing messages plan will be "wrapped" and embedded into media vehicles, such as advertisements. The messages will also be conceptually reflected in all possible visual and written elements of the product such as: packaging, logo, tagline, user manual, and tutorials.

6.12 Summary

This chapter described the underlying concepts of the value marketing method, a part of the product marketing discipline of the marketing domain, and outlined how to perform value marketing through the use of marketing messages.

As with any marketing method, results are not guaranteed. This is because marketing methods attempt to foretell and alter human behavior, and therefore their outcome is most challenging and least predictable. Marketing is an inexact science and since humans are considered emotional and irrational by their own fabric, the results of all marketing activities are probabilistic and unpredictable, and typically there are no definitive best practices.

By understanding the concepts, definitions and structures introduced in this chapter, those responsible for marketing now have a complete and clear framework for creating marketing messages that pertain to the product's positioning and value propositions.

Carefully formed clear and targeted marketing messages are the basis for virtually all promotions, communications, advertising, sales, and other marketing activities. These messages will help promote a more efficient use and management of the company's marketing function with the aim of properly appealing to potential customers. The outcome will be marketplace success.

Chapter 7
Extending Product Life Cycle Stages

Exploring the Product Life Cycle Model and Ways to Extend the Life of a Product

7.1 Introduction

Businesses are always seeking better ways to grow profits and maximize revenue from the sale of products or services. Revenue allows a company to maintain viability, invest in new product development and improve its workforce; all in an effort to acquire additional market share and become a leader in its respective industry.

A consistent and sustainable revenue stream from product sales is key to any long-term investment, and the best way to attain a stable revenue stream is a "Cash Cow"[1] product. Cash cows are leading products that command a large market share in mature markets. Cash cows display a "Return On Investment" (ROI) that is greater than the market growth rate, and thus produce more cash than they consume. The question is therefore: How can a company develop a cash cow product? One way of doing so is by applying relevant product planning and/or product marketing strategies, a.k.a. competitive moves, at the various stages that make a "Product Life Cycle" (PLC).

The PLC Model is a relatively new theory which identifies the distinct stages affecting sales of a product, from the product's inception until its retirement. Companies that successfully recognized those stages and subsequently applied a custom "Marketing Mix" (combination of product, pricing, promotion, and place [distribution] activities) at each stage, were able to sustain sales and defend or win market share. By deliberately extending the length of time spent at each of the PLC stages through different tactics, companies were also able to realize much of the revenue potential a product can offer.

---

[1]The BCG Growth Share Matrix Boston Consulting Group, www.bcg.com

G. Steinhardt, *The Product Manager's Toolkit*,
DOI 10.1007/978-3-642-04508-0_7, © Springer-Verlag Berlin Heidelberg 2010

7.2 Product Life Cycle Model Assumptions

At the core of the PLC Model are the following simple assumptions:

- All products have limited life spans.
- Product sales pass through different and distinct stages.
- Each stage presents a different challenge, which calls for the application of a customized marketing mix.

7.3 Product Life Cycle Model Stages

A PLC is traditionally viewed, from a marketing perspective, as being comprised of four distinct stages: Introduction, Growth, Maturity and Decline.

In the "Introduction" stage, the product is introduced to the market through a focused and intense marketing effort designed to establish a clear identity and promote maximum awareness. Many trial or impulse purchases will occur at this stage. Next, consumer interest will bring about the "Growth" stage, distinguished by increasing sales and the emergence of competitors. The "Growth" stage is also characterized by sustaining marketing activities on the vendor's side, with consumers engaged in repeat purchase behavior patterns. Arrival of the product's "Maturity" stage is evident when competitors begin to leave the market, sales velocity is dramatically reduced, and sales volume reaches a steady state. At this point in time, mostly loyal consumers purchase the product. Continuous decline in sales signals entry into the "Decline" stage. The lingering effects of competition, unfavorable economic conditions, new fashion trends, etc. often explain the decline in sales (Fig. 7.1).

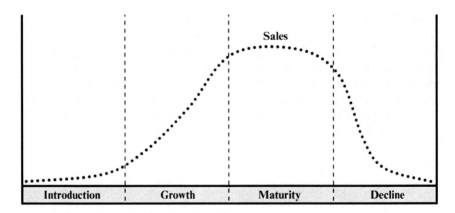

Fig. 7.1 Timeline and PLC Stages

7.4   Reasons for Extending the PLC

Understanding and extending the PLC stages allows a company to fully exploit market opportunities, and defend or establish a competitive advantage through a lasting market presence. The main business reason for extending the PLC is to gain more sales through longer presence in the marketplace. The main marketing reason is since not all consumers are alike; certain consumer types will adopt a product at different stages of the product life cycle. By extending each stage of the PLC there is a better chance of exposure to the relevant consumer group. Extending the PLC should not be confused with extending the life of the product, which applies to enhanced durability, reliability or technical quality.

7.5   Strategies for Extending the PLC

The nature and type of applicable strategies to extend the PLC will vary with each stage, and the level of variation depends on the product type, market conditions, consumer audience and projected PLC timeline. It is hard to predict a transition from one PLC stage to another (because of measurement lags) and proactively react to the change with targeted action. However, through proper marketing mix design and contingency planning, it is possible to apply various product planning and product marketing strategies at the beginning of a particular stage when it arrives. The underlying approach with any of the strategies is Targeted Improvement.[2]

7.6   Product Planning Strategies for Extending the PLC

* Product Diversification – Creating different product variants.

Microsoft's family of Windows 9x operating systems allowed the software giant to continuously extend the life cycle of this desktop computer operating system. Windows 95, Windows 98, Windows 98SE, and Windows ME are among the better-known variants. Coca-Cola's vanilla flavored drink is an example and a variant to the venerable Classic Coca-Cola drink.

* New Product Uses – Applying the core product to different uses.

Apple Computer has been very innovative and successful by finding additional uses for its Macintosh computer, such as desktop publishing and strong graphics/animation capabilities. Apple's Digital Hub concept extends the Macintosh's functionality even further to serve as a center for managing

---

[2]The PDMA HandBook of New Product Development, Milton D. Rosenau.

multimedia files from cameras, DV recorders, scanners, and MP3 devices.[3] On the retail side, in the world of "Consumer Packaged Goods" (CPG), Arm and Hammer had devised over several decades a multitude of deodorizing uses for their core product, baking soda.

- Changing Product Layers – Altering the product features and creating different product families.

Hewlett-Packard's InkJet and LaserJet printers are examples of product families that share the same technological core. In addition are Jell-O's product families of puddings, colored gelatins, and snacks which are all based on raw gelatin.

7.7   Product Marketing Strategies for Extending the PLC

- Re-Positioning – Changing the product's perceived values and intent in the mind of the consumer.

Microsoft's Windows NT was designed as a multi-tasking, multi-threaded, multi-functional desktop operating system. It was based on work done by Microsoft for IBM's OS/2 and in terms of its feature set resembled Unix more than it did Novell's NetWare. NetWare, a "Network Operating System" (NOS) and Novell's flagship product dominated the File&Print server market in the early 1990s to the tune of 75% market share. Through massive and prolonged positioning efforts, Microsoft was able to persuade corporate information technology departments that Windows NT could be more than just a powerful desktop operating system, and could replace NetWare as the departmental File&Print server. Novell tried unsuccessfully to shield NetWare from Windows NT by attempting to position UnixWare (Novell's Unix based operating system) against Windows NT.[4]

- Co-Branding – Enhancing (or diluting) the product's brand equity by association with another strong brand.

In an attempt to boost sales, IBM announced in 2001 a joint effort with J.D. Edwards and Company to market a specialized IBM eServer called the IBM eServer for J.D. Edwards, optimized to run J.D. Edwards' collaborative commerce software for small to medium size businesses. These types of co-branding initiatives are nearly always an attempt to capitalize on synergy between brands and products.

- Re-Packaging – Literally placing the product in a new package as to revive its appeal.

---

[3]Welcome to the digital lifestyle – Apple's Digital hub, www.apple.com/imac/digitalhub.html

[4]Networking Wars: Is Novell Finally Finished?, By Robyn Weisman, www.newsfactor.com/perl/story/17803.html

This is common practice in retail markets with the introduction of new labels, different container sizes and different container types, such as Colgate's toothpaste in a tube or pump dispenser. In the computer software world, virtual repackaging is done through the introduction of a new visual "Graphical User Interface" (GUI) while application functionality remains relatively unchanged.

- Re-Branding – A drastic and costly measure used to disassociate the brand from the previous values with which the brand has been associated.

The key concern with such a move is maintaining existing market share. For example, in 2000, IBM re-branded its eCommerce software application, Net.Commerce to WebSphere Commerce. It also re-branded its line of servers as eServer (formerly Netfinity). This was an attempt by IBM to make a fresh entry and position itself as a competitor in the world of Unix and Intel based servers dominated by Sun Microsystems and Dell Computers. Sometimes companies re-brand themselves in an effort to build new reputation and brand equity – Datsun/Nissan vehicles, Borland/Inprise software products, and GTE/Verizon telecomm services.

- Increasing Frequency of Use – Encouraging consumers to break away from traditional molds of product usage.

Chivas Regal was always considered a fine Scotch whisky to be consumed on special occasions such as weddings, or given as a gift. Through a worldwide advertising campaign, Chivas was able to increase consumption by delivering a consistent message about the brand's broader appeal.

- New Markets and Segments – This strategy is an attempt to penetrate non-traditional markets or consumer segments.

Companies are able through exploratory research to discover the potential of geographically remote markets (Asia, Africa, and former Soviet Bloc) or new consumer segments (seniors, minorities, and women). During 2001, Subaru specifically targeted women as a new automotive consumer segment, realizing their strong potential as first-owner buyers.

- Pricing and Special Offers – Pricing is a positioning tool and a way to influence sales through the use of various price, payment schemes and models.

Price manipulation can take place at all stages of the PLC, including the "Introduction" phase. For example, only six months after its launch in November 2001, Microsoft reduced the price of the xBox game console in North-America by about 30%.

7.8 Strategy Application within the PLC Model

Planning which product planning and product marketing strategies to apply, and when, should be part of any long-term approach. Since there are so many diverse products, markets and companies, it is difficult to provide a definitive, single methodology for strategy selection and application.

Table 7.1 Strategy Application within the PLC Model

Introduction	Growth	Maturity	Decline
• Increasing frequency of use • Pricing	• Product diversification • New product uses • Changing product layers • Pricing	• Re-packaging • Co-branding • Product diversification • New product uses • Pricing	• Re-branding • Re-positioning • Increasing frequency of use • New markets and segments • Pricing

However, some general guidelines can be followed to help ensure marketing mix effectiveness in promoting a PLC stage extension. Once a decision to extend a PLC stage has been made, the following elements must be factored into the planning:

- The company's product line's business strategy – leader, follower, innovator.
- The company's marketing policies – soft or hard product launches, traditional choice of media vehicles, pricing policies, sales channels selection, etc.
- External constraints – government regulations, distribution networks, cultural barriers, politics, tariffs and taxes, etc.

Sometimes a certain strategy may seem applicable to all PLC stages. Price manipulation is an example of something that can be used at all stages of the PLC to help influence sales and serve as a flexible way to rapidly react to competition. The drawback of repeatedly applying a certain strategy or using several strategies at once is that it may confuse the consumers. Exercising any such combined approach should be well justified.

Table 7.1 notes the strategies considered most applicable to their respective PLC stage.

7.9 Limitations of the PLC Model

It is difficult to foresee transitions in PLC stages since the key indicator are sales which are always calculated with some lag. Therefore, the realization that a stage transition has occurred is nearly always in retrospect. In addition, fluctuations in sales will produce erroneous conclusions, therefore declining sales do not necessary mean the product has reached the decline phase and the resulting conclusion to retire the product and divert resources is wrong.

Products, companies and markets are different; therefore not all products or services go through every stage of the PLC. There have been many cases where products have gone straight from introduction to decline, usually because of bad marketing, misconceived features, lack of value to the consumer or simply a lack of need for such a product. However, even if products would go through every stage of the PLC, not all products and services spend the same length of time at each stage. This adds another level of complexity in determining which PLC stage the product is in and consequently, which strategy to apply.

Finally, the PLC Model is inefficient when dealing with brands or services. "Brand" is an identity, made of symbols and ideas, which portray a specific offering from a known source. Brands apply to both companies and products. Brands have a life cycle of their own, and products belonging to a certain brand will experience a very different life cycle than the brand itself. For example, Dell and Mercedes-Benz are very strong brands whose life cycle is marginally affected by the failure of any of the products which they hold. Apple Computer's Lisa, Newton (market failures) and iMac (market success) are proof that brands and products have different PLC's although they are closely related.[5]

7.10   Benefits of the PLC Model

Managers are always in need of predictive tools to help them navigate a seemingly chaotic market, and the PLC Model gives managers the ability to forecast product directions on a macro level, and plan for timely execution of relevant competitive moves.

Coupled with actual sales data, the PLC Model can also be used as an explanatory tool in facilitating an understanding of past and future sales progression. The PLC Model aids in making sense of past events as part of any extrapolatory and interpretive approach to building strategy. Once a product strategy or product line strategy has been formulated, the PLC Model can be used as part of an ongoing strategy validation process, since it reflects on market trends, customer issues and technological advancement.

Companies always anticipate the emergence of new competitors and therefore must prepare in advance to battle the competition and strengthen their product's position. The PLC Model is advantages in planning long-term offensive marketing strategies, particularly when markets and economies are stable. Nevertheless, most products die and once products are dead they hold no substantial revenue potential and represent a toll on a company's resources. By combining the elements of time, sales volume and notion of evolutionary stages, the PLC Model helps determine when it becomes reasonable to eliminate dead products.

7.11   Conclusion

Keeping a product alive for decades is a sign of successful PLC extensions, and brand/product combinations such as Heinz Ketchup, Hershey Chocolate and Gillette's Safety Razor are clear indicators of such extensions. Through consistent PLC management, a company will be able to improve products and become a marketplace leader. The role of the product marketing department is to understand the Product Life Cycle theory and identify the critical PLC stages. This will aid the

---

[5]Product Life Cycle Management, AICPA, www.aicpa.org/cefm/plcm/index.htm

planning and execution of an effective marketing mix, designed to support business (revenue, profit) and marketing (market share, loyalty, growth) objectives.

The PLC Model can and has been effectively used by business managers to support decision-making at every stage of a product's life cycle. Although the PLC Model itself is subject to many interpretations with some advocates theorizing five or even six stages, it will always remain fairly flexible and adaptive to many product categories.

The PLC Model is yet another tool managers have when dealing with dynamic and complex situations that abound in the world of proactive product planning and product marketing.

Chapter 8
Product Management Glossary

Clear Definitions that Establish a Common Understanding, Better Internal Cooperation, and Standard Corporate Processes

8.1 Product Management Terms and Definitions

Term	Definition
Actual relative value	The ratio of benefits and costs(customer) the product factually delivers to customers
Actual resultant value	A fixed combination of gains in time, cost and status the product factually delivers to customers
Actual value	The measured and validated worth that the customer or similar customers factually obtain from owning and using the product
Actual value formula	Actual value = actual resultant value + actual relative value
Advertising	Non-personal communication from an identified sponsor using mass media
Allowances (Pricing)	A conditional refund only in form of a deduction from the list price in exchange for customer action. Allowances are often accomplished in two forms: Trade-in (Pricing) – An item of property given in part payment upon purchase. Rebate (Pricing) – Customer receives reimbursement for a portion of the purchase price, in exchange for customer information
Analyst relations	The bi-directional information exchange with financial analysts and industry analysts to inform and favorably influence them
Bait pricing	Pricing that aims to attract customers with low prices with intent to sell higher priced items
Base price	Initial price of a product before any alteration
BDM buyer	"Business Decision Maker" buyer. The person who has the ultimate decision making power to purchase a product or not
Benefits	Product features that are desirable to the customer
Blackblot product frames model	A descriptive model that demonstrates how product functionality is built and how, in total, the product solves the market problem
Blackblot Product Manager's Toolkit™ (PMTK)	PMTK is a comprehensive set of tools and accompanying methodology, that illustrates notable best practices and processes which help create successful market-driven products

(continued)

G. Steinhardt, *The Product Manager's Toolkit*,
DOI 10.1007/978-3-642-04508-0_8, © Springer-Verlag Berlin Heidelberg 2010

Term	Definition
Brand	An identity, made of symbols and ideas, which portray a specific offering from a known source
Business case	Examination of a potential market opportunity on a product level
Business competence	Set of professional skills and knowledge that relate directly to performing product management
Business development	Actions that improve the performance of the enterprise, its access to markets, and its ability to compete by creating strategic relationships with logistical, content and technological partners
Business plan	Examination of a potential business opportunity on a company level
Business products	Products intended for resale, for use in producing other products, or for providing services in an organization. Business Products are used for making money
Business strategy	Decisions that support being a leader, follower or innovator in a specific line of business
Business to business	The transaction of goods or services between businesses (B2B)
Business to consumer	The transaction of goods or services between businesses and private individuals (B2C)
Buyer	The entity that decides to obtain the product
Captive product (Pricing Tactic)	An imbalanced price ratio between product's components which are sold separately. The main system component is under-priced and the consumables or support services are over-priced. The "Captive Product" pricing tactic can be quickly and easily accomplished via product system decoupling
Client	The entity that is the receiver of goods or services
Company core competency	A company's unique ability to deliver value, while differentiating itself from the competition
Competitive advantage	A depiction that the company or its products are each doing something better than their competition in a way that could benefit the customer
Competitive advantage formula	Competitive advantage = corporate quality + product quality
Conditional license	Expiring ownership and usage rights to a product. Can be renewable and non-renewable
Consumer	An individual or household that buy and use goods and services created by industries
Consumer problem	A marketplace situation in which consumer needs remain unsatisfied (B2C). The solution is a whole product
Consumer products	Products intended for use by household consumers for non-business purposes. Consumer Products are used for personal gain
Consumers	Individuals or households that buy and use goods and services created by industries
Corporate branding	The process of building and maintaining a brand at the institutional level
Corporate marketing	An outbound activity aimed at generating awareness and differentiation to the company
Corporate mission statement	A formal statement that a company makes about their reason for existing and briefly describes the company's general

(*continued*)

Term	Definition
	business direction and depiction of the value customers should expect to receive
Corporate quality	A state in which the company delivers a relationship more rewarding than customers expected
Corporate vision statement	A message that summarizes the company's purpose and intent and describes how, in the future, its products and activities shall affect the world
Costs(Customer)	The aggregate expenses incurred by the customer from buying and using the product (essentially Total Cost of Ownership or TCO)
Credibility	The quality of being believable or trustworthy
Credit terms	Schedule for delayed payment(s)
Customer	The entity (consumer or company) that takes (financial) responsibility for purchasing the product. Often the realm to which the buyer and user belong
Customers expectations	The hopes for deriving benefits from the product and establishing a rewarding relationship with the vendor
Demand (Economics)	Quantity of a product that will be bought in the market at various prices for a specified period
Demand (Marketing)	Wants for specific products coupled by an ability to pay for them. The demand formula is Demand = Want + Buying Power
Demand-based pricing (Pricing Tactic)	Rapidly adjust prices per customer according to market characteristics
Derived price	Price that is determined based on attributed benefit
Disclaimer	Denial of responsibility to events occurring during product ownership to discourage current or future legal action
Discrimination (Pricing Tactic)	Charging different market segments with different prices for same product. There are several levels of discrimination: First Level – Price discrimination that is based on the ability to pay (charge per income). Second level – Price discrimination that is based on artificial obstacles (same price yet coupons, advance purchase, restricted use). Third level – Price discrimination that is based on external factors (gender, age, geography, or profession)
Diversification (Pricing Tactic)	Creating product variants with distributed price points
Domain expertise	Knowledge in the technical and business aspects of the product, industry, market, and technology
Durability (Product)	How long the product maintains a level of performance without degradation
Dynamic pricing (Pricing Tactic)	Rapidly adjust prices per customer according to customer characteristics
End-user license agreement (EULA)	Perimeters of usage and ownerships rights granted to the customer
Expert	A user that has considerable experience with the product and utilizes many advanced features (power user)
Functional expertise	Knowledge in processes, tools, and techniques to plan/market products
Global discount	Universal, non-discriminatory, non-conditional deduction from the list price, for enticement purposes
Goods	Tangible products we can possess. Segmented to durable and non-durable

(*continued*)

Term	Definition
Graphic arts	The conception and copywriting of all collateral material
High-tech company	A business entity that either develops technology that is incorporated in a product or is used in the assembly or manufacturing of a product, or manufactures a product that contains technology and that same product relies on that technology to perform its core function
Impact	A positive or negative consequence that will most likely occur when embarking on a product development and delivery project
Industry	A group of companies which produce and sell a particular product type
Innovation	The introduction of a product that is new or substantially improved. Innovation is the process of converting and commercializing an invention into a product
Innovation (Formula)	Innovation = Invention + Utilization
Invention	An idea which represents a revolutionary or evolutionary change. Invention is an idea that improves an existing solution or offers a conceptually new solution to a problem
Licensing	A method of providing rights to usage and ownership to a product, for a specified price and/or term
Licensing mix	A combination of perpetual and term licenses relative to a particular product
Longevity (Product)	How long a product lasts
Loss leader	A product that is priced below cost to attract consumers to buy other items
Management by objectives (MBO)	A systematic approach for instilling flow and structure in one's work by setting clear, achievable, measurable and challenging goals
Manufacturer	The entity that produces the product or service
Margins	Direct financial gains by selling
Market intelligence	An ongoing real-time market data collection and analysis process. Market intelligence builds a body of knowledge
Market opportunity	A lucrative, lasting and sizable market problem. Market Problem + Volume + Duration + Earning Potential = Market Opportunity
Market plan	A description of the long-term goals and messages delivered to the target market relative to a particular company or product
Market problem	A "consumer", "product" or "technology" problem in the target market
Market requirement	An aggregate unit of information which represents with sufficient detail the functionality that is sought to address a specific facet of a particular market problem
Market requirements document (MRD)	A written representation of the overall functionality that users seek in order to address a particular market problem
Market segmentation	A division of the overall market for a product, into groups of common characteristics
Market strategy	Decisions that define target markets, set marketing objectives, and outline how to build a corporate competitive advantage
Market-driven	A product delivery strategy that is based on producing and delivering products that the market needs
Marketing	An instructive business domain that serves to inform and educate target markets about the value and competitive advantage of a company and its products

(*continued*)

Term	Definition
Marketing communications	The employment of a mix of media vehicles that support marketing objectives
Marketing mix	A combination of product, price, place (distribution), and promotion activities that are applied to a particular target market
Marketing plan	A description of the selection and application of marketing mixes in the target market
Marketing program	A short-term marketplace effort designed to obtain a specific marketing goal
Marketing strategy	The decisions that determine how to achieve marketing's goal in a particular target market, through the selection and application of marketing mixes
MSRP	The price the manufacturer recommends that the seller offers the product for. MSRP = Manufacturer's Suggested Retail Price
Need	A state of felt deprivation (condition or motivation in which something is sought after to affect a change)
Niche market	A small overall market or small market segment
Novice	A user that is new to the product (newbie)
Odd/even pricing	Ending the price with certain numbers to influence buyers' perceptions of the price or product
Onetime fee (Licensing)	A onetime fixed charge that enables constant use of the product
Overall market	All customers who share a common need
Payment	The actual economic sacrifice a customer makes to acquire certain rights to a product
Payment forms	Means of payment such as cash, credit card, check, or wire transfer
Payment terms	Payment conditions as currency type, letter of credit and purchase prerequisites
Penetration (Pricing Tactic)	Briefly charging a relatively low price upon product launch
Perceived value	An unsubstantiated estimation of worth that the customer obtains or could potentially obtain from owning and using the product
Perceived value formula	Perceived value = resultant value proposition + relative value proposition
Perpetual license	Non-expiring ownership and usage rights to a product
Personal competence	The set of individual personality traits which enable individuals to manage themselves independently and capably
PMTK MVP model	A market-value centric pricing process which guides sets of managerial decisions that help determine a product's price. The "PMTK MVP Model" is comprised of three distinct components that effectively act as sequential stages in the pricing process: Pricing Scheme, Pricing Formula, and Price Mix
Positioning	The customer's unique psychological placement of the relative qualities of a product or company with respect to its competitors
Price	A specification of what a seller wants in exchange for granting right of ownership or use to a product. The price formula is Price = Costs + Margins
Price discounts	Deductions from the list price

(continued)

Term	Definition
Price elasticity of demand	Percentage change in quantity demanded that occurs in response to a percentage change in price
Price lining	Pricing of products in a product family with corresponding price points
Price mix	A price related aggregate of information and conditions that the customer is presented with
Price modifiers	Conditional deduction from the list price
Price psychology	Dynamic human reasoning process which infers from a product's price, price comparisons and price changes, diverse messages about the product and company; and accordingly influences buying decisions
Price reductions	Universal, non-discriminatory and non-conditional official list price decreases
Price variables	Price changes based on product characteristics
Pricing	The act of setting a price
Pricing formula	A calculatory structure that allows the application of pricing changes to specific markets or competitive regions
Pricing objectives	A description of what a company wants to achieve through pricing its products
Pricing scheme	An outline of the overall pricing approach which encompasses the principles for pricing the specific product
Pricing strategies	The primary method to pricing that relies on a particular pricing decision factor
Pricing tactics	Pricing actions which are dependent on the particular life cycle stage of the product that is being priced
Problem	A difficulty. A situation that requires change
Product	Any offering that satisfies needs. Represents a collection of tangible and intangible assets
Product attribute	A real characteristic or property of the product
Product branding	The process of building and maintaining a brand at the product level
Product bundling	An aggregate of products sold collectively at a price that is lower than the sum of their prices. The price of the set of products is lower than the total of individual products. Bundling is often accomplished in two forms: Direct Bundling – Customer must buy the entire package. Indirect Bundling – Customer cannot buy product X without also buying Y, in fixed proportions
Product category or class (ification)	A term synonymous to "product line" in the context of competing products
Product family	A set of derived products that share the same technological foundation. Members of a product family are called "product variants"
Product feature	A product capability that satisfies a specific user/buyer need
Product group	A set of products coupled or packaged together to form a new unified offering. Members of a product group are called "product members"
Product line	A set of products that are technologically different yet provide similar functionality that serves the same target market needs

(continued)

Term	Definition
Product management	An occupational domain which contains two professional disciplines: product planning and product marketing. Expanded definition: Occupational domain that is based on general management techniques that are focused on product planning and product marketing activities
Product marketing	Outbound activities aimed at generating product awareness, differentiation and demand
Product mix	An entire set of products offered by a company. Collection of product units, product lines, product families, and product groups
Product planning	The ongoing process of identifying and articulating market requirements that define a product's feature set
Product portfolio	A product line in which the products are properly diversified and balanced along the timeline and stages of the product life cycle model
Product problem	An industry situation in which product requirements' are unmet (B2B). The solution is a product component
Product quality	The market's perception of the degree at which the product can consistently meet or exceed customers' expectations
Product requirements document (PRD)	A high level description of the solution, intended use, and the set of features it provides that address the market problem and satisfy needs
Product review	An independent inspection, analysis and evaluation of a product by a trusted industry thought leader (often a journalist)
Product roadmap	A high level schedule of future product releases with brief descriptions of market requirements and features for those releases
Product strategy	Decisions that build and enhance products to fit market needs, and outline how to build a product competitive advantage
Product type	A set of products that serve the same specific target market needs, which are technologically and functionally similar
Product unit	An individual product that may be offered separately from any other product
Productivity (Product)	The product's scope of useful features
Professionalism	The characteristic of being a skilled practitioner; an expert
Project documents	The basic documents for managing the development project. Includes: schedules, project milestone criteria, test plans, development plans, and resources
Public relations	The actions that promote and distribute information for a company. Focused on encouraging media coverage of the company and its products and building a virtual relationship between the company and its target audience
Quality	A market's perception of the degree at which the company or product can consistently meet or exceed customers' expectations
Quality (Marketing)	The market's perception of the degree at which the company or product can consistently meet or exceed customers' expectations
Quality (Technological)	The highest MTBF (mean time between failures) and lowest MTTR (mean time to repair) of a product
Recurring fee (Licensing)	A fixed charge that enables limited time use of the product, but is renewed periodically at regular intervals

(*continued*)

Term	Definition
Relative value Proposition	An implicit promise a product holds for customers to deliver a desired ratio of benefits and costs(customer)
Reliability (Product)	How long before the product malfunctions
Reliability (Service)	The company's record of promising and delivering
Resultant value proposition	An implicit promise a product holds for customers to deliver a fixed combination of gains in time, cost and status
Risk	A factor or event that may jeopardize the product/project from achieving the anticipated benefits or increase the cost and/or schedule of the product/project
Risk contingency	Actions and incurring cost to be used in the future should the risk occur, thereby ceasing to be a risk and becoming a fact (after damage had occurred)
Risk mitigation	Actions and incurring cost to proactively change exposure to a risk while it is still a risk (before damage occurs)
Sales	The act of interacting with and persuading potential customers to buy the product
Sales-driven	A product delivery strategy that is based on producing and delivering products that a customer wants
Scenario	A succession of uses cases
Seller	The entity that sells the product or service
Services	Intangible products that we pay for and use but can never own
Site license discount	Discount provided to a large quantity purchase. The number of product licenses acquired is estimated
Skilled	A user that is comfortable using the product to perform job tasks (average user)
Skimming (Pricing Tactic)	Briefly charging a relatively high price upon product launch
Social competence	The set of human interaction skills which relate directly to communicating and managing relationships with others in a professional environment's social structure
Soft skills	Non-technical, communicative and personal abilities used in business
Solution	An answer which removes or controls the problem
Strategic aptitude	The long-term planning and decision making abilities that help achieve corporate objectives
Strategy	A coordinated set of long-term decisions that help achieve corporate objectives. Two common goals of any strategy are to: (1) Provide more value than the competition. (2) Help build a sustainable competitive advantage
Subscription fee (Licensing)	A onetime fixed charge that enables limited time use of the product
Superior perceived value	A state where customers perceive the product gives a net value more positive than its alternatives
Superior perceived value formula	Superior perceived value = competitive advantage + value
Supply	Quantity of a product that will be offered to the market by suppliers at various prices for a specific period
Tactical activities	Assignments, usually self-contained and specific that fulfill short-term business needs
Tactics	A set of actions taken to fulfill a strategy
Target market(s)	The group or groups of customers selected by a firm to sell to
TDM buyer	"Technology Decision Maker" buyer. The person who has the authority to decide what technology will be used by the company to do work or to develop products

(continued)

Term	Definition
Technical specification (Tech. Spec.)	A highly detailed description of the solution's design, attributes and standards
Technology problem	Challenges in applied science. The solution is scientific research
Technology-driven	A product delivery strategy that is based on producing and delivering products that we conceive
Unique selling proposition (USP)	A key "statement" that describes the distinct and compelling value of the product, which sets the product apart from other competing products
Usability	Ease of operation
Usage fee (Licensing)	A charge per unit of measure that is tallied at regular intervals
Use case	A specific way of using the product by performing some part of its functionality
User	The entity that interacts with the product
Value	The worth derived by the customer from owning and using the product
Value formula	Value = benefits − costs(customer)
Voice of the customer (VOC)	The process for eliciting needs from customers. It embodies a market-driven approach that involves spending time with current and future customers to determine past, present and future market problems that customers need to solve in order to meet their business goals and objectives
Volume price (Discount)	Discount provided to a large quantity purchase. The exact number of product licenses acquired is stated
Want	A request for specific objects that might satisfy the need

8.2 Product Management Glossary Description

Many perspectives abound as to what the marketing and product management disciplines are responsible for and how to define them. These interpretations vary significantly to a point where job titles and their associated responsibilities are interpreted very differently by different companies. This diversity also influences the professional terminology that shapes corporate processes.

It is therefore useful to have a set of clear definitions that help establish a common understanding. This glossary presents term definitions as they are used throughout the "Blackblot Product Manager's Toolkit™" (PMTK).

Part II
Product Manager's Toolkit

Chapter 9
PMTK Introduction

9.1 PMTK Index

Contents of the "Blackblot Product Manager's Toolkit™" (PMTK)

PMTK Methodology

- PMTK Core Models
  - PMTK Action Model – Reference framework which governs the sequence of using PMTK templates.
  - PMTK Flow Model – Applying the PMTK Action Model in a stage-gate like fashion.
  - PMTK Task Model – Synchronizing PMTK templates with Blackblot's concepts of a product management team and a product definition team.
- PMTK Support Models
  - PMTK Action-Team Model – Synchronization of "PMTK Action Model" with "Blackblot Product Management Team Model."
  - PMTK MVP Pricing Model – Illustration of a practical product pricing process.
  - PMTK PRM Model – Illustration of a market requirement's internal structure.
  - PMTK Problem Echelon Model – Illustration and mapping of the various problems handled by the industry and the market.
  - PMTK Product Tree Model – Illustration of the ways product functionality can be divided or grouped to make a better offering.
- Blackblot Concept Models
  - Blackblot Product Management Team Model – Illustration of the responsibilities and makeup of the product management team.
  - Blackblot Product Definition Team Model – Illustration of the responsibilities and makeup of the product definition team.
  - Blackblot Product Frames Model – Illustration that demonstrates how product functionality is built.

G. Steinhardt, *The Product Manager's Toolkit*,
DOI 10.1007/978-3-642-04508-0_9, © Springer-Verlag Berlin Heidelberg 2010

– Blackblot Marketing Model – Illustration that maps the various marketing activities within the marketing domain.

PMTK Product Planning

- Requirements Management
  - PRM Market Requirements – Description of the market opportunity, market problem and the resulting market requirements. Part of the "Procedural Requirements Management™" seminar.
  - PRM Product Requirements – High-level description of the functional solution, intended use and the set of features it provides, that addresses the market problem and satisfies needs. Part of the "Procedural Requirements Management™" seminar.
  - PMTK Market Requirements – Describing the product and the market into which the product will be introduced. An "inclusive" approach in which business information, market and product requirements are all bundled together in the same document.
- Use Cases – Ways various users put the product to use and under which scenarios.
- Features Matrix – Managing actual product characteristics (Microsoft Excel – Fee, available online).
- Product Roadmap – Plan or vision that describes a product's evolution.
- Pricing Model
  - Pricing Model – Building a product pricing model.
  - Pricing Model Spreadsheet – Tool for establishing a market-value driven base price (Microsoft Excel – Fee, available online).
- Win/Loss Analysis
  - Win/Loss Analysis Questionnaire – Information gathering tool in a process whose output helps to improve products and develop better sales functions.
  - Win/Loss Analysis Report – Summary results reporting tool in a process whose output helps improve products and develop better sales functions.
- Customer Visit – Planning customer visits with the intent of better understanding their needs.

PMTK Product Marketing

- Business Case
  - Business Case – Examination of a potential market opportunity on a product level.
  - Business Case Presentation – Concise overview of a business case for presentation to stakeholders (Microsoft PowerPoint – Fee, available online).
- Competitor Analysis – Analysis of competing companies, partially via their products.
- Product Comparison – Tabular comparison of competing products.
- Corporate Mission – General business direction and company purpose.

- Product Positioning – Basis for clear and focused marketing messages that communicate the product's value proposition to multiple audiences.
- Value Documents
  - Sales Axioms – Fundamental concepts the product is built upon.
  - Problem/Solution/Feature/Benefit – Outlining a product's ability to address the overall customer problem by merit of its feature scope and capabilities.
  - Unique Selling Proposition – Key value differentiator which sets the product apart from other competing products.
- Market Plan – Description of the long-term goals, and messages delivered to the target market, relative to a particular product.
- Marketing Communications
  - Company Profile – Overview description of a company.
  - Product Backgrounder – Product/service overview information at a glance.
  - Collateral Matrix – List of various marketing communications collateral items.
  - Press Release Questionnaire – Eliciting targeted information for creating meaningful press releases.
- Sales Support
  - Company Presentation – Broad company overview for internal and external audiences (Microsoft PowerPoint – Fee, available online).
  - Product Presentation – Broad product overview for internal and external audiences (Microsoft PowerPoint – Fee, available online).
  - Lead Generation – Process to discover and qualify prospective customers.

PMTK Process Efficiency

- Meeting Rules – Rules and general guidelines for conducting productive corporate meetings.
- Management by Objectives – Intelligent form of self-management.
- Decision Making – Driving an effective process of decision making within a project.
- Deliverable Sign-Off – Tool for securing acceptance and commitment to deliverables.
- Generic Templates
  - Generic Document – General Microsoft Word document template.
  - Generic Presentation – General Microsoft PowerPoint presentation template based on the format used in Blackblot courses (Microsoft PowerPoint – Fee, available online).
- Bundle Book
  - Bundle Book – Central repository of documents related to a particular product.
  - Bundle Book Folder – Product bundle book folder structure for organizing product documents or deliverables (Fee, available online).
- Gap Analysis – Procedure for assessing how well product management tasks are being performed.

- Performance Review
  - Performance Review – Product management merit and performance measurement process and tool.
  - Performance Review Matrix – Product management merit and performance measurement process and tool (Microsoft Excel – Fee, available online).

PMTK Personnel Management

- PMTK Career Development
  - Curriculum Vitae – Individual's professional history, skills sets, and specific key contributions to convey one's value to an organization.
  - Professional Development Plan – Process to develop or increase the professional competencies of product management professionals.
- PMTK Team Management
  - PMTK Role Descriptions – Framework for the roles which conform to the PMTK methodology.
  - PMTK Job Description – Framework for preparing a PMTK team model compliant job description.
  - PMTK Interview Process – Framework for administering a product management oriented interview process.

PMTK Implementation

- PMTK Implementation Plan – Phased process for introducing and implementing PMTK methodology within a company.

9.2   PMTK Overview

Description of the "Blackblot Product Manager's Toolkit™" (PMTK)

9.2.1   PMTK Synopsis

PMTK is a comprehensive set of tools and accompanying methodology, that illustrates notable best practices and processes which help create successful market-driven products. It is a systematic, non-mathematical, managerial approach to the planning and marketing of new products, and life-cycle management of existing products.

PMTK covers the major concerns in each phase of the product planning and product marketing processes. PMTK emphasizes managerial issues, concepts, tools and methods that can be directly used in product planning and product marketing.

9.2.2   PMTK Background

There is a myriad of product management templates available to product managers via the Internet. These templates were created by individuals or companies and are distributed for free or for a fee. However, templates created by individuals are either rudimentary or excessive and are often cryptic since they evolved from internal needs within a specific enterprise. Conversely, templates created by companies, for profit, aspire to be both tutorials and templates at the same time and thus miss both objectives and become complex, hard to engage and time consuming. They can also be very expensive with price tags running into hundreds of dollars per template.

Compounding the issue is the true lack of consistency and uniformity in the appearance, instruction tone, and general workflow of the various templates on the market; even those emanating from the same entity. Working with many templates that drastically differ from each other is confusing and extremely frustrating for any product manager.

The solution is a set of intermediate templates designed for product managers by product managers, which are consistent, uniform and focused on being a template – not a tutorial. A template is a template and no more.

9.2.3   PMTK Scope

PMTK, originally written by Blackblot as work tools for internal use, provides flow with structure and allows the product manager to focus on content (what to write) and not on the method (how to write). Most documents in the toolkit are fill-in-the-blanks templates. Several documents are general guideline documents that help instill better process management and process efficiency. The templates were written based on actual work experience and a variety of sources including books, articles and other content available in the public domain.

There are countless books, articles and educational opportunities on virtually every topic addressed by these templates. Product managers will be able to use the PMTK templates to do their work but will need to learn the product management discipline through professional training seminars or books, since these templates are not tutorials and contain few explanations or examples. The templates can be extremely useful, but some form of professional product management training is often needed in order to understand and properly use the templates.

The templates are intentionally broad and general in nature because every business is different. Product managers will need to modify the templates in varying degrees so that they fit their specific needs and particular reading audience.

9.2.4   PMTK Use Convention

All templates are similar in appearance, structure and follow the same simple work convention.

Pointed brackets colored in light blue contain instructions regarding content that should be entered into the document. For example: <Enter product name.> or

<Define and describe the market problem the product is trying to solve>. These instructions are subsequently deleted and replaced with relevant content.

Pointed brackets with italicized text colored in violet, contain comments or examples. For example: *<Comment: This section is the last task and is done once the MRD is complete.>*. These comments and examples are ultimately deleted from the document. The colored text of light blue or violet is evident in the "Blackblot Product Manager's Toolkit™" (PMTK) digital templates which are part of the PMTK Commercial Package (see the Addendum).

Chapter 10
PMTK Models

10.1 PMTK Core Models

10.1.1 PMTK Action Model

Figure 10.1

10.1.1.1 PMTK Action Model Description

The "PMTK Action Model" is a reference framework which governs the sequence of using "Blackblot Product Manager's Toolkit™" (PMTK) templates. It is also an operational framework that demonstrates the process and phases of performing and correlating product planning tasks with product marketing tasks.

The top section of the "PMTK Action Model" illustrates product planning tasks and the bottom illustrates product marketing tasks. Overlapping the product planning and the product marketing tasks allows seeing how these respective tasks can be correlated for maximum effect. The overlapping also allows proper sequencing and job planning.

In the "PMTK Action Model" the flow of events (or phases) is from left to right, and the flow of tasks is from top to bottom. The "PMTK Action Model" contains a component that depicts tools which promote process efficiency since product management is comprised of extremely well-ordered and well-disciplined processes.

10.1.2 PMTK Flow Model

Figure 10.2

G. Steinhardt, *The Product Manager's Toolkit*,
DOI 10.1007/978-3-642-04508-0_10, © Springer-Verlag Berlin Heidelberg 2010

PMTK Action Model

▼Product Planning ▼

(left margin: RESEARCH — right margin: LEARNING)

Planning▶	Definition▶	Development▶	Maintenance▶
Describe market problems and needs	*Define solutions to market problems*	*Build solutions that solve market problems*	*Sales channels support and product revisions*
Market Requirements	Features Matrix	Pricing Model	Win/Loss Analysis
Use Cases	Product Roadmap	Product Evangelism	Customer Visit

▼Product Marketing ▼

Evaluation▶	Strategy▶	Readiness▶	Execution▶
Examine opportunities to serve the market	*Formulate the market approach*	*Prepare market tactics and MarCom activities*	*Deliver value and build competitive advantage*
Business Case	Corporate Mission	Company Profile	Company Presentation
Competitor Analysis	Product Positioning	Product Backgrounder	Product Presentation
Product Comparison	Value Documents	Collateral Matrix	Lead Generation
	Market Plan	Launch Plan	Marketing Review

▼Process Efficiency ▼

(left margin: EXMPT — right margin: FORMAL)

People▶	Decisions▶	Deliverables▶	Learning▶
Instill flow and structure at work	*Bring closure and secure commitment*	*Present and share work output*	*Assess and measure performance*
Meeting Rules	Decision Making	Generic Templates	Gap Analysis
Management By Objectives	Deliverable Sign-Off	Bundle Book	Performance Review

Fig. 10.1 PMTK Action Model

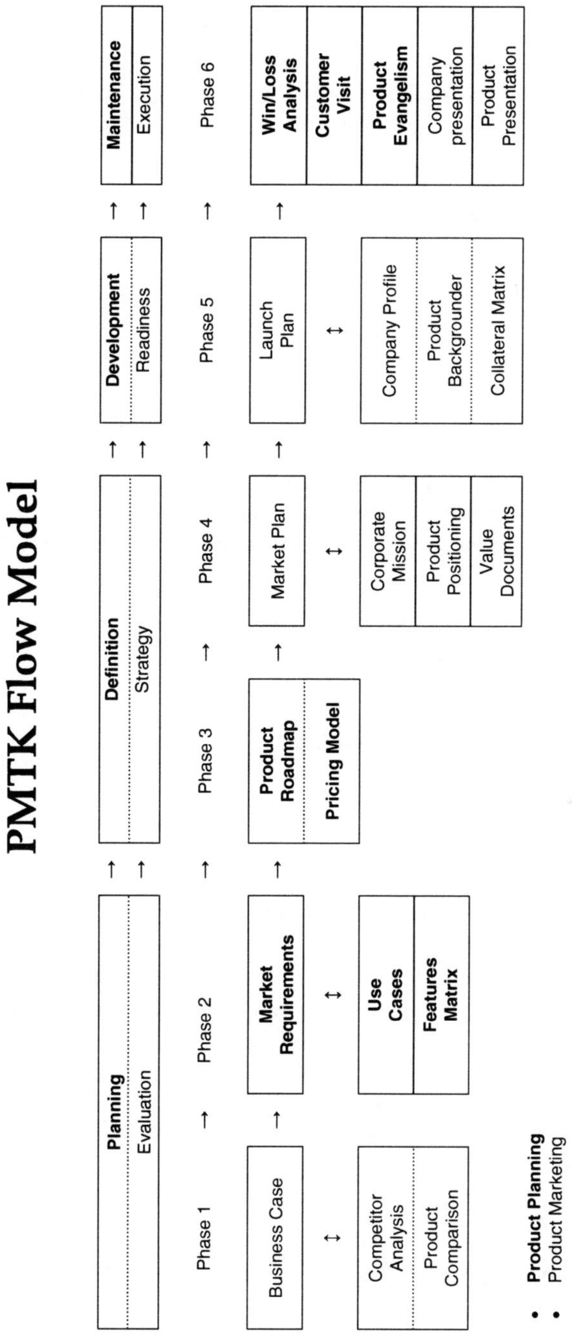

PMTK Flow Model

Planning		Definition		Development	Maintenance	
Evaluation	Strategy			Readiness	Execution	
Phase 1	Phase 2	Phase 3	Phase 4	Phase 5	Phase 6	

| Business Case | Market Requirements | Product Roadmap | Market Plan | Launch Plan | Win/Loss Analysis | |
| | | Pricing Model | | | Customer Visit | |

Competitor Analysis	Use Cases		Corporate Mission	Company Profile	Product Evangelism	
Product Comparison	Features Matrix		Product Positioning	Product Backgrounder	Company presentation	
			Value Documents	Collateral Matrix	Product Presentation	

- **Product Planning**
- Product Marketing

Fig. 10.2 PMTK Flow Model

10.1.2.1 PMTK Flow Model Description

The "PMTK Flow Model" demonstrates the internal flow and interaction between product planning and product marketing deliverables, and maps them to the entire product management process. The goal of this model is to help managers apply the "PMTK Action Model" in a traditional milestone or stage-gate like fashion.

10.1.3 PMTK Task Model

Tables 10.1 and 10.2

10.1.3.1 PMTK Task Model Description

The "PMTK Task Model" synchronizes various PMTK templates with the "Blackblot Product Management Team Model" and "Blackblot Product Definition Team Model". The goal of this model is to help managers assign tasks to the appropriate team roles by defining the owner, writer and contributor(s) of every PMTK document.

10.2 PMTK Support Models

10.2.1 PMTK Action-Team Model

Figure 10.3

10.2.1.1 PMTK Action-Team Model Description

The "PMTK Action-Team Model" is a graphic representation that maps and synchronizes the "PMTK Action Model" with the "Blackblot Product Management Team Model".

10.2.2 PMTK MVP Model

Figure 10.4

10.2.2.1 PMTK Market-Value Pricing Model Description

Developed by Blackblot, the "PMTK Market-Value Pricing Model" (MVP Model) is a market-value centric pricing process which guides sets of managerial decisions

Table 10.1 PMTK Task Model

Documents and Tasks

PMTK Documents	(O)wner/(W)riter	Contributor(s)	Audience	Audience Dept.
Product planning				
Market requirements				
PRM Market Requirements – Description of the market opportunity, market problem and the resulting market requirements. Part of the "Strategic Product Management for Planners™" course.	Product planner	Product architect	Internal	● Development ● Executive management ● Product marketing ● Product planning ● Program management ● Quality assurance ● Sales force ● User experience
PRM Product Requirements – High-level description of the functional solution, intended use and the set of features it provides, that addresses the market problem and satisfies needs. Part of the "Strategic Product Management for Planners™" course.	Product architect	Lead developer	Internal	● Development ● Product planning ● Program management ● Quality assurance
PMTK Market Requirements – Describing the product and the market into which the product will be introduced. An "inclusive" approach in which business information, market and product requirements are all bundled together in the same document.	Product planner	Product architect	Internal	● Development ● Executive management ● Product marketing ● Product planning ● Program management ● Quality assurance ● Sales force ● User experience
Use Cases – Ways various users put the product to use and under which scenarios.	Product planner	Product architect	Internal	● Development ● Product planning ● Program management ● Quality assurance
Features Matrix – Managing actual product characteristics.	Product architect	Product planner	Internal	● Development ● Product planning

(continued)

Table 10.1 (continued)

Documents and Tasks

PMTK Documents	(O)wner/(W)riter	Contributor(s)	Audience	Audience Dept.
Product Roadmap – Plan or vision that describes a product's evolution.	Product planner	Product architect	Internal	• Development • Executive management • Product marketing • Product planning • Program management • Quality assurance • Sales force • User experience
			External	• Customers • Sales channels
Pricing Model – Building a product pricing model. Part of the "Market-Value Pricing™" course.	Product planner	Product marketer Product architect	Internal	• Executive management • Product marketing • Product planning • Program management • Quality assurance • Sales force • User experience
			External	• Partners • Sales channels
Win/Loss analysis Win/Loss Analysis Questionnaire – Process whose output helps to improve products and develop better sales functions.	Product planner	Sales engineer	Internal	• Executive management • Product planning • Program management • Sales force
Win/Loss Analysis Report – Process whose output helps improve products and develop better sales functions.	Product planner	Sales engineer	Internal	• Executive management • Product planning • Program management • Sales force
Customer Visit – Planning customer visits with the intent of better understanding their needs. Product marketing	Product planner	Sales engineer	Internal	• Product planning

Document	Owner (O) / Writer (W)	Additional roles	Internal / External	Audiences
Business Case – Examination of a potential market opportunity on a product level. Part of the "Strategic Product Management for Marketers™" course.	Director of products (O) Product marketer (W)	Product planner Product architect Sales engineer	Internal External	• Development • Executive management • Product marketing • Product planning • Program management • Investors • Partners
Competitor Analysis – Study of competing companies, partially via their products.	Product marketer	Product planner	Internal	• Corporate marketing • Executive management • Product marketing • Product planning • Program management • Sales force
Product Comparison – Tabular comparison of competing products.	Product marketer (O) Product planner (W)	Product architect	Internal	• Corporate marketing • Executive management • Product marketing • Product planning • Program management • Sales force
Corporate Mission – General business direction and company purpose.	Product marketer	Director of products	Internal	• Corporate marketing • Executive management • Product marketing • Product planning • Program management • Customers
Product Positioning – Clear and focused messages that communicate the product's value proposition to multiple audiences.	Product marketer	Director of products Product planner	External Internal	• Corporate marketing • Executive management • Product marketing • Product planning • Program management

(continued)

Table 10.1 (continued)

Documents and Tasks

PMTK Documents	(O)wner/(W)riter	Contributor(s)	Audience	Audience Dept.
Value documents				
Sales Axioms – Fundamental concepts the product is built upon.	Product marketer (O) Product planner (W)	Product architect	Internal	• Product marketing • Product planning
Problem/Solution/Feature/Benefit (PSFB) – Outlining a product's ability to address the overall customer problem by merit of its feature scope and capabilities.	Product marketer (O) Product planner (W)	Product architect	Internal	• Product marketing • Product planning
Unique Selling Proposition (USP) – Key value differentiator which sets the product apart from other competing products.	Product marketer	Product planner	Internal	• Product marketing • Product planning
Market Plan – Description of the long-term goals, and messages delivered to the target market, relative to a particular product. Part of the "Strategic Product Management for Marketers™" course.	Product marketer	Product planner	Internal	• Executive management • Corporate marketing • Product marketing • Product planning • Program management • Sales force
Marketing communications				
Company Profile – Overview description of a company.	Product marketer (O) MarCom manager (W)	Product planner	Internal External	• Corporate marketing • Executive management • MarCom • Product marketing • Sales force • Job applicants • Customers • Investors
Product Backgrounder – Product/service overview information at a glance.	Product marketer (O) MarCom manager (W)	Product planner	Internal External	• Corporate marketing • Executive management • MarCom • Product marketing • Product planning • Program management • Sales force • Customers

Deliverable	Owner	Approver	Audience Type	Audience
Collateral Matrix – List of various marketing communications collateral items.	Product marketer (O) MarCom manager (W)	Product planner	Internal	• MarCom • Product marketing • Program management
Press Release Questionnaire – Eliciting targeted information for creating meaningful press releases. Sales support	Product marketer (O) MarCom manager (W)	Product planner	Internal	• MarCom • Product marketing • Program management
Company Presentation – Broad overview of a company for internal and external audiences.	Product marketer	Director of products	Internal External	• Corporate marketing • Executive management • MarCom • Product marketing • Sales force • Customers • Investors
Product Presentation – Broad overview of a product for internal and external audiences.	Product marketer (O) Sales engineer (W)	Product planner	Internal External	• Executive management • MarCom • Product marketing • Product planning • Program management • Sales force • Customers • Investors
Lead Generation – Process to discover and qualify prospective customers.	Director of sales	Product marketer MarCom manager	Internal	• MarCom • Product marketing • Program management • Sales force

Table 10.2 PMTK Task Model – Teams and Roles

Teams and Roles			
Product Management Team Model			
Role	Responsibility	Goal	Expertise
Product planner (Strategic Role)	Identify and articulating market requirements.	Satisfied product buyers and users.	Market expert
Product marketer (Strategic Role)	Generate awareness, differentiation and demand.	Satisfied Sales Force.	Marketing expert
Sales engineer (Tactical Role)	Outbound product-centric activities, i.e., pre-sale support and product demos.	Customer knowledge of product value and functionality.	Advocacy expert
MarCom manager (Tactical Role)	Conception and copywriting of all collateral material.	Consistent company image and positioning in the marketplace.	Media expert
Director of products (Strategic Role)	Balancing corporate goals with long-term market trends and opportunities.	Successful formulation and execution of market and product strategies.	Strategy and process expert
Product Definition Team Model			
Role	Responsibility	Deliverable	Expertise
Product planner (Strategic Role)	Articulate market problem.	Market requirements document ("What to solve?")	Market expert
Product architect (Tactical Role)	Devise functional solution.	Product requirements document ("How to solve?")	Product expert
Lead developer (Technical Role)	Design product implementation.	Technical specification ("How to build?")	Technology expert

that help determine a product's price. Price is the specification of what a seller wants in exchange for granting right of ownership or use to a product. Pricing is the act of setting a price.

The "PMTK MVP Model" is comprised of three distinct parts that effectively act as sequential stages in the pricing process:

1. "Pricing Scheme" – outline of the overall pricing approach which encompasses the principles for pricing the specific product (how to achieve).
2. "Pricing Formula" – calculatory structure that allows the application of pricing changes to specific markets or competitive regions (how to calculate).
3. "Price Mix" – price related aggregate of information and conditions that the customer is presented with (how to present).

The "PMTK MVP Model" is designed to be used in conjunction with the "MVP Pricing Model" spreadsheet and the "MVP Pricing Model" template.

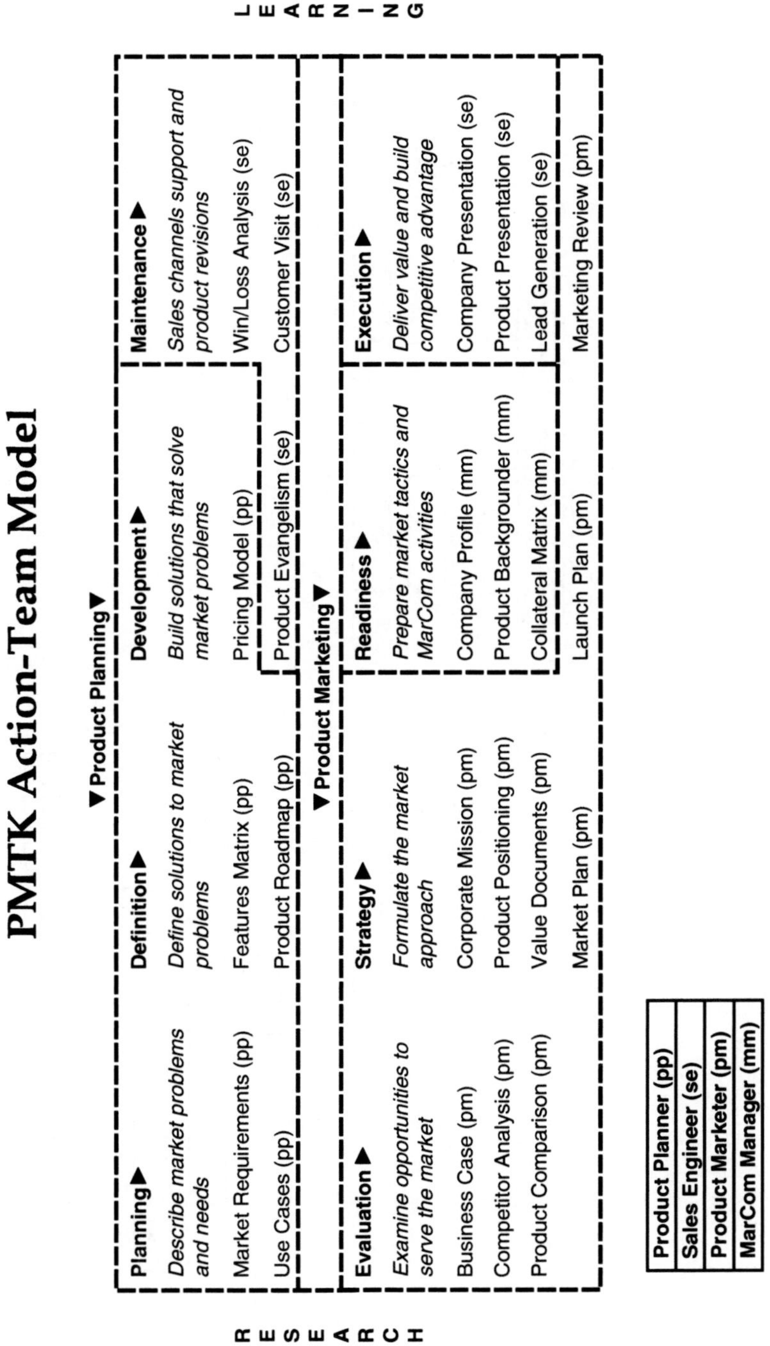

PMTK Action-Team Model

LEARNING

REACH

▼ Product Planning ▼

Planning ▶	Definition ▶	Development ▶	Maintenance ▶
Describe market problems and needs	*Define solutions to market problems*	*Build solutions that solve market problems*	*Sales channels support and product revisions*
Market Requirements (pp)	Features Matrix (pp)	Pricing Model (pp)	Win/Loss Analysis (se)
Use Cases (pp)	Product Roadmap (pp)	Product Evangelism (se)	Customer Visit (se)

▼ Product Marketing ▼

Evaluation ▶	Strategy ▶	Readiness ▶	Execution ▶
Examine opportunities to serve the market	*Formulate the market approach*	*Prepare market tactics and MarCom activities*	*Deliver value and build competitive advantage*
Business Case (pm)	Corporate Mission (pm)	Company Profile (mm)	Company Presentation (se)
Competitor Analysis (pm)	Product Positioning (pm)	Product Backgrounder (mm)	Product Presentation (se)
Product Comparison (pm)	Value Documents (pm)	Collateral Matrix (mm)	Lead Generation (se)
	Market Plan (pm)	Launch Plan (pm)	Marketing Review (pm)

Product Planner (pp)
Sales Engineer (se)
Product Marketer (pm)
MarCom Manager (mm)

Fig. 10.3 PMTK Action–Team Model

PMTK MVP Model

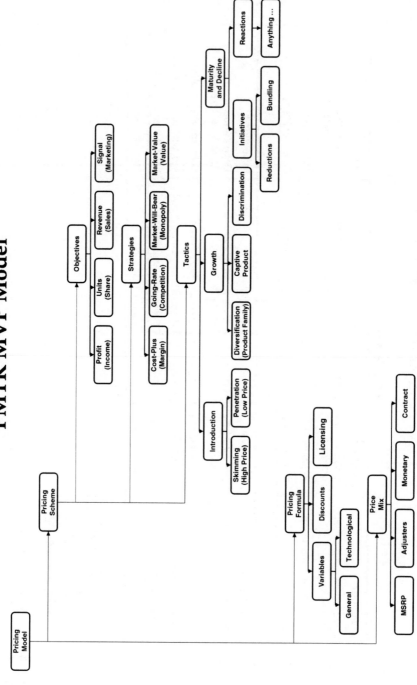

Fig. 10.4 PMTK Market-Value Pricing Model

10.2.3   PMTK PRM Model

Figure 10.5

10.2.3.1   Blackblot Procedural Requirements Management Model Description

A market requirement is an aggregate unit of information, which represents with sufficient detail, the functionality sought by users to address a specific facet of a particular market problem. This is the full and comprehensive definition of a market requirement.

Developed by Blackblot, the "Blackblot Procedural Requirements Management Model" (PRM Model) is a methodology to create high-quality, usable market requirements. This model serves several objectives:

- Provide a structured approach to crafting market requirements.
- Establish a market requirement's internal structure.
- Validate a market requirement's integrity.

By understanding the overall functionally that is described by the sum of market requirements, it is possible to construe the scope of the market problem. Essentially, the market problem is described by the sum of market requirements, and the market problem scope is described by the overall functionality that is in the market requirements.

PMTK PRM Model

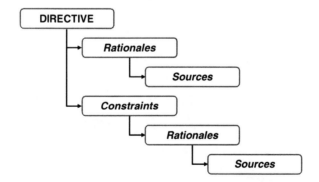

PRM MODEL ELEMENT	DESCRIPTION
Directive	Instruction that guides what is to be accomplished.
Constraints	Limitations imposed on the solution.
Rationales	Reasoning that supports a claim.
Sources	Information that validates a claim.

Fig. 10.5 PMTK Procedural Requirements Management Model

Market requirements are built using four components: directive, constraints, rationales and sources. The essential component of a market requirement, that must be present in any market requirement, is the directive.

For more information, please see the "Crafting Market Requirements" chapter. Also review the corresponding "Content Retention Tool" (see the Addendum).

10.2.4   PMTK Problem Echelon Model

Figure 10.6

10.2.4.1   PMTK Problem Echelon Model Description

Developed by Blackblot, the "PMTK Problem Echelon Model" is a descriptive model that demonstrates the inner workings of value-chains and helps to map the various problems handled by the industry and the market.

This model serves several objectives: structure and simplify the analysis of market problems in product management, explain how technology finds uses and applications, and demonstrate the sequence of events in which market dynamics generate market problems which are then followed by products and technology that solve them.

For more information, please see the "Who's Driving Your Company?" chapter. Also review the corresponding "Content Retention Tool" (see the Addendum).

PMTK Problem Echelon Model

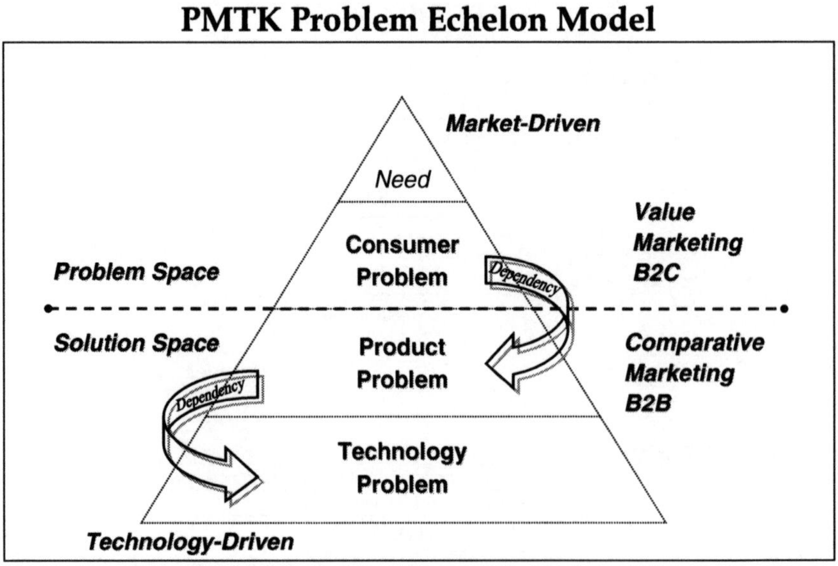

Fig. 10.6 PMTK Problem Echelon Model

10.2.5   PMTK Product Tree Model

Figure 10.7 and Table 10.3

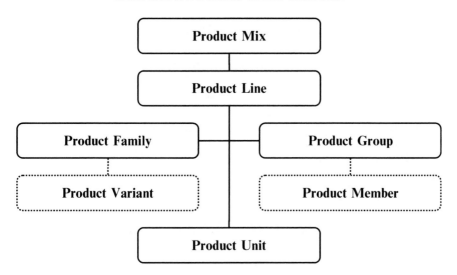

Fig. 10.7 PMTK Product Tree Model

Table 10.3

Term	Definition
Product	Any offering that satisfies needs. Represents a collection of tangible and intangible assets.
Product unit	Individual product that may be offered separately from any other product.
Product mix	Entire set of products offered by a company. Collection of product units, product lines, product families, and product groups.
Product line	Set of products that are technologically different yet provide similar functionality that serves the same target market needs.
Product family	Set of derived products that share the same technological foundation. Members of a product family are called "product variants".
Product group	Set of products coupled or packaged together to form a new unified offering. Members of a product group are called "product members".
Product portfolio	Product line in which the products are properly diversified and balanced along the timeline and stages of the product life cycle model.
Product type	Set of products that serve the same specific target market needs, and are technologically and functionally similar.
Product category or class(ification)	Synonymous to "product line" in the context of competing products.

10.2.5.1 PMTK Product Tree Model Description

The "PMTK Product Tree Model" serves as the basis for discussion on the ways product functionality can be divided or grouped to make a better offering.

10.2.5.2 PMTK Product Tree Model Relationships

- Product unit is not a container entity.
- Product unit, product family and product group; may also be viewed as being a "Product Member" or "Product Variant".
- Product unit can be part of a product line, product family (product variant), or product group (product member).
- Product families contain products designated as "Product Variants".
- Product groups contain products designated as "Member Products".
- Product lines can contain product families, product groups and product units.
- Product mix can contain several product lines.
- Product mix, line, family and group; are all container entities.

10.3 PMTK Concept Models

10.3.1 Blackblot Product Management Team Model

Figure 10.8

10.3.1.1 Blackblot Product Management Team Model Description

The product management team is a task group, comprised of four distinct roles, which organizationally reside in the product management department. The four roles in the "Blackblot Product Management Team Model" are the product planner, product marketer, sales engineer, and marketing communications (MarCom) manager. These four roles are the basic providers of the planning, deliverables, and actions that guide the inbound oriented product definition and the outbound marketing efforts.

The "Blackblot Product Management Team Model" addresses the organizational challenges faced by modern high-tech product managers and resolves them by formalizing and structuring the responsibilities and makeup of the product management team.

For more information, please see the "Product Management Team" chapter. Also review the corresponding "Content Retention Tool" (see the Addendum).

Blackblot Product Management Team Model

Sales
Engineer
*Advocacy
Expert*

MarCom
Manager
*Media
Expert*

Product
Planner
*Market
Expert*

Product
Marketer
*Marketing
Expert*

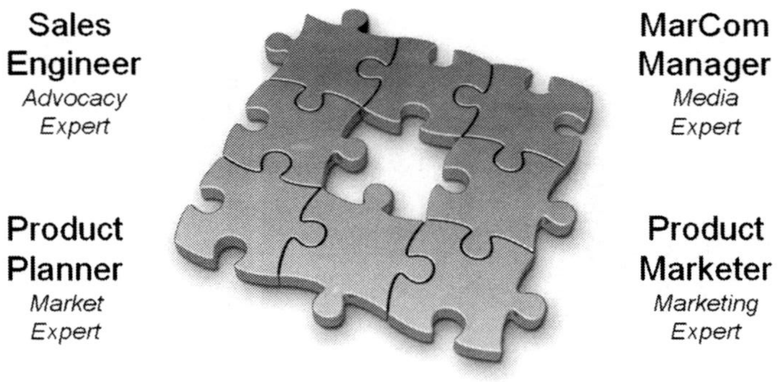

Role	Responsibility	Goal	Expertise
Product Planner (Strategic Role)	Identify and articulating market requirements	Satisfied product buyers and users	Market Expert
Product Marketer (Strategic Role)	Generate awareness, differentiation and demand	Satisfied sales force	Marketing Expert
Sales Engineer (Tactical Role)	Outbound product-centric activities, i.e., pre-sale support and product demos	Customer knowledge of product value and functionality	Advocacy Expert
MarCom Manager (Tactical Role)	Conception and copywriting of all collateral material	Consistent company image and positioning in the marketplace	Media Expert
Director of Products (Strategic Role)	Balancing corporate goals with long-term market trends and opportunities	Successful formulation and execution of market and product strategies	Strategy and Process Expert

Fig. 10.8 Blackblot Product Management Team Model

10.3.2   Blackblot Product Definition Team Model

Figure 10.9

10.3.2.1   Blackblot Product Definition Team Model Description

Different roles are required to create a product. These roles require different skills sets, and in some cases, even a different psychological make up to successfully plan, define and build a product that meets customers' expectations.

Extreme due diligence needs to be performed during the product planning and product definition processes to properly and accurately define a product. This requires people that possess different skills, abilities, backgrounds, experience, education, personalities, and other qualities or characteristics. Professional and distinct roles are needed to create the foundation documents required to accurately define the product. Hence, in order to be successful, a team approach is implemented, bringing together a cohesive set of individuals that have unique qualities to perform all that is needed to define a successful product.

There are three key roles that all product definition teams must have:

1. "Product Planner" – a market expert who is able to articulate the market problem and needs.
2. "Product Architect" – a product expert who is able to create a high-level design for the solution.
3. "Lead Developer" – a technology expert who is able to describe how to build and implement the solution's design.

For more information, please see the "Product Definition Team" chapter. Also review the corresponding "Content Retention Tool" (see the Addendum).

10.3.3   Blackblot Product Frames Model

Figure 10.10

10.3.3.1   Blackblot Product Frames Model Description

Product planning is the ongoing process of identifying and articulating market requirements from which the product's feature set is ultimately defined. Developed by Blackblot, the "Blackblot Product Frames Model" is a descriptive model that demonstrates how product functionality is built and how, in total, the product solves the market problem. This model serves several objectives: to validate the product's functional completeness with respect to the market problem; to synchronize user/buyer needs with product features; and to provide a backbone for a product definition process.

Blackblot Product Definition Team Model

Role	Responsibility	Product Frame	Deliverable	Expertise
Product Planner (Strategic Role)	Articulate market problem	Market Requirements	MRD ("What to solve?")	Market Expert
Product Architect (Tactical Role)	Devise functional solution	Product Requirements	PRD ("How to solve?")	Product Expert
Lead Developer (Technical Role)	Design product implementation	Product Attributes and Specifications	Tech. Spec. ("How to build?")	Technology Expert

Fig. 10.9 Blackblot Product Definition Team Model

Blackblot Product Frames Model

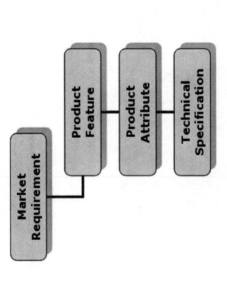

Product Frame Element	Description
Market Requirement	A user/buyer need.
Product Feature	Something the product does or has.
Product Attribute	An actual trait of the product.
Technical Specification	The attribute's implementation.

Fig. 10.10 Blackblot Product Frames Model

Blackblot Marketing Model

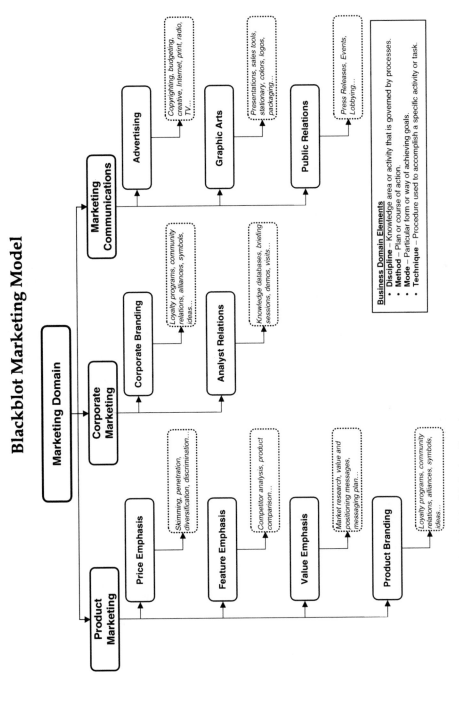

Fig. 10.11a Blackblot Marketing Model – Marketing Domain

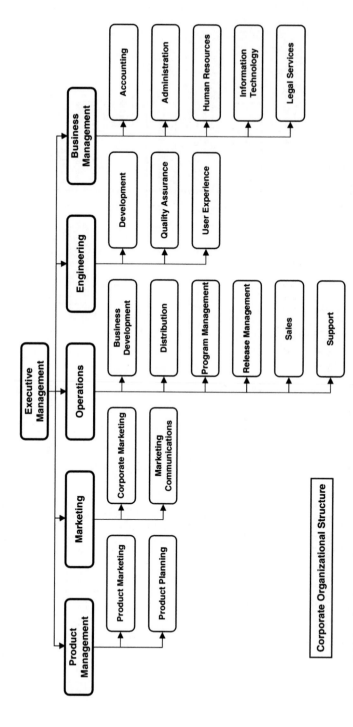

Fig. 10.11b Blackblot Marketing Model – Corporate Organizational Structure

The inner workings of a single product frame show how a certain product feature addresses a particular facet of the market problem. The sum of all of the product frames defines a product that has overall functionality that solves the entire scope of issues presented by a market problem. A product frame is comprised of four elements: market requirement, product feature, product attribute, and technical specification.

For more information, please see the "Product Definition Team" chapter. Also review the corresponding "Content Retention Tool" (see the Addendum).

10.3.4 Blackblot Marketing Model

Figures 10.11a and 10.11b
    Tables 10.4–10.8

10.3.4.1 Blackblot Marketing Model Description

Marketing is an instructive business domain that serves to inform and educate target markets about the value and competitive advantage of a company and its products.

Table 10.4 Blackblot Marketing Model – Marketing Domain Elements (Tabular Form)

Marketing Disciplines	Marketing Methods	Marketing Modes	Marketing Techniques
Product marketing	Value emphasis	Messaging model	Market research, value and positioning messages, messaging plan...
	Feature emphasis	Feature comparison	Competitor analysis, product comparison...
	Price emphasis	Cost-plus, going-rate	Skimming, penetration, diversification, discrimination...
	Product branding	Uniqueness, labeling	Loyalty programs, community relations, alliances, symbols, ideas...
Corporate marketing	Corporate branding	Personification	Loyalty programs, community relations, alliances, symbols, ideas...
	Analyst relations	Engagements, resources	Knowledge databases, briefing sessions, demos, visits...
Marketing			communications
	Advertising	Entertainment, information	Copyrighting, budgeting, creative, Internet, print, radio, TV...
	Graphic arts	Signals, imagery, perception	Presentations, sales tools, stationary, colors, logos, packaging...
Public relations	Relationship, media coverage	Press releases, events, lobbying...	

Additional elements can be added to this component of the "Blackblot Marketing Model"; however, the current mapping is relatively whole and effectively encompasses the essence of the marketing domain

Table 10.5 Blackblot Marketing Model – Corporate Organizational Structure (Tabular Form)

Product Management	Marketing	Operations	Engineering	Business Management
"Product marketing"	"Corporate marketing"	Business development	Development	Accounting
Product planning	"Marketing communications"	Distribution	Quality assurance	Administration
		Program management	User experience	Executive management
		Release management		Human resources
		Sales		Information technology
		Support		Legal services

Framed in quotes are the three marketing domain disciplines

Table 10.6 Blackblot Marketing Model – Marketing Domain Strategies (Summary Table)

Strategy	Coordinated set of long-term decisions that help achieve corporate objectives
Market strategy	Decisions that define target markets, set marketing objectives, and outline how to build a corporate competitive advantage
Marketing strategy	Decisions that determine how to achieve marketing's goal in a particular target market, through the selection and application of marketing mixes
Product strategy	Decisions that build and enhance products to fit market needs, and outline how to build a product competitive advantage. (Product strategy belongs to the product management business domain)

Table 10.7 Blackblot Marketing Model – Marketing Domain Plans (Summary Table)

Market plan	Description of the long-term goals and messages delivered to the target market relative to a particular company or product
Marketing plan	Description of the selection and application of marketing mixes in the target market
Marketing program	Description of the short-term marketplace effort designed to obtain a specific marketing goal

Table 10.8 Blackblot Marketing Model – Marketing Domain Plan/Strategy/Department Mapping (Summary Table)

Plan type	Market plan	Marketing plan
Strategy type	"Market strategy" and elements of the "Product strategy"	"Marketing strategy"
Corporate department	• Product marketing (relative to the product) • Corporate marketing (relative to the company)	Marketing communications

The goal of marketing is to build and maintain a preference for a company and its products within the target markets.

The "Blackblot Marketing Model" maps the marketing activities within the marketing domain, presents the division and location of departments identified with marketing in the corporate organizational hierarchy, and describes the types of strategies and plans related to the marketing domain.

For more information, please see the "Concept of Marketing" chapter. Also review the corresponding "Content Retention Tool" (see the Addendum).

Chapter 11

PMTK

TEMPLATES

G. Steinhardt, *The Product Manager's Toolkit*,
DOI 10.1007/978-3-642-04508-0_11, © Springer-Verlag Berlin Heidelberg 2010

11.1 PRODUCT PLANNING

11.1.1 PRM Market Requirements Document (MRD) – Template V. 4.0

Company Name: <Enter company name>

- Date: <Enter date>
- Contact: <Enter your name>
- Department: <Enter department name>
- Location: <Enter location>
- Email: <Enter email address>
- Telephone: <Enter telephone number>

Document Revision History:

Date	Revision	Revised By	Approved By
<Enter date>	<Revision #>	<Enter your name>	<Enter name>

Table of Contents

7.   SUPPORTING DATA

1. Introduction

1.1. Document Objective

The Market Requirements Document (MRD) focuses on describing the market problem, market opportunity and the resulting market requirements that help design a solution that addresses the market problem and realizes the market opportunity.

<Comment: This document is presented to Engineering for solution planning and design.>

1.2. Executive Summary

<Write the executive summary. Provide a concise report of the pertinent facts, assumptions and suggestions noted throughout this document.>

<Comment: This section is the last section to be filled in and is to be done once the MRD is complete. Focus on the key elements in each document section and do not exceed two pages. The executive summary is a miniature version of the entire document.>

2. Market Problem and Opportunity

2.1. Section Objective

This section describes the market problem and resulting market opportunity.

2.2. Market Problem

<Identify and justify the specific market problem. Explain any other interlinking market problems.>

<Comment: The market problem is a "consumer" or "product" or "technology" problem in the target market. The market problem is essentially a situation (difficulty) that exists in the target market and requires change.

- *Consumer Problem – A marketplace situation in which consumer needs remain unsatisfied (B2C). The solution to a consumer problem is a whole product.*
- *Product Problem – An industry situation in which product requirements' are unmet (B2B). The solution to a product problem is a product component.*
- *Technology Problem – Challenges in applied science. The solution to a technology problem is scientific research.*

2.3. Market Opportunity

<Provide a statement detailing the specific market opportunity. Size and substantiate the market opportunity as much as possible. Document the assumptions and facts that validate and justify the market opportunity. Explain any other interlinking market opportunities.>

<Comment: The market opportunity is a lucrative, lasting and sizable market problem. Market Opportunity = Market Problem + Volume + Duration + Earning Potential.>

3. Market Overview

3.1. Section Objective
This section describes the target market into which the solution will be introduced.

3.2. Target Market Description
<Describe the market at which the solution is targeted.>

3.2.1. Target Market Characteristics
<List and describe key characteristics of the target market.>

3.2.2. Target Market Trends
<List and describe influential trends taking place in the target market. Note the technological, economic, political, and competitive landscape.>

3.2.3. Target Market Segmentation
<Define and describe any form of applicable market segmentation such as geographical, demographical, behavioral, or sociological classifications. In addition, complete the table below.>

Market Segment	Key Characteristics

3.2.4. Target Market Time Constraints
<Describe any timeline constraints affecting the introduction of the marketplace solution. Note constraints such as: seasonal restrictions, competition, technological obsoleteness, or other major events.>

4. Customers and Buyers

4.1. Section Objective
This section describes the customers and buyers.

<Comment: The customer is the entity that takes (financial) responsibility for the product. The buyer is the entity that decides to obtain the product (solution). The user is the entity that interacts with the product. Users are described in the "Users and Personas" section.>

4.2. Target Customer Description
<Define and describe the general customer profile towards which the solution is targeted.>

4.2.1. Target Customer Segmentation
<Define and describe any form of applicable segmentation such as geographic, demographic, and behavioral. How many distinct customer categories are there and what are their characteristics? In addition, complete the table below.>

Customer Segment	Key Characteristics

4.2.2. Target Customer Motivators
<Define and describe the reasons why customers will buy the solution. Why would customers prefer the solution over the competition?>

4.2.3. Target Customer Influencers
<Define and describe any tangible and non-tangible influencers on the customer's buying decision. Note influencers such as: price sensitivity, selectivity, culture, peer interactions, fashion, trends, or income level.>

4.2.4. Target Customer Goals
<Define and describe customer goals in obtaining the solution. Customer goals in obtaining the solution are often to serve corporate business goals.>

4.3. Target Buyers Description
<Define and describe the buyers; the entities that decide to obtain the product.>

4.3.1. BDM (Business Decision Maker) Buyers
<List, define and describe the BDM buyers.>

4.3.1.1. BDM Motivators
<Define and describe the reasons why BDM buyers will buy the solution. Why would BDM buyers prefer the product over the competition?>

4.3.1.2. BDM Goals
<Define and describe BDM buyer goals in obtaining the solution. BDM buyer goals are often focused on issues such as: improving the organization, increasing productivity, or reducing costs.>

4.3.2. TDM (Technical Decision Maker) Buyers
<List, define and describe the TDM buyers.>

4.3.2.1. TDM Motivators
<Define and describe the reasons why TDM buyers will buy the solution. Why would TDM buyers prefer the product over the competition?>

4.3.2.2. TDM Goals
<Define and describe TDM buyer goals in obtaining the solution. TDM buyer goals are often focused on issues such as: reliability, simplicity, integration, install-ability, support, or scalability.>

5. Users and Personas

5.1. Section Objective
This section describes Personas relative to the market problem and planned solution.

5.2. Personas
<Create and fill a persona description table per each possible persona relative to the market problem and planned solution.>
<Comment: The user is the entity that interacts with the product. Personas are a set of fictional, representative user archetypes with well understood skills, attitudes, environment, behavior patterns, and goals.>

Parameter	Description
Persona name	
Background	
Skills	
Environment	
Attitudes	
Behavior	
Goals	
Notes	

<Comment: To illustrate the concept of personas, the following is an example of a network administrator persona.

Example:

Parameter	Description
Persona name	*John Smith*
Background	*37 years old network administrator*
Skills	*10 years experience, BS EE, CCNA*
Environment	*Corporate network with several servers and Internet gateway*
Attitudes	*Customer focused attitude; passion for technology*
Behavior	*Monitors traffic and does troubleshooting*
Goals	*Seeks decision support and system auto-management*
Notes	*Usually work 50 hours per week*

>

5.3. **Persona Needs in the Present**

<Describe what the personas are presently doing to satisfy their needs.>

5.4. **Persona Linkage**

<Describe how and which personas link back to the Customer and Buyer. This link helps establish the persona's relevance to the solution.>

6. Market Requirements

6.1. **Section Objective**

This section describes the market requirements that are drawn from the market problem.

<Comment: Market Requirements are facets of the market problem. In the entire requirements section, avoid defining a product and avoid providing detailed design or implementation specifications. If there are no objectives or relevant discussion for a specific requirement category or section, then the requirement category or section must still be included, with the notation 'N/A' (not applicable) and a short explanation.

All market requirements describe the solution from the user's perspective and effectively depict what the user wishes to accomplish.>

6.2. <u>Glossary and Definitions</u>

<Provide a list of any market problem related terms and their definitions, which will be used as part of describing the various market requirements.>

Term	Definition
<Term>	<Provide a definition for the term.>

6.3. <u>Functional Category</u>

<Provide a list of the operational characteristics; the working capabilities required of the solution. Write each market requirement separately in its own table.>

Field	Description
MR Identifier	<Provide a unique identifier using a consistent name convention.>
MR Name	<Provide a short name for easy reference to the market requirement.>
Directive	<Provide the instruction that guides and directs functionality being sought by the user. Each directive addresses a facet of the market problem. The directive format is: *"User [persona] <shall/should[(high/medium/low)]> be able to <functionality>.">* <Comment: The special conventions used in the directive are:* • Square *brackets "[ ]" denote optional arguments* • Pointed *brackets "<>" denote mandatory arguments* • Slash *symbol "/" denote the "OR" logical operator.>*
Priority	<Indicate the level of priority attributed to this market requirement: • "Shall" directive conditioning – critical functionality. • "Should" directive conditioning – desirable functionality (high, medium, low).>
• Rationales	<Provide a list of all possible rationales; the reasons that support the introduction of this market requirement.>
o Sources	<Each rationale must be supported by a source. Sources are a list of references and information origins that validate the market requirement.>
Constraints	<Provide a list of all possible constraints; the limitations imposed on the solution relevant to this particular market requirement. Each constraint should be supported by its own rational and source.>
• Rationales	<Provide a list of all possible rationales; the reasons that support the introduction of this constraint.>
o Sources	<Each rationale must be supported by a source. Sources are a list of references and information origins that validate the market requirement.>
Persona	<List names of all personas applicable to this market requirement.>
Use Case	<Provide a use case statement or use case identifiers applicable to this market requirement. Entry of use case information is applicable only if a product or product concept actually exists.>
Buying Criterion	<Indicate via this Boolean indicator (Yes/No/NA) whether this market requirement will foster a product feature used as a buying criterion.>
Differentiator	<Indicate via this Boolean indicator (Yes/No/NA) whether this market requirement will foster a product feature that is a key differentiator, relative to competing products.>

<Comment: Recommended name convention is product initials followed by .MR. (e.g., SLC.MR200) and followed by other market requirement component initials. Introduce numerical gaps into the identifiers in order that future market requirements can be inserted without need for renumbering. Following is an example of a functional market requirement. Note the identifier name convention used for the rationales and constraints.*

Field	Description
MR Identifier	MGL.MR200
MR Name	Dropped Flashlight.
Directive	User shall be able to find dropped flashlight.
Priority	Critical Functionality.
• Rationales	MGL.MR200.R10 – loss of flashlight impairs critical navigational abilities and limits spotting by rescue force in 75% of cases.
o Sources	MGL.MR200.R10.S10 – Red Cross report, 2001.
Constraints	• MGL.MR200.C10 – terrain: snow (one foot deep) • MGL.MR200.C20 – recovery time: ten seconds • MGL.MR200.C30 – visibility: darkness
• Rationales	• MGL.MR200.C10.R10 – 20% of users have lost flashlight in snow.
o Sources	• MGL.MR200.C10.R10.S10 – USFS Survey, 2001.
Persona	John Pro (professional hiker), Tim Easy (weekend hiker)
Use Case	MGL.UC500 (weekend travel), MGL.UC900 (wilderness survival)
Buying Criterion	Yes. Buyers: Mike Slide (Ski Patrol), John Fire (Rescue Force). This is a buying criterion because individuals in these organizations rely on flashlights to save lives.
Differentiator	Yes. Functionality not found in any other commercially available flashlight.

>

6.4. Development Category
<Provide a list of the engineering demands placed by the user on the solution. These market requirements constitute the solution's development environment. With regard to software these are often the development tools and API sets. Write each market requirement separately in its own table.>

6.5. Compatibility Category
<Provide a list of the conformance demands placed by the user on the solution. These can be conditions that support the solution and constitute the environment in which the solution will operate. With regard to software, these are elements such as: operating system platforms, GUI interfaces, or supported standards. Write each market requirement separately in its own table.>

6.6. Performance Category
<List the quantitative and qualitative demands placed by the user on the solution. These market requirements reflect the need for certain levels of speed, usability,

capacity, or scalability. These market requirements are sometimes referred to as non-functional market requirements. Write each market requirement separately in its own table.>

6.7. Internationalization Category

<List the language and cultural demands placed by the user on the solution. These market requirements reflect the need to tailor the solution to the nuances imposed by different global markets. These market requirements impact the solution's design as to accommodate for culturally diverse markets. Write each market requirement separately in its own table.>

6.8. Documentation Category

<List the written support demands placed by the user on the solution. Write each market requirement separately in its own table.>

6.9. Physical Category

<If applicable, provide a list of market requirements that detail the solution's desired physical attributes such as size, weight, color, dimensions, or construction materials. Write each market requirement separately in its own table.>

6.10. Distribution Category

<List the market requirements which are based on implications that affect the solution's distribution channels. These market requirements deal with how the solution is transported to the customer's possession, and include elements such as: regulatory barriers, legal restrictions on export, or transport limitation (e.g., land only). Write each market requirement separately in its own table.>

6.11. Support and Training Category

<List the market requirements which are based on implications that affect the need for user support and training structures because of the solution. Write each market requirement separately in its own table.>

6.12. Miscellaneous Product Category

<List all market requirements not covered in other sections. Write each market requirement separately in its own table.>

6.13. Solution Overview

<Only if truly applicable, provide a very general description of the solution, its purpose and functionality. Explain how the solution fits in to the overall corporate product strategy. This section is relevant only if a product or product concept already exists.>

6.14. Solution Technology Overview

<Only if truly applicable, provide a general description of the technology and innovation found in the solution itself, and in the technology which will be

employed in producing the solution. This section is relevant only if a product or product concept already exists.>

6.15.   Market Requirements Summary Table

<The table below is a summary of all market requirements. It provides an overview of the problem that will be solved by the proposed functional solution. Enter into the table the various market requirements in concise form and sort the table by Category (primary) and Priority (secondary).>

Identifier	Directive	Constraints	Rationales	Persona	Category	Priority

7. Supporting Data

7.1. Section Objective

The section provides data in support of claims, assertions, assumptions, and statements made throughout this document.

7.2. MRD Assumptions

<Describe any assumptions made when writing this document. Be specific about the assumptions that if changed will alter the direction of the MRD and resulting solution.>

7.3. Research Information

<If relevant, describe and list the type and scope of research conducted in the course of writing this document.>

7.4. Product Diagram/Architecture

<If relevant, describe the solution's architecture and modules accompanied by a schematic diagram.>

11.1.2 PRM Product Requirements Document (PRD) – Template V. 4.0

Company Name: <Enter company name>
Product Name: <Enter product name>

- Date: <Enter date>
- Contact: <Enter your name>
- Department: <Enter department name>
- Location: <Enter location>
- Email: <Enter email address>
- Telephone: <Enter telephone number><

Document Revision History:

Date	Revision	Revised By	Approved By
<Enter date>	<Revision #>	<Enter your name>	<Enter name>

Table of Contents

1. Introduction

1.1. Document Objective
The Product Requirements Document (PRD) provides a complete requirements definition of a product, based on the market requirements. The PRD describes the features and functions of a product without regard to implementation.

1.2. Market Problem
<Identify and justify the specific market problem. Explain any other interlinking market problems.>
<Comment: The market problem is a "consumer" or "product" or "technology" problem in the target market. The market problem is essentially a situation (difficulty) that exists in the target market and requires change.
- *Consumer Problem – A marketplace situation in which consumer needs remain unsatisfied (B2C). The solution to a consumer problem is a whole product.*
- *Product Problem – An industry situation in which product requirements' are unmet (B2B). The solution to a product problem is a product component.*
- *Technology Problem – Challenges in applied science. The solution to a technology problem is scientific research.*

1.3. Market Opportunity
<Provide a statement detailing the specific market opportunity. Size and substantiate the market opportunity as much as possible. Document the assumptions and facts that validate and justify the market opportunity. Explain any other interlinking market opportunities.>
<Comment: The market opportunity is a lucrative, lasting and sizable market problem. Market Opportunity = Market Problem + Volume + Duration + Earning Potential.>

1.4. Product Concept
<Describe in general terms the proposed product, its functions and capabilities.>

1.5. Sales Axioms
<Describe the product's suggested sales axioms. See the "PMTK Sales Axioms" template.>

1.6. Unique Selling Proposition (USP)
<Describe the product's suggested Unique Selling Proposition (USP). See the "PMTK Unique Selling Proposition" template.>

2. Product Project Overview

2.1. Section Objective
This section provides macro information about the environment into which the product will be introduced.

2.2. **Target Market Description**
<Describe in very general terms the market to which the solution is targeted.>

2.3. **Target Customer Description**
<Define and describe the general customer profile for which the product is targeted. Also, describe the buyer and user.>

3. Product Environment

3.1. **Section Objective**
This section provides macro information on the constraints and assumptions that guide and limit the product's scope, functionally, and impact on its future design.

3.2. **General Constraints**
<Identify and enumerate any core elements that will limit the developers' options in building the system. These are typically hardware/software limitations and interfaces to other systems.>

3.3. **Assumptions and Dependencies**
<Create a numbered list of all the assumptions that affect the product. Include all dependency issues resulting from development efforts with other products, the need for output from other product projects, or the need-to-know decisions made by other development groups.>

4. Product Requirements

4.1. **Section Objective**
This section describes the functional and feature requirements of the product.
<Comment: Each product requirement must be written as a clear and concise statement, rather than in a long narrative or paragraph form. Do NOT describe the product design in the product requirements document. The PRD is a description of 'what' the product is from an external viewpoint. The PRD does not state 'how' the product does what it does. Avoid providing detailed design or implementation specifications. Rational and sources are optional within each product requirement.>

4.2. **Functional Requirements**
<List the features and functions provided by the product. This effectively is a list of what the product does or has. Write each requirement separately in its own table.>

Requirement	Description
PR Identifier	<Provide a unique identifier for the product requirement. Recommended name convention is product initials followed by .PRxxx (i.e. SLC.PR200). Introduce gaps into the identifiers so future requirements can be inserted without need for renumbering.>
Directive	<Provide the requirement's directive; a statement that describes a facet of the product. The directive is an instruction, guiding what the product does or has. Directives are phrased as follows: *"Product shall/should provide...".*>
Constraints	<Provide all possible constraints; the design limitations imposed on the product, relevant to this particular product requirement.>
MR Identifier	<Provide reference to the market requirement identifier, listed in the MRD, which is the cause for introducing this product requirement.>

<Comment: Recommended name convention is product initials followed by .PR with the product requirement's number (i.e. SLC.PR200) and followed by other product requirement's component's initials and numbers. Introduce gaps into the identifiers in order that future product requirements can be inserted without need for renumbering. Following is an example of a functional product requirement. Note the identifier name convention used for the rationales and constraints.

Requirement	Description
PR Identifier	*SLC.PR200*
Directive	*Product shall provide an electrical output signal.*
Constraints	• *SLC.PR200.C10 – amplitude of the output shall be less than 1.0 volts peak-to-peak.* • *SLC.PR200.C20 – output signal shall be limited 20,000 hertz.* • *SLC.PR200.C30 – output impedance shall be no more than 20 ohms.*
MR Identifier	*SLC.MR239*

>

4.3. Development Requirements
<Provide a list of the engineering demands that shape the solution. These requirements constitute the solution's development environment. With regard to software, these are often the development tools and API sets. Write each requirement separately in its own table.>

4.4. Compatibility Requirements
<Provide a list of the conformance demands that shape the solution. These can be conditions that support the solution and constitute the environment in which the solution will operate. With regard to software, these are elements such as: operating system platforms, GUI interfaces, or supported standards. Write each requirement separately in its own table.>

4.5. Performance Requirements

<List the quantitative and qualitative demands that shape the solution. These requirements reflect the need for certain levels of speed, usability, capacity, or scalability. These requirements are sometimes referred to as non-functional requirements. Write each requirement separately in its own table.>

4.6. Internationalization Requirements

<List the language and cultural demands that shape the solution. These requirements reflect the need to tailor the solution to the nuances imposed by different global markets. These requirements impact the solution's design as to accommodate for culturally diverse markets. Write each requirement separately in its own table.>

4.7. Documentation Requirements

<List the written support demands that shape the solution. Write each requirement separately in its own table.>

4.8. Physical Requirements

<If applicable, provide a list of product requirements that detail the solution's desired physical attributes such as size, weight, color, dimensions, or construction materials. Write each requirement separately in its own table.>

4.9. Distribution Requirements

<List the product requirements which are based on implications that affect the solution's distribution channels. These requirements deal with how the solution is transported to the customer's possession, and include elements such as: regulatory barriers, legal restrictions on export, or transport limitation (i.e., land only). Write each requirement separately in its own table.>

4.10. Support and Training Requirements

<List the product requirements which are based on implications that affect the need for user support and training structures because of the solution. Write each requirement separately in its own table.>

4.11. Miscellaneous Product Requirements

<List all requirements not covered in other sections. Write each requirement separately in its own table.>

4.12. Solution Overview

<Provide a general description of the solution, its purpose and functionality. Explain how the solution fits in to the overall corporate product strategy.>

4.13. Solution Technology Overview

<Provide a description of the technology and innovation found in the solution itself, and also in those technologies which will be employed in producing the

solution. This section is relevant only if a product or product concept already exists.>

4.14. Product Requirements Summary Table

<The table below is a summary of all product requirements. It provides an overview of the functional solution. Enter into the table the various product requirements in concise form and sort the table by Category (primary) and Priority (secondary).>

PR Identifier	Directive	Constraints	MR Identifier	Category	Priority

5. Supporting Data

5.1. Section Objective

The section provides data in support of claims, assertions, assumptions, and statements made throughout this document.

5.2. PRD Assumptions

<Describe any assumptions made when writing this document. Be specific about the assumptions that if changed will alter the direction of the PRD and resulting solution.>

5.3. Research Information

<If relevant, describe and list the type and scope of research conducted in the course of writing this document.>

5.4. Product Diagram/Architecture

<If relevant, describe the solution's architecture and modules accompanied by a schematic diagram.>

11.1.3 PMTK Market Requirements Document (MRD) – Template V. 4.0

Company Name: <Enter company name>

Product Name: <Enter product name>

- Date: <Enter date>
- Contact: <Enter your name>
- Department: <Enter department name>
- Location: <Enter location>
- Email: <Enter email address>
- Telephone: <Enter telephone number>

Document Revision History:

Date	Revision	Revised By	Approved By
<Enter date>	<Revision #>	<Enter your name>	<Enter name>

Table of Contents

1. Introduction

1.1. <u>Document Objective</u>

The Market Requirements Document (MRD) describes the product and the market into which the product will be introduced.

<Comment: This document represents an "inclusive" approach to writing an MRD in which business information, market and product requirements are all bundled together in the same document. The information contained in this document is also used for business worthiness and technological feasibility approval.>

1.2. <u>Executive Summary</u>

This section provides a concise report of the pertinent facts, assumptions and suggestions noted throughout this document.

<Comment: This section is the last section to be filled in and completed once the rest of the MRD is complete. Focus on the key elements of the product and do not exceed two pages.>

1.2.1. <u>Business Objectives</u>
<Based on the corresponding section, describe the product's strategic business objectives and overall fit with the company's corporate mission.>

1.2.2. <u>Market/Customer Overview</u>
<Based on the corresponding section, describe the target markets and customer profile to which the product is targeted.>

1.2.3. <u>Customers Use Cases</u>
<Based on the corresponding section, describe how various users will put the product to use.>

1.2.4. <u>Product Requirements</u>
<Based on the corresponding section, describe the general product functional requirements.>

1.2.5. <u>Success Criteria</u>
<Based on the corresponding section, describe the criteria used to define and measure the product's level of success.>

1.2.6. <u>Financial Data</u>
<Based on the corresponding section, describe financial and budgetary issues associated with the product from both cost and revenue perspectives.>

1.2.7. <u>Product Schedule</u>
<Based on the corresponding section, describe the estimated product delivery timeline.>

1.2.8. <u>Risks And Consequences</u>
<Based on the corresponding section, describe the risks and consequences associated with the decision to develop and market the product.>

1.2.9. <u>Supporting Data</u>
<Based on the corresponding section, describe data in support of claims, assertions, assumptions, and statements made throughout this document.>

2. Business Objectives

2.1. Section Objective
This section describes the product's strategic business objectives and overall fit with the company's vision and mission statements.

2.2. Background
<Describe the rationale for building the new product, such as environment, history and decisions that lead to the recognition that the product should be built.>

2.3. Market Problem and Opportunity
<Describe the market opportunity that exists or which will be created. Outline the relevant market problem that will be solved with the help of the product.>
<Comment: The market problem is a situation (difficulty) that exists in the marketplace and requires change. The market opportunity is a lucrative, lasting and sizable marketplace situation in which customer needs remain unsatisfied.>

2.4. Product Problem and Opportunity
<Only if relevant, describe the product problem and product opportunity.>
<Comment: The product problem is an industry situation in which product requirements' are unmet. The product opportunity is a market opportunity dependent, lucrative, lasting, and sizable industry situation in which product requirements' are unmet.>

2.5. Technology Problem and Opportunity
<Only if relevant, describe the technology problem and technology opportunity.>
<Comment: The technology problem is challenges in applied science. The technology opportunity is a product opportunity dependent challenges in applied science.>

2.6. Business Objectives
<Describe what the product is supposed to do for the company. Be specific about the product's strategic purpose and how it helps the enterprise achieve its long term business objectives. Will the product: Demonstrate a new technology? Defend existing markets? Penetrate new markets? Be a "me-too" product?>

2.7. Value and Benefits to Company
<Describe the value or benefits the product will generate for the company (not the customer). These include repositioning, improved offering, market penetration, or demonstrating technology.>

2.8. Value and Benefits to Customer
<Describe the value or benefits the product will generate for the customer. Describe the value in terms such as: productivity, automation, cost savings, efficiency, marketability, profit, new or improved abilities, and conformance to standards.>

3. Market/Customer Overview

3.1. Section Objective

This section describes the target markets and customer profile to which the product is targeted.

3.2. Target Market Description

<Describe the market to which the product is targeted.>

3.2.1. Target Market Characteristics

<List and describe the key characteristics of the target market.>

3.2.2. Target Market Trends

<List and describe influential trends taking place in the target market. Note the technological, economic, political, and competitive landscape.>

3.2.3. Target Market Segmentation

<Complete the table below. Define and describe any form of applicable market segmentation, such as geographic, demographic, and behavioral.>

Market Segment	Key Characteristics

3.2.4. Target Market Size and Demand Projection

< Complete the table below. Describe the estimated market volume and the projected demand for product units, per each segment.>

Market Segment	Projected Demand

3.2.5. Target Market Time Constraints

<Describe any timeline constraints affecting the introduction of the product to the market. Note any special constraints, such as seasonal restrictions, competition, technological obsoleteness, or major events.>

3.3. Target Customer Description

<Define and describe the customer profile to which the product is targeted.>

3.3.1. Target Customer Needs

<Complete the table below and rank the needs in order of importance. Outline the target customer needs and explain how those needs will be met by the product. Describe what the customer is presently doing to satisfy the needs.>

Need	Description	Present Method of Satisfying the Need

3.3.2. Target Customer Segmentation

<Complete the table below. Define and describe any form of applicable segmentation such as geographic, demographic, and behavioral. Describe

any distinct customer categories are there and what their characteristics are.>

Customer Segment	Key Characteristics

3.3.3. Target Customer Profile
<Complete the table below. List and describe the target customer profile. If applicable, describe the typical customer profile.>

Customer Segment	Customer Profile	Valued Features	Notes

3.3.4. Target Customer Motivators
<Define and describe the reasons why customers will buy the product on its own right. Explain why customers would prefer the product over the competition.>

3.3.5. Target Customer Influencers
<Define and describe any tangible and intangible influencers on the customer's buying decision. Note any specific influencers, such as price sensitivity, selectivity, culture, peer interactions, fashion, trends, or income level.>

3.4. The Competitive Landscape
<Complete the table below. Describe the range of competing products that have similar applications to the product. Also detail products which are not similar or direct competitors to the product but are being used to perform functions of the product.>

Competing Product	Description	Key Functional and Feature Differences	Price	Strengths and Weaknesses	Market Share/ Dominance

4. Customer Use Cases

4.1. Section Objective
This document describes how various users will put the product to use and under which scenarios.

4.2. Use Cases
<Describe the various scenarios in which users will employ the product or are currently employing similar products.>

5. Product Requirements

5.1. Section Objective
This section describes the product's functional specification.
<Comment: In the entire requirements section, avoid providing detailed design or implementation requirements.>

5.2. Product Overview
<Provide a general description of the product and its purpose and functionality. Explain how the product fits in to the overall corporate product strategy.>

5.3. Product Technology Overview
<Provide a general description of technology and innovation found in the product itself, as well as those which will be employed in the making of the product.>

5.4. General Product Requirements
<Complete the table below. Provide a list of requirements that support the product and constitute the environment in which the product will operate. With regard to software, these are elements such as API sets, development tools, operating system platforms, GUI interfaces, compatibility and conformance issues, or supported standards.>

Requirement Name	Description	Priority Level

5.5. Physical Product Requirements
<Complete the table below. If applicable, provide a list of requirements that detail the product's physical attributes such as size, weight, color, dimensions, or construction materials.>

Requirement Name	Description	Priority Level

5.6. Functional Product Requirements
<Complete the table below. Provide a list of the product's operational characteristics and its abilities. This is effectively a list of what the product "can do". Write each functional requirement separately.>

Requirement Name	Description	Priority Level

5.7. Performance Product Requirements
<Complete the table below. List the quantitative and qualitative demands placed on the product. These requirements reflect the need for certain levels of speed, usability, capacity, or scalability. These requirements are sometimes referred to as non-functional requirements.>

Requirement Name	Description	Priority Level

5.8. **Product Process Requirements**
<Complete the table below. List the internal procedures and routines which govern how various modules or parts of the product interact with each other. These requirements explain an internal course of action within the product itself.>

Requirement Name	Description	Priority Level

5.9. **Product Distribution Requirements**
<Complete the table below. List all implications that affect the product's distribution channels and the resulting requirements. These requirements deal with how the product is transported to the customer's possession, and include elements such as regulatory barriers, legal restrictions on export, or transport limitation (e.g., land only).>

Requirement Name	Description	Priority Level

5.10.   **Support and Training Requirements**
<List all implications that affect the need for support and training structures because of the product.>

5.10.1. **Internal Support and Training Requirements**
<Complete the table below. List all support and training requirements that internal company functions will require. These function departments are usually sales, business development, consulting, customer service and support.>

Requirement Name	Description	Priority Level

5.10.2. **External Support and Training Requirements**
<Complete the table below. List all support and training requirements that external company functions will require. These entities are usually the customer, partners, external/indirect sales channel, consulting companies, VAR's or solution providers.>

Requirement Name	Description	Priority Level

5.11.   **Miscellaneous Product Requirements**
<Complete the table below. List all requirements not covered in other sections.>

Requirement Name	Description	Priority Level

5.12. **Product Features and Benefits**

<Complete the table below with the key benefits and their supporting features. Map the notable benefits the customer will get to the product's major features sets. See the section titled "Value and Benefits to Customer" for a list of benefits the product will generate for the customer. In addition, complete the table below.>

Customer Benefits	Supporting Features

6. Success Criteria

6.1. **Section Objective**

This section describes the criteria used to define and measure the product's level of success.

6.2. **Success Criteria and Metrics**

<Describe the applicable and chosen success criteria and metrics that will be used in evaluating the product's performance. Commonly used criteria are unit price, unit production cost, deviance from budget or timeline or feature set, time-to-market, feature set scope, sales volume, sales velocity, market penetration, or market share.>

6.3. **Factors of Impact**

The following are factors which have the greatest impact on the product's potential success.

<Comment: These factors may also be considered as constraints and dependencies.>

6.3.1. **Internal Factors of Impact**

<Describe factors that are likely to affect the product's success and are under the direct control of the company.>

6.3.2. **External Factors of Impact**

<Describe factors that are likely to affect the product's success and are **not** under the direct control of the company. These are factors such as third-party vendors, marketplace competition, user acceptance, implementation challenges, specific technologies, development partners, or other business relationships.>

7. Financial Data

7.1. **Section Objective**

This section describes all financial and budgetary issues associated with the product from both cost and revenue perspectives. <Present, at a minimum, a two year timeline.>

7.2. Sales and Revenue Forecast

This section describes the estimated sales volume and revenue the product will produce for the company.

7.2.1. Direct Sales Channel Forecast

<Describe the sales and revenue forecast for the direct sales channel.>

7.2.2. Indirect Sales Channel Forecast

<Describe the sales and revenue forecast for the indirect sales channel.>

7.3. Cost and Budget Estimates

<Describe the cost and budget estimates for the product. Present, at a minimum, a two year timeline.>

7.3.1. Product Development Costs

<Describe the cost and budget estimates associated with designing and developing the product.>

7.3.2. Product Production Costs

<Describe the cost and budget estimates associated with the ongoing production costs of the product once design and development are completed.>

7.3.3. Product Marketing Costs

<Describe the cost and budget estimates associated with all product marketing and marketing communication activities including product launch.>

7.3.4. Product Education and Training Costs

<Describe the cost and budget estimates associated with the education and training of internal and external entities.>

7.3.5. Product Service and Support Costs

<Describe the cost and budget estimates associated the product service and support functions.>

8. Product Schedule

8.1. Section Objective

This section describes the estimated product timeline.

8.2. Product Schedule and Critical Milestones

<Describe the estimated product timeline. The period reflected in the schedule for the purpose of this document should begin at the start of the design and development stage and end when the product launch stage is officially complete.>

9. Risks and Consequences

9.1. Section Objective

This section describes the risks and consequences associated with the decision to develop and market the product.

9.2. Product Risks and Consequences

<Complete the table below. Describe what could **negatively** happen to the company if it does decide to develop the product. Explain if product failure in the marketplace will have far reaching strategic consequences to the company. Explain how the risks could be mitigated. For clarification, this section does not deal with threats affecting the development process such as resource constraints.>

Risk Name	Description	Severity	Mitigation Options

10. Supporting Data

10.1. Section Objective

The section provides data in support of claims, assertions, assumptions and statements made throughout this document.

10.2. MRD Assumptions

<Describe any assumptions made when writing this document. Be specific about the assumptions that if changed will alter the direction of the MRD and resulting solution.>

10.3. Research Information

<If relevant, describe and list the type and scope of research conducted in the course of writing this document.>

10.4. Product Diagram/Architecture

<If relevant, describe the product's architecture and modules accompanied by a schematic diagram.>

11.1.4 Use Cases – Template V. 4.0

Company Name: \<Enter company name\>
Product Name: \<Enter product name\>

- Date: \<Enter date\>
- Contact: \<Enter your name\>
- Department: \<Enter department name\>
- Location: \<Enter location\>
- Email: \<Enter email address\>
- Telephone: \<Enter telephone number\>

Document Revision History:

Date	Revision	Revised By	Approved By
\<Enter date\>	\<Revision #\>	\<Enter your name\>	\<Enter name\>

Table of Contents

1. Introduction

1.1. **Document Objective**

This document describes how different personas put a solution to use and in which events.

<Comment: There are several scenarios to writing use cases:

- *The Market Requirements Document (MRD) exists but there is no product concept and no Product Requirements Document (PRD). In this scenario no use cases are written by anyone.*

- *The Market Requirements Document (MRD) exists and there is a general product concept, but no Product Requirements Document (PRD) exists so actual features are not documented. In this scenario the owner/writer of the Use Cases document is the product planner who may prepare (with the product architect as a contributor) high-level and descriptive use cases which describe how possible future features in the product would be possibly employed by different personas. These descriptive uses cases are included with the Market Requirements Document (MRD) document.*

- *The Market Requirements Document (MRD) and the Product Requirements Document (PRD) exist, and consequently there is a definitive product concept and documented actual features. In this scenario the owner/writer of the Use Cases document is the product architect who prepares (with the product planner as a contributor) detailed use cases which describe how actual features in the product would be employed by different personas. These detailed use cases are included with the Product Requirements Document (PRD) document.>*

2. The Product

2.1. **Section Objective**

This section describes the product.

2.2. **Product Overview**

<Provide a general description of the product relating to its purpose and functionality.>

2.3. **Product Technology Overview**

<Provide a general description of the technology and innovation found in the product itself.>

3. Personas Overview

3.1. **Section Objective**

This section describes the personas that will use the product.

<Comment: Throughout this section you may reference or copy relevant information from the "Users and Personas" section in the PMTK "PRM Market Requirements Document" (MRD).>

3.2. Primary Persona Description
<Define and describe the primary persona that uses the product.>

3.2.1. Primary Persona Needs
<Outline the primary persona needs and explain how those needs will be met by the product. Describe what the persona is presently doing to satisfy those needs. In addition, complete the table below and rank the needs in order of importance.>

Rank	Need	Need Description	Present Method of Satisfying the Need

3.3. Secondary Persona(s) Description
<Define and describe the secondary personas of the product.>

3.3.1. Secondary Persona(s) Needs
<Outline the secondary personas' needs and explain how those needs will be met by the product. Describe what the persona is presently doing to satisfy those needs. In addition, complete the table below and rank the needs in order of importance.>

Rank	Need	Need Description	Present Method of Satisfying the Need

3.4. Personas Goals
<List and describe the goals of the various personas.>
<Comment: Personas are distinguished by their goals. Goals are what the persona wishes to accomplish. Goals are not tasks.>

Persona	Goal

4. Use Cases

4.1. Section Objective
This section describes the various use cases relative to the personas that use the product.

*<Comment: Use cases describe how different personas put a solution to use and for which events. Use cases define **events** (specific instances of usage) and describe **who** (persona) does **what** (interaction) with the product and for what **purpose** (goal). In more precise terms, a Use Case is a specific way of using the system by performing some part of the functionality. Each use case constitutes a complete course of action initiated by a persona, and it specifies the interaction*

that takes place between a persona and the system. The collected use cases specify all the existing ways of using the system. Use cases focus on single instances of use. Combining several use cases forms a "Scenario". A scenario is a succession of use cases, and is sometimes presented using a "Storyboard". In several published books covering the topic of use cases; the "Persona" may be referred to as the "Actor", and the "Product" may be referred to as the "System". These terms are and can be used alternately.>

4.2. <u>Use Case Specification</u>

Use cases define *events* (specific instances of usage) and describe *who* (persona) does *what* (interaction) with the solution and for what *purpose* (goal).

<Comment: Prepare use cases for the primary and secondary personas. The following is a general tabular structure that can be used in describing each use case.>

Item	Description
Use Case Name	<Title given to the specific use case.>
Use Case Statement	<Summary description of the use case that encompasses and defines the *event* (specific instance of usage) and describes *who* (persona) does *what* (interaction) with the solution and for what *purpose* (goal).>
Priority	<Level of priority for implementing the specific functionality needed to realize this use case.>
Persona	<Entity that interacts with the product and uses it.>
Persona's Capabilities	<Framework of the persona's knowledge and abilities. The competence level that can be expected from the persona.>
Responsibility	<Scope of responsibility the persona has relative to the product.>
Persona Goal	<Purpose for using the product. What the persona wishes to achieve by using the product.>
Pre-Conditions	<State of things before the persona begins using the product.>
Trigger	<Event that causes the persona to use the product in the specific way.>
Interaction and Primary Flow	<Most common and primary use for the product as used by the persona.>
Alternative Flow #n	<Variation of the main flow or different use for the product.>
Post-Conditions	<State of things after the persona had completed using the product.>
Frequency	<Number of times the use case will be executed by the persona in a given time period.>
Assumptions	<Assumptions or stipulations made in support of the use case.>
Miscellaneous	<Additional comments and notes about the use case.>

<Example: The following are proper examples of use case statements. Note that it is clear to recognize from each statement "Who" does "What" with the product for which "Event(s)" and for what "Purpose".
- *"Professional Hikers use light signals to signal rescue airplanes in case of emergency so that their lives can be saved."*
- *"Homeowners use alternate light sources to navigate their home during power blackouts so they do not fall and injure themselves."*

- *"Mechanics use light sources to peer into vehicle nooks and crannies so they can easily search for and retrieve lost parts."*>

5. Supporting Data

5.1. Section Objective
The section provides data in support of claims, assertions, assumptions, and statements made throughout this document.

5.2. Assumptions
<Describe any assumptions made when writing this document.>

5.3. Research Information
<If relevant, describe and list the type and scope of research conducted in the course of writing this document.>

5.4. Product Diagram/Architecture
<If relevant, describe the product's architecture and modules accompanied by a schematic diagram.>

11.1.5 Product Roadmap – Template V. 4.0

Company Name: <Enter company name>

Product Name: <Enter product name>

- Date: <Enter date>
- Contact: <Enter your name>
- Department: <Enter department name>
- Location: <Enter location>
- Email: <Enter email address>
- Telephone: <Enter telephone number>

Document Revision History:

Date	Revision	Revised By	Approved By
<Enter date>	<Revision #>	<Enter your name>	<Enter name>

Table of Contents

1. Introduction

1.1. Document Objective

This document describes a product roadmap for the <Enter the name of the product or product line>. A product roadmap is a plan or vision that describes the company's long-term strategy for the product's evolution during the course of time.

2. Market/Technology Overview

2.1. Section Objective

This section describes the market to which the product is targeted towards and the technological landscape that affects the product.

2.2. Market Overview

<Define and describe the target markets and customer profile to which the product is targeted. List key characteristics of the target market and the customer. Note market trends and size as well as the economic, political and competitive landscape.>

2.3. Technology Overview

<Define and describe technologies that affect the product, such as foundational, competitive and emerging technologies. Note trends, standards, and dominance. Address technologies in the product and those used to manufacture the product.>

3. Product Roadmap

3.1. Section Objective

This section describes the product roadmap for <Enter name of product or product line>.

3.2. Product Roadmap

Roadmap	<Enter Year>	<Enter Year+1>	<Enter Year+2>
Product Location (Line, Family, Group, Unit)			
Product Name/Code Name			
Target Market			
Market Strategy			
Product Strategy			
Unique Selling Proposition			
Value Proposition			
Enhancements and Added Features			
Technologies Used in Product			

Roadmap	<Enter Year>	<Enter Year+1>	<Enter Year+2>
MSRP †			

† Manufacturer's suggested retail price

<Example:

Microsoft Windows Roadmap		
Roadmap	*2001*	*2007*
Product Location (Line, Family, Group, Unit)	*Desktop Operating Systems /Windows*	*Desktop Operating Systems /Windows*
Product Name/Code Name	*Windows XP (Whistler)*	*Windows Vista (Longhorn)*
Target Market	*SMB and consumers*	*SMB and consumers*
Market Strategy	*Complete global market dominance. Competitive advantage: brand, product proliferation and availability*	
Product Strategy	*Productivity (standards compliant and feature-rich)*	
Unique Selling Proposition	*Compatibility*	*Compatibility*
Value Proposition	---	---
Enhancements and Added Features	*Stability, domains, memory management, remote admin*	*Security, stability, Aero GUI, shell, account control*
Technologies Used in Product	*Multiprocessing, EFS, NTFS, hyper-threading, ClearType*	*WIM, WinFX, Speech recognition IPv6, MSH, WPF*
MSRP †	*$200 (Pro)*	*$400-$500 (?)*

† Manufacturer's suggested retail price
>

4. Supporting Data

4.1. Section Objective

This section provides data in support of claims, assertions, assumptions, and statements made throughout this document.

4.2. Assumptions

<Describe any assumptions made when writing this document.>

4.3. Research Information

<If relevant, describe and list the type and scope of research conducted in the course of writing this document.>

4.4. Product Diagram/Architecture

<If relevant, describe the product's architecture and modules accompanied by a schematic diagram.>

11.1.6 MVP Pricing Model – Template V. 4.0

Company Name: <Enter company name>

Product Name: <Enter product name>

- Date: <Enter date>
- Contact: <Enter your name>
- Department: <Enter department name>
- Location: <Enter location>
- Email: <Enter email address>
- Telephone: <Enter telephone number>

Document Revision History:

Date	Revision	Revised By	Approved By
<Enter date>	<Revision #>	<Enter your name>	<Enter name>

Table of Contents

1. Introduction

1.1. **Document Objective**

The purpose of this document is to provide a pricing model for the <Enter product name>.

<Comment: The "MVP Pricing Model Template" is designed to be used in conjunction with the "MVP Pricing Model Spreadsheet" and the "PMTK MVP Model Flowchart". Price is the specification of what a seller wants in exchange for granting right of ownership or use to a product. Pricing is the act of setting a price. Knowledge prerequisites to building a pricing model are:

- *Body of Knowledge – customers, competitors, complimentary.*
- *Knowledge of Costs – cost of goods, cost of selling, and overhead cost; (fixed or variable).*

The "PMTK MVP Model" is comprised of three distinct parts that effectively act as sequential stages in the pricing process (see the "PMTK MVP Model Flowchart"):

- *Pricing Scheme – outline of the overall pricing approach that encompasses the principles for pricing the specific product (how to achieve).*
- *Pricing Formula – calculatory structure that allows the application of pricing changes to specific markets or competitive regions (how to calculate).*
- *Price Mix – price related aggregate of information and conditions that the customer is presented with (how to present).*

This template implements the "PMTK MVP Pricing Process". The steps in this process are as follows:

1. *Secure knowledge prerequisites.*
2. *Determine pricing objectives.*
3. *Select pricing strategy.*
4. *Choose life cycle stage pricing tactics.*
5. *Devise a pricing formula.*
6. *Assemble a price mix.>*

1.2. **Product**

<Define and describe the product for which the pricing model is being developed.>

<Comment: Remember that the price a customer will ultimately pay should reflect the value and functionality that were given to the customer and not the resources invested in the product.>

2. Pricing Scheme

2.1. **Section Objective**

The purpose of this section is to determine the pricing scheme which is an outline of the overall pricing approach.

<Comment: The pricing scheme encompasses the principles for pricing the specific product. The pricing scheme is comprised of three distinct components that effectively act as sequential stages in the pricing process:
- *Objectives – description of what a company wants to achieve through pricing its products.*
- *Strategies – primary method to pricing that relies on a particular pricing decision factor.*
- *Tactics – pricing actions which are dependent on the particular life cycle stage of the product that is being priced.>*

2.2. Pricing Objectives

<Describe the pricing model's objectives. Explain why the particular objective or objectives are sought.>
<Comment: "Pricing Objectives" describe what a company wants to achieve through the pricing of its products. Common pricing model objectives are:
- *Profit (Income) – most financial gain.*
- *Units (Share) – biggest market share.*
- *Revenue (Sales) – largest volume of sales.*
- *Signal (Marketing) – indication to market or industry.>*

2.3. Pricing Strategies

<Describe the strategy that will be used in the pricing model. Explain why the particular strategy was selected.>
<Comment: Common pricing model strategies are:
- *"Cost-Plus" (Margin) – uses costs as the primary pricing decision factor.*
- *"Going-Rate" (Competition) – uses competitors' prices as the primary pricing decision factor.*
- *"Market-Will-Bear" (Monopoly) – uses unfair competitive advantages and market dependencies as the primary pricing decision factor.*
- *"Market-Value" (Value) – relies on customers' relative importance and paying propensity as the primary pricing decision factor.>*

2.3.1. Base Price

<Determine the "*Base Price*" that is recommended for this product.>
<Comment: "Base Price" is the initial price of a product before any alteration. This section is conditional on selecting either the "Cost-Plus" or "Going-Rate" or "Market-Will-Bear" pricing model strategy. Delete this section if not applicable.>

2.3.2. Market-Value Price (Base Price)

<Determine the "*Market-Value Price*" that is recommended for this product. The "*Market-Value Price*" will serve as the "*Base Price*".>
<Comment: "Base Price" is the initial price of a product before any alteration. This section is conditional on selecting the "Market-Value" pricing model strategy. Delete this section if not applicable.
Methods for performing "Market-Value Pricing" include:

- *"Inferred Price" (Implicit) – asking customers "How important to you is this product relative to [other products]?", and the price is concluded based in their answers.*
- *"Declared Price" (Explicit) – asking customers "How much are you willing to pay for this product?", and the price is explicitly declared by them.*
- *"Derived Price" (Determined) – price is determined based on attributed benefit. Determination of the "Derived Price" is preformed using the "MVP Pricing Mode" Spreadsheet".>*

2.4. **Pricing Tactics**
- <Determine and note the present life cycle stage the product is conceivably at.
- Describe the tactic or tactics that will be used in the pricing model, at the present lifecycle stage and possibly at later lifecycle stages.
- Explain why the particular tactic or tactics were selected.
- When relevant, determine the alteration applied to the base price, based on tactic selected.>

<Comment: Pricing model tactics are pricing actions which are dependent on the particular life cycle stage of the product that is being priced, relevant to the "Product Life Cycle Model" (PLC Model). For additional information about the PLC Model, see the "Extending Product Life Cycle Stages" chapter in this book. Common pricing model tactics are:
- *Introduction PLC Model Stage*
  - *Skimming (High Price) – briefly setting a high price for a new product to gain maximum revenues from segments willing to pay the high price.*
  - *Penetration (Low Price) – briefly setting a low price for a new product in order to attract a large number of buyers and a large market share.*
- *Growth PLC Model Stage*
  - *Diversification (Product Family) – create product variants with new price points.*
  - *Captive Product – offer an imbalanced price ratio of a product's components which are sold separately.*
  - *Discrimination – charge different market segments with different prices for same product.*
- *Maturity and Decline PLC Model Stages*
  - *Initiatives:*
    - *Reductions – universal, non-discriminatory and non-conditional official list price decreases.*
    - *Bundling – price of a set of products is lower than the sum total of the individual products purchased separately.*
  - *Reactions:*
    - *Anything ...>*

3. Pricing Formula

3.1. Section Objective

The purpose of this section is to determine the elements of a pricing formula used to calculate the price. The pricing formula allows the application of pricing changes to specific markets or competitive regions.

<Comment: The pricing formula is comprised of three distinct sections:
- *Variables – price changes based on product characteristics.*
- *Discounts – deductions from the list price.*
- *Licensing – variations in rights to usage and ownership.>*

3.2. Pricing Variables

<Describe the pricing variables that will be used in the pricing model. Select the variables relevant to your market and product. Pricing variables are not applicable to all products.>

<Comment: Pricing variables allow the application of pricing changes to specific markets or competitive regions. Pricing variables are usually characteristics of the product on which different price adjustments can be made. Pricing variables can also be viewed as being deliverable-based or quantum-based. The following are commonly used pricing variables:
- *General Pricing Variables*
  - o *Scale – Number of users.*
  - o *Schedule – Pace at which the project is to be completed.*
  - o *Implementation Challenges – Any unique implementation issues.*
  - o *Transactions – Number of transactions (commerce applications).*
- *Technological Pricing Variables*
  - o *Security Issues – Companies have different levels of security needs and different preferences where security is the issue.*
  - o *Remote Management – Charges can be presented if a company demands additional or complex management layers.*
  - o *Reserved Capacity – Some clients will need granted service levels in terms of performance, response times. The charge for this service is usually fixed and dependent on service level.>*

3.3. Discounts

<Describe the pricing discounts that will be used in the pricing model.>

<Comment: Pricing discounts are commonly applied in the following ways:
- *Modifiers – conditional deduction from the list price.*
  - o *Cash – immediate payment (via bank notes or cheque).*
  - o *Volume – large quantity purchase.*
  - o *Time-frame – purchase made within prescribed periods.*
- *Allowances – conditional refund only in form of a deduction from the list price in exchange for customer action.*
  - o *Trade-in – item of property given in part payment upon purchase.*
    - ☐ *Upgrade – form of trade-in that grants a reduced price of new product releases for current customers to maintain customer loyalty.*

   ☐   *Competitive Upgrade – form of trade-in that grants a reduced price of new product for relinquishing the license or ownership to a competing product.*

   o *Rebate – reimbursement for a portion of the purchase price, in exchange for customer information.*

- *Global – universal, non-discriminatory, non-conditional deduction from the list price, for enticement purposes.>*

3.4. Licensing

<Describe the licensing scheme that will be used in the pricing model.>

<Comment: Licensing is commonly applied in the following ways:

- *Perpetual License – non-expiring ownership and usage rights to a product.*
- *Conditional License – expiring ownership and usage rights to a product (renewable and non-renewable). Also known as "Term License".*
- *Licensing Mix – combination of perpetual and term licenses relative to a particular product.*

A "Perpetual License" is often based on a onetime fee. A "Term License" is often based on reoccurring fees. Licensing fees may be applied singly or in combination, and can complement or substitute a base price. Licensing fees commonly include the following options:

- *Onetime Fee – onetime fixed charge that enables constant use of the product. Often applied to a tangible product.*
- *Subscription Fee – onetime fixed charge that enables limited time use of the product. Often applied to an intangible product (service).*
- *Recurring Fee – fixed charge that enables limited time use of the product, but is renewed periodically at regular intervals.*
- *Usage Fee – charge per unit of measure that is tallied at regular intervals.>*

4. Price Mix

4.1. Section Objective

The purpose of this section is to determine the price mix presented to the customer.

4.2. Price Mix

<Describe the price mix that will be used in the pricing model.>

<Comment: The "Price Mix" is comprised of the following elements:

- *MSRP – manufacturer's suggested retail price.*
- *Adjusters – variations to the MSRP.*
  - o *Variables – price changes based on product characteristics.*
  - o *Discounts – deductions from the list price.*
  - o *Tax – levies imposed by law.*
  - o *Shipping – product transporting charges.*
- *Monetary – payment terms and conditions.*

o *Payment Forms – means of payment as cash, credit card, check, or wire transfer.*
o *Payment Terms – payment conditions as currency type, letter of credit and purchase prerequisites.*
o *Credit Terms – schedule for delayed payment(s).*
- *Contract – granted rights to usage, ownership and benefits.*
  o *End-User License Agreement (EULA) – perimeters of usage and ownerships rights granted to the customer.*
  o *Terms and Conditions – setting of requirements and obligations for the parties.*
  o *Disclaimer – denial of responsibility to events to discourage legal action.>*

5. <Product Name> Pricing Model

5.1. Section Objective
The purpose of this section is to describe the pricing model structure that will be applied to <Enter product name>.

5.2. <Product Name> Pricing Model
<Describe the entire actual pricing model that will be applied to the product. This is in effect a summary and concise aggregate of the preceding sections.>
<Comment: This pricing model should be described in an actionable and realistic way in order that it may be implemented.>

5.3. Pricing Model Clarity
<Define and list principals used to promote clarity within the pricing model.>
<Comment: Customers always expect to be presented with an easy to understand price model. Intricate price models may serve the vendor well as they cover many revenue options, but tend to create disengagement at the customer's end.>

6. Market/Customer Data

6.1. Section Objective
The purpose of this section is to describe the market, competition and customer data used in support of creating the pricing model.

6.2. Market/Customer Data
<Describe and list market and customer data that was used. When relevant, detail how the data directly supports the decision made regarding the pricing model.>

6.3. Competitor's Pricing
<Describe and list any relevant pricing information (pricing, rates, models, mix) used by the competition.>

7. Pricing Model Assumptions

7.1. Section Objective
Describe assumptions made in support of creating the pricing model.

7.2. Pricing Model Assumptions
<Describe and list any assumptions whatsoever made in support of creating the pricing model.>

8. Supporting Data

8.1. Section Objective
The section provides data in support of claims, assertions, assumptions, and statements made throughout this document.

8.2. Assumptions
<Describe any assumptions made when writing this document.>

8.3. Research Information
<If relevant, describe and list the type and scope of research conducted in the course of writing this document.>

8.4. Product Diagram/Architecture
<If relevant, describe the product's architecture and modules accompanied by a schematic diagram.>

11.1.7 Win/Loss Analysis Questionnaire – Template V. 4.0

Company Name: <Enter company name>

Product Name: <Enter product name>

- Date: <Enter date>
- Contact: <Enter your name>
- Department: <Enter department name>
- Location: <Enter location>
- Email: <Enter email address>
- Telephone: <Enter telephone number>

Document Revision History:

Date	Revision	Revised By	Approved By
<Enter date>	<Revision #>	<Enter your name>	<Enter name>

Table of Contents

1. Introduction

1.1. __Document Objective__

The purpose of this document is to present a sales process and product oriented questionnaire, used to elicit unbiased feedback from company employees and customers involved in the sales effort and buying decision process, after winning or losing a deal.

<Comment: Win/Loss Analysis is a process whose output helps improve products and develop better sales functions.>

2. Win/Loss Analysis Objectives

2.1. __Section Objective__

This section describes the objectives of the Win/Loss analysis process.

<Comment: This section helps more clearly define what Win/Loss analysis is trying to obtain. It serves as a reminder/guideline to the interviewer and helps readers understand the purpose of the analysis.>

2.2. __Win/Loss Analysis Objectives__

- Analysis of customer purchase decision factors
- More information on the actual buyer/decision maker
- Uncover the true reasons for winning and losing deals
- Improve sales force performance with targeted sales tools and information
- Improve understanding of the target market trends and needs at any given time
- Understand marketing reaction levels to marketing mix changes
- General exploration of key issues in marketing and sales that need revision
- Mapping the competitive landscape and the company's perceived positioning
- Gaining a customer perspective on which product features are most important or critical to make a sale

2.3. __Win/Loss Analysis Desired Outcomes__

- Developing and reinforcing best practices in the sales cycle
- Identifying, correcting or eliminating any obstacles, stages or practices in the sale cycle that are perceived as ineffective or inappropriate

3. Product/Market Overview

3.1. __Section Objective__

This section provides a general overview of the product and market.

<Comment: This section helps clearly define baseline information for the reader and interviewer, before doing the actual Win/Loss analysis interview.>

3.2. **Market/Customer Description**
<Define and describe the target market and customer profile the product is targeted at. Also list the key characteristics of the target market and customer.>

3.3. **Product Description**
<Define and describe the product which solves the market problem.>

4. Win/Loss Analysis Questionnaire/Form

4.1. **Section Objective**
This section describes the general process of querying a customer regarding the specific business deal and the buying decision.

4.2. **Win/Loss Analysis Questionnaire/Form**

Background Information	Details
Date	<Enter text.>
Company Name	<Enter text.>
Company Address	<Enter text.>
Interviewee #1 (Name, Title, Phone, Email)	<Enter text.>
Interviewee #2 (Name, Title, Phone, Email)	<Enter text.>
Interviewer Details	<Enter text.>
Relevant Product(s) or Product Line	<Enter text.>
Original Deal Outcome (Win/Loss)	<Enter text.>
Comments:	<Enter text.>

Interview Questions	Answer
Corporate Identity and Perception	
How do you perceive our company (leader, follower, innovator)?	<Enter text.>
What is your general opinion or impression of our company?	<Enter text.>
What is your general opinion or impression of our products?	<Enter text.>
What are our company's merits?	<Enter text.>
What are our company's faults?	<Enter text.>

Sales Force Evaluation	
Rate your overall level of satisfaction with the company's salesperson(s) you interacted with?	<Enter text.>
Rate your overall level of satisfaction with the product information provided to you by the salesperson?	<Enter text.>
What could the salesperson improve in the next engagement with you?	<Enter text.>

Were you satisfied with the product demonstration?	<Enter text.>
How could have the product demonstration been improved?	<Enter text.>
Are you satisfied the offer that was made to you? Its presentation? Wording? Clarity? Price? Projected Value? Extras?	<Enter text.>

Buying and Evaluation Information	
What factors were used to select the competing products? (price, availability, innovativeness, support, personal contact, previous experience, reputation, and functionality)	<Enter text.>
Who evaluated the products?	<Enter text.>
What process was used to evaluate the products?	<Enter text.>
What were the top three criteria used to evaluate the products?	<Enter text.>
What sources were used to gather information on the products?	<Enter text.>
Who made the buying decision?	<Enter text.>
What criteria/process was used to achieve a buying decision?	<Enter text.>
What sources were used to gather information on the products?	<Enter text.>

Win/Loss Outcome	
What were the reasons for our win (or loss)?	<Enter text.>
What were the reasons for our competitor's win (or loss)?	<Enter text.>
What were our strongest/weakest points in the entire process?	<Enter text.>
What were our competitors' strongest/weakest points in the entire process?	

<Comment: Many additional topics and questions can be added to the questionnaire, subject to necessity. In the actual interview, make sure you constantly focus on the main points you wish to illicit and be concise. Avoid developing a questionnaire that is overbearing and/or excessively granular.>

4.3. **Parameters List**

The following are a list of parameters that can be used to assist (or confine) the interviewee when answering the Win/Loss analysis questionnaire.

- Company – Financial viability
- Company – Key partnership

- Company – Local presence
- Company – Visibility
- Price – ROI
- Price – Structure/Model
- Price – Total deal price
- Product – Features
- Product – Installation
- Product – Scalability
- Product – Security
- Product – Stability/Robustness
- Product – Usability
- Product – User Management – TCO
- Relationship – Existing customer/vendor relationship
- Relationship – Personal relationship with customer
- Service – Deployment
- Service – Support
- Service – Training

<Comment: As a matter of preference when conducting a Win/Loss analysis interview, it is possible to present the interviewee with open-ended or multiple-choice questions. There are obvious advantages and disadvantages to either approach.>

4.4. <u>Competition Summary Table</u>

Competitor	Their Top 3 Advantages	Their Top 3 Disadvantages	Comment / Recommendation for Improvement
<Competitor Name.>	<1. Advantage.> <2. Advantage.> <3. Advantage.>	<1. Disadvantage.> <2. Disadvantage.> <3. Disadvantage.>	<Enter Recommendation for Improvement.>

<Comment: This table allows you to review the competitors who participated in bidding for the deal, and draw recommendations regarding your own company.>

5. Supporting Data

5.1. <u>Section Objective</u>
The section provides data in support of claims, assertions, assumptions, and statements made throughout this document.

5.2. <u>Assumptions</u>
<Describe any assumptions made when writing this document.>

5.3. **Research Information**

<If relevant, describe and list the type and scope of research conducted in the course of writing this document.>

5.4. **Product Diagram/Architecture**

<If relevant, describe the product's architecture and modules accompanied by a schematic diagram.>

11.1.8 Win/Loss Analysis Report – Template V. 4.0

Company Name: <Enter company name>

Product Name: <Enter product name>

- Date: <Enter date>
- Contact: <Enter your name>
- Department: <Enter department name>
- Location: <Enter location>
- Email: <Enter email address>
- Telephone: <Enter telephone number>

Document Revision History:

Date	Revision	Revised By	Approved By
<Enter date>	<Revision #>	<Enter your name>	<Enter name>

Table of Contents

1. Introduction

1.1. Document Objective

The purpose of this document is to present sales process and product oriented recommendations and data derived from unbiased feedback from company employees and customers involved in the sales effort and buying decision process after winning or losing a deal.

<Comment: Win/Loss Analysis is a process whose output helps to improve both products and sales functions.>

2. Win/Loss Analysis Report Form

2.1. Section Objective

This section describes the information obtained during win/loss analysis interviews and the resulting conclusions.

2.2. Win/Loss Analysis Report Form

Information	Details
Customer's Perception of Company	
Customer's opinion of the company:	<Enter text.>
Customer's opinion of the products:	<Enter text.>
Customer's opinion of the sales process:	<Enter text.>
Customer's key buying decision factors:	<Enter text.>
Customer's Perception of Competition	
Customer's opinion of the competition:	<Enter text.>
Customer's opinion of the competing products:	<Enter text.>
Customer's opinion of the competitor's sales process:	<Enter text.>
Analysis and Results	
Overall assessment of the company's customer engagement process:	<Enter text.>
Relevant conclusions:	<Enter text.>
Resulting recommendations:	<Enter text.>
Action items:	<Enter text.>
General Comments:	<Enter text.>

3. Supporting Data

3.1. Section Objective

The section provides data in support of claims, assertions, assumptions, and statements made throughout this document.

3.2. Assumptions

<Describe any assumptions made when writing this document.>

3.3. Research Information

<If relevant, describe and list the type and scope of research conducted in the course of writing this document.>

3.4. Product Diagram/Architecture

<If relevant, describe the product's architecture and modules accompanied by a schematic diagram.>

11.1.9 Customer Visit – Guidelines V. 4.0

Company Name: <Enter company name>
Product Name: <Enter product name>

- Date: <Enter date>
- Contact: <Enter your name>
- Department: <Enter department name>
- Location: <Enter location>
- Email: <Enter email address>
- Telephone: <Enter telephone number>

Document Revision History:

Date	Revision	Revised By	Approved By
<Enter date>	<Revision #>	<Enter your name>	<Enter name>

Table of Contents

1. Introduction

1.1. **Document Objective**

This document describes how to plan a customer visit. The core purpose of a customer visit is to meet customers and listen closely to them with the intent of better understanding their needs.

2. Customer Visit Planning

2.1. **Section Objective**

This section describes the stages and steps for building an effective customer visit plan.

2.2. **Visit Purpose**

- Establish a reason and need for the customer visit.
- Establish scope of visit or visits (e.g. exploratory, in-depth).
- Establish the key deliverables that the visit should produce (such as: customer visit report, decision, approval, information, contract, follow-up, schedule, and budget).

2.3. **Visit Planning**

- Alert management to the process and seek approval, if necessary.
- Establish timing and duration of the visit.
- Identify key corporate team members and alternates.
- Assign key individuals to meet at customer site and alternates.
- Establish what information to present to the customer.
- Establish what information to elicit from the customer.
- Establish main discussion points in the meeting with the customer.
- Create a visit schedule/appointment and meeting agenda.

2.4. **Visit Strategy**

- Convene team for a briefing about the visit.
- Establish team member roles.
- Set proper internal and customer expectations of the visit.
- Address potential visit positives and pitfalls.

2.5. **Visit Rollout**

- Note: All communications with the customer are done via the account manager.
- Create a "visit request email" and send it to the appropriate account manager.
- The account manager will forward the "visit request email" to the customer and return with the customer's response and possible dates.
- Secure travel and accommodations for the corporate team.
- Conduct the visit.

2.6. Visit Follow-Up

- Have team members submit customer visitation reports.
- Receive additional feedback from the customer (via account manager) on the visit.
- Compile/synthesize reports into the major deliverables.
- If necessary, produce executive summary and propagate.
- Follow-up with the customer on agreed upon action items or promises.

3. Supporting Data

3.1. Section Objective

The section provides data in support of claims, assertions, assumptions, and statements made throughout this document.

3.2. Assumptions

<Describe any assumptions made when writing this document.>

3.3. Research Information

<If relevant, describe and list the type and scope of research conducted in the course of writing this document.>

3.4. Product Diagram/Architecture

<If relevant, describe the product's architecture and modules accompanied by a schematic diagram.>

11.2 PRODUCT MARKETING

11.2.1 Business Case – Template V. 4.0

Company Name: \<Enter company name>
Product Name: \<Enter product name>

- Date: \<Enter date>
- Contact: \<Enter your name>
- Department: \<Enter department name>
- Location: \<Enter location>
- Email: \<Enter email address>
- Telephone: \<Enter telephone number>

Document Revision History:

Date	Revision	Revised By	Approved By
\<Enter date>	\<Revision #>	\<Enter your name>	\<Enter name>

Table of Contents

1. INTRODUCTION

    1.1.   DOCUMENT OBJECTIVE

2. EXECUTIVE SUMMARY

    2.1.   SECTION OBJECTIVE
    2.2.   THE EXECUTIVE SUMMARY

3. MARKET PROBLEM AND OPPORTUNITY

    3.1.   SECTION OBJECTIVE
    3.2.   MARKET PROBLEM
    3.3.   MARKET OPPORTUNITY

4. PRODUCT DESCRIPTION

    4.1.   SECTION OBJECTIVE
    4.2.   PRODUCT DESCRIPTION
    4.3.   SOLVING THE PROBLEM

5. MARKET OVERVIEW

    5.1.   SECTION OBJECTIVE
    5.2.   MARKET OVERVIEW
    5.3.   CUSTOMER OVERVIEW
    5.4.   MARKET/CUSTOMER SEGMENTATION
    5.5.   MARKET/CUSTOMER SEGMENTS
    5.6.   MARKET/PRODUCT SEGMENTATION
    5.7.   COMPETITION

6. BUSINESS ADVANTAGES

    6.1.   SECTION OBJECTIVE
    6.2.   EXISTING ADVANTAGES – COMPANY
    6.3.   GAINED ADVANTAGES – COMPANY
    6.4.   INTRINSIC ADVANTAGES – PRODUCT

7. BARRIERS TO ENTRY

    7.1.   SECTION OBJECTIVE
    7.2.   MARKETPLACE BARRIERS TO ENTRY
    7.3.   ADVANTAGEOUS BARRIERS TO ENTRY

8. MARKET STRATEGY

    8.1.   SECTION OBJECTIVE
    8.2.   MARKETING OBJECTIVES
    8.3.   MARKET STRATEGY
    8.4.   MARKETING MIX
    8.4.1.   TARGET CUSTOMER
    8.4.2.   PRODUCT POSITIONING
    8.4.3.   PRODUCT
    8.4.4.   PRICE
    8.4.5.   PROMOTION
    8.4.6.   PLACE [DISTRIBUTION]
    8.5.   SUPPORTING STRATEGIES
    8.5.1.   GROWTH STRATEGY
    8.5.2.   CONVERGENCE STRATEGY

1. Introduction

1.1. Document Objective

This document outlines a business case, a key document, used to define, assess and evaluate the best approach to either proceed or not proceed with a product delivery program or initiative. This business case is an examination of a potential market opportunity on a product level.

<Comment: Throughout the document, keep your writing short, clear and simple.>

2. Executive Summary

2.1. Section Objective

This section provides an executive summary – a concise overview of the business case.

<Comment: The executive summary should enable the reader to understand the market opportunity, the role of the proposed product in the company's business plan/direction, and the business justification for delivering the proposed product to market. The executive summary is prepared once the entire document is complete. Focus on the key elements of the business case and do not exceed two pages.

The Executive Summary must address the following issues:
- *The current state of the market problem and resulting market opportunity.*
- *The offering and the competitive environment.*
- *A brief description of the line of business and financial impacts.*
- *The risks of undertaking the proposed product delivery project.*
- *Recommendations.>*

2.2. The Executive Summary

<Enter the executive summary.>

3. Market Problem and Opportunity

3.1. Section Objective

This section describes the market problem and the resulting market opportunity that are the subject of this business case.

3.2. Market Problem

<Identify and justify the specific market problem. Explain any other interlinking market problems.>

<Comment: The market problem is a "consumer" or "product" or "technology" problem in the target market. The market problem is essentially a situation (difficulty) that exists in the target market and requires change.

- *Consumer Problem* – *A marketplace situation in which consumer needs remain unsatisfied (B2C). The solution to a consumer problem is a whole product.*
- *Product Problem* – *An industry situation in which product requirements' are unmet (B2B). The solution to a product problem is a product component.*
- *Technology Problem* – *Challenges in applied science. The solution to a technology problem is scientific research.*

3.3. Market Opportunity

<Provide a statement detailing the specific market opportunity. Size and substantiate the market opportunity as much as possible. Document the assumptions and facts that validate and justify the market opportunity. Explain any other interlinking market opportunities.>

<Comment: The market opportunity is a lucrative, lasting and sizable market problem. Market Opportunity = Market Problem + Volume + Duration + Earning Potential.>

4. Product Description

4.1. Section Objective

This section explains how the proposed product addresses the market problem and market opportunity.

<Comment: It is possible that no actual product or even a product concept presently exist. Consequently, explain that the market problem and market opportunity have been identified, and why no actual product or even a product concept presently exist.>

4.2. Product Description

<Define and describe the proposed product which solves the market problem. Describe the product concept if no actual product exists.>

4.3. Solving the Problem

<Describe how the proposed product solves the market problem.>

5. Market Overview

5.1. Section Objective

This section describes the market and customer profile that the proposed product is targeted towards.

5.2. Market Overview

<Define and describe the target markets that the proposed product is targeted at. Also list the target market key characteristics. Comment on market size, market growth, and any technological, regulatory, cultural, supply conditions, economic, and political trends.>

5.3. <u>Customer Overview</u>
<Define and describe the customer profile that the proposed product is targeted at. Also list the customers' key characteristics.>

5.4. <u>Market/Customer Segmentation</u>
<Define and describe the most applicable way to segment the market, using factors such as geographical location, industry, size, or technology.>

5.5. <u>Market/Customer Segments</u>
<Describe which market/customer segments were selected and explain the rational supporting why these segments should be pursued.>

5.6. <u>Market/Product Segmentation</u>
<Describe and explain which market/product segmentation approach is likely to be most realistic and/or successful. Relevant segmentation approaches are: single segment, selective specialization, product specialization, market specialization, full market coverage. Reflect on the applicability of presenting product groups and product families as the main offering.>

5.7. <u>Competition</u>
<Describe the competitive landscape and key competitors. Provide a brief overview.>

6. Business Advantages

6.1. <u>Section Objective</u>
This section defines and describes the unique value-added characteristics the company and product provide customers, and how these combined characteristics translate into a significant business advantage.

6.2. <u>Existing Advantages – Company</u>
<Define and describe the business advantages that the company presently has that will help in delivering the product.>
<Comment: Existing advantages include: first to market, patents pending, cost advantages, price advantages, partnerships formed, alliances formed, key customer contacts, and industry expert management team.>

6.3. <u>Gained Advantages – Company</u>
<Define and describe the business advantages that the company expects to gain by delivering the product.>
<Comment: Existing advantages include: first to market, market presence, fending competitors, and establishing leadership.>

6.4. <u>Intrinsic Advantages – Product</u>
<Describe any business advantage intrinsic to the product itself.>

<Comment: Business advantages can be any number of distinctive competencies, such as superior customer value, lower total cost of ownership, lower price, greater market share and profitability, superior technology, broader distribution network, and higher operational efficiency.>

7. Barriers to Entry

7.1. Section Objective
This section outlines barriers to entry which are obstacles designed to block potential entrants from profitably entering the market.

7.2. Marketplace Barriers to Entry
<Define and describe barriers to entry that presently exist in the marketplace. These barriers are often introduced by the competition and work against the company.>

<Comment: marketplace barriers could also be local/global legal, political, cultural, geographical, language, sociological, religious, national, and technological availability. These barriers are not due to the competition of the market per se but deserve mentioning if relevant.>

7.3. Advantageous Barriers to Entry
<Define and describe barriers to entry that the company has or will create in order to protect the product from the competition.>

<Comment: Examples of barriers to entry include: patents, pricing, cost advantages, customer loyalty, and cost of research and development.>

8. Market Strategy

8.1. Section Objective
This section describes the market strategy and marketing mix which will be used to help achieve the business and marketing objectives.

<Comment: This document does not need the level of detail as a market plan would; therefore, be extremely brief and concise when writing this section.>

8.2. Marketing Objectives
<Describe the marketing objectives the company wishes to achieve by delivering the proposed product.>

<Comment: This section outlines what will be accomplished by delivering the proposed product in clear and measurable terms within a specified time frame. Marketing objectives should focus on goals, not operations, and on outputs, not production. Marketing objectives include: market penetration, market share acquisition, establishing leadership of any kind, demonstrating technology, building an identity, and exhibiting commitment to customers; but not revenue or profit.>

8.3. <u>Market Strategy</u>
<Describe the chosen market strategy.>
<Comment: Market strategy is decisions that define target markets, set marketing objectives, and outline how to build a corporate competitive advantage. Focus and elaborate on how to build a corporate competitive advantage since the target market and marketing objectives were previously defined.>

8.4. <u>Marketing Mix</u>
8.4.1. <u>Target Customer</u>
<Define the customer who will buy the product and the main reason why they will buy it. Briefly describe the Buyer and User entities.>
8.4.2. <u>Product Positioning</u>
<Define and describe the product positioning statement.>
8.4.3. <u>Product</u>
<Define and describe the product's physical characteristics, quality, functionality, and the value it brings to the customer. Use the product concept as a guide if no actual product exists.>
8.4.4. <u>Price</u>
<Define and describe how you intend to charge customers for the product. Describe the pricing model and any major considerations affecting it. Address the competition's pricing.>
8.4.5. <u>Promotion</u>
<Define and describe any promotions, incentives, advertising, events, public relations and other marketing programs which will be used to generate awareness, differentiation and demand for the product.>
8.4.6. <u>Place [Distribution]</u>
<Define and describe the sales and distribution channels that will be used to deliver the product to the customer. Refer to any form of market segmentation that will be used in the process.>

8.5. <u>Supporting Strategies</u>
8.5.1. <u>Growth Strategy</u>
<Define and describe any applicable growth paths based on: product diversification, product development, market development, and market diversification.>
8.5.2. <u>Convergence Strategy</u>
<Define and describe any applicable product line convergence paths based on: market constriction, product or product line feature reduction, and product termination.>

8.6. <u>Strategic Alignment</u>
<Describe how the proposed product is aligned with the company's overall business strategy. Identify and explain the level of influence that delivery of the proposed product will have on achieving the various corporate business goals.
Explain how the product helps the company establish a leader, innovator or follower position.>

9. Impact Assessment

9.1. Section Objective

This section lists the business and operational impacts (implications) that will most likely occur when embarking on the product delivery project.

<Comment: Impacts are any consequences that will most likely occur when embarking on the product delivery project. Identify all business (external, long-term focused) and operational (internal, detailed focused) impacts that may arise by delivering the product. Although highly subjective, consequences can be categorized in three ways: those most likely to occur, those most likely to not occur, and those that will occur. There is always a range of probabilities that any of these categories will occur. It is not always easy to know which consequences will most likely occur at any given time. The impact assessment may include the subjective assessment (probability) that a particular impact will or will not occur.>

9.2. Business Impacts

<Define and describe the business impacts that may occur by delivering the product.>

<Comment: Examples of business impacts are:
- *Change in service and/or products being provided.*
- *Change in focus or direction of the division.*
- *Change in company image.>*

9.3. Operational Impacts

<Define and describe the operational impacts that may occur by delivering the product.>

<Comment: Examples of operational impacts are:
- *Staff training required.*
- *Reduction of staff resources.*
- *Manufacturing capacity.>*

10. Risk Assessment

10.1. Section Objective

This section provides an understanding of the risks related to the product/project and how these risks may vary by viable alternatives. This section includes mitigation and contingency planning for each risk.

<Comment: Identify all product/project risks that may relate to the product.
- *Risk – A factor or event that may jeopardize the product/project from achieving the anticipated benefits or increase the cost and/or schedule of the product/project.*
- *Risk Mitigation – Actions, and incurring cost, to pro-actively reduce exposure to a risk while it is still considered a risk.*

> • _Risk Contingency_ – _Actions, and incurring cost, to be used in the future should the risk occur, thereby ceasing to be a risk and becoming a fact._>

10.2.   **Product/Project Risk Table**

Risk	Description	Probability	Effect	Mitigation	Contingency
1.					
2.					
3.					
4.	_<Example: Partner fails to provide needed technology_	_Low_	_High_	_Provide partner with line of credit_	_Identify alternative partners_>

10.2.1.   **Probability of Risk**
   • High – The risk is highly likely to occur.
   • Medium – The risk is likely to occur.
   • Low – The risk is not likely to occur.

10.2.2.   **Effect of Risk**
   • High – The risk can significantly affect on the product.
   • Medium – The risk can somewhat affect the product.
   • Low – The risk can have relatively minor affect on the product.

<Comment: Examples of risks are:
• _Legislative changes._
• _Conflicting priorities._
• _Lack of competencies._
• _Lack of contingency budget._
• _Lack of required technology._
• _Lack of executive management support._
• _Inability to free-up critical business resources._
• _Insufficient funds or time provided for training._>

11. Financial Outlook

11.1.   **Section Objective**
This section depicts the financial outlook and costs relative to the product.

11.2.   **Market Analysis**
   <Fill the table below.>

Potential Customers	Growth	Year 1	Year 2
Consumer	%	0	0
Small Business	%	0	0
Large Business	%	0	0
Government	%	0	0
Other	%	0	0

Potential Customers	Growth	Year 1	Year 2
Total	%	0	0

<Example:

Potential Customers	Growth	Year 1	Year 2
Consumer	2%	12,000	12,240
Small Business	5%	15,000	15,750
Large Business	8%	33,000	35,640
Government	-2%	36,000	35,280
Other	0%	19,000	19,000
Total	2.78%	115,000	117,910

Develop a basic Market Analysis table, with a simple list of market segments. Fill in the total potential customers estimated and the annual growth rate expected for each segment.>

11.3.   Break Even Analysis
<Fill the table below.>

Break-even Analysis	
Monthly Units Break-even	0
Monthly Sales Break-even	$
Assumptions	
Average Per-Unit Sales Price	$
Average Per-Unit Variable Cost	$
Estimated Monthly Fixed Cost	$

<Example:

Break-even Analysis	
Monthly Units Break-even	1175
Monthly Sales Break-even	$381,875
Assumptions	
Average Per-Unit Sales Price	$325
Average Per-Unit Variable Cost	$245
Estimated Monthly Fixed Cost	$94,000

The Break-even Analysis Table is an illustration of where it is estimated the business will actually begin to make money. The Break-even Analysis table calculates a break-even point based on total fixed costs, total variable costs per unit of sales, and revenue per unit of sales.>

11.4.   Financial Costs
<Fill the table below.>

Financial Analysis	Year 1	Year 2
Revenue:	$	$

Financial Analysis	Year 1	Year 2
Costs:		
Analysis	$	$
Design	$	$
Development	$	$
Implementation	$	$
Ongoing Operational Costs:		
Human Resources	$	$
Administration	$	$
Net Benefit or Cost:	$	$
Net Present Value (xx% Discount Rate)	$	$

<Comment: Ascertain the relevant costs incurred over the chosen timeframe:
- *Cost of goods.*
- *Cost of selling.*
- *Overhead cost.*

Note that each of the relevant costs possesses a fixed and variable component.

Consideration should be given to:
- *When the costs will be incurred.*
- *Who will incur the costs.*
- *Certainty of costs.*

Do not intentionally underestimate costs or any capital requirements. It is better to ask for all necessary funding the first time rather than to have to go back and ask for more.>

12. Conclusions and Recommendations

12.1.   Section Objective

This section provides specific recommendations regarding the product delivery program.

12.2.   Conclusions

<Identify and describe any conclusions reached during the preparation of the business case.>

12.3.   Recommendations

<Make specific recommendations on proceeding with product delivery.>

<Comment: The extent of the recommendation may range from recommending approval for a full product delivery program to recommending a more detailed requirements analysis be done to validate some key business case components.>

12.4. Product Delivery Program Responsibility
<Recommend who should be the Program Manager and the assigned scope of responsibility. Also recommend who should be the product delivery program sponsor having overall accountability to ensure the program is completed.>

12.5. Exit Strategy
<Describe and recommend an exit strategy for the team, product and technology; should the product commercially fail. Common exit options are: sale, merger, spin-off, or public offering.>

13. Review and Approval

13.1. Section Objective
This section describes how the business case is reviewed and approved, and who is responsible for the process and the decision making.
<Comment: This section also contains the final outcome of the business case. If the business case is approved, then evidence of the approval should be included. If the business case is not approved, then the business decision behind either rejecting the product or deferring the delivery program should be documented.>

13.2. Review Process
<Describe who will review the business case, what is the approval process and by when should the business case be approved or not.>
<Comment: Ultimately note in this document whether or not the business case is approved. If applicable, approval conditions should be identified and documented. If the business case is not approved, reasons for the decision should be documented.>

14. Supporting Data

14.1. Section Objective
The section provides data in support of claims, assertions, assumptions, and statements made throughout this document.

14.2. Assumptions
<Describe any assumptions made when writing this document.>

14.3. Research Information
<If relevant, describe and list the type and scope of research conducted in the course of writing this document.>

14.4. **Product Diagram/Architecture**

<If relevant, describe the product's architecture and modules accompanied by a schematic diagram.>

11.2.2 Competitor Analysis – Template V. 4.0

Company Name: <Enter company name>
Product Name: <Enter product name>

- Date: <Enter date>
- Contact: <Enter your name>
- Department: <Enter department name>
- Location: <Enter location>
- Email: <Enter email address>
- Telephone: <Enter telephone number>

Document Revision History:

Date	Revision	Revised By	Approved By
<Enter date>	<Revision #>	<Enter your name>	<Enter name>

Table of Contents

1. Introduction

1.1. Document Objective

The purpose of this document is to evaluate <Enter the competing company name>, its products, services, strengths and weaknesses versus <Enter your company name>. <Enter the competing company name> is a competitor to <Enter your company name>.

Comparative competitor analysis provides input that is used in the preparation of marketing collateral and sales tools, and helps gain a better understanding of the competitive landscape. It is also used in support of decision making during strategic planning and product management.
<Comment: For clarification purposes, the Comparative Competitor Analysis is not a Product Comparison Table – it is an analysis of competing companies, partially via their products. Compare your company to (at least) the top three competitors.>

2. <Your Company Name>

2.1. Section Objective

This section provides background information on <Enter your company name>.
<Comment: In order to avoid hindsight errors, this section is designed to reflect the baseline information and perspectives that were in place when the document was prepared. It is also provided so that diverse audiences will be brought to the same level of baseline information.>

2.2. Company – <Your Company Name>

<Describe your company and its product line. Provide a short paragraph.>

2.3. Product – <Your Product Name>

<Provide a short, general description of your product, its purpose and functionality. Explain how the product fits in to the overall corporate product strategy.>

2.4. Target Market Description

<Concisely describe the market at which your product is targeted.>

2.5. <Your Company Name> Information Matrix

Parameter	<Your Company Name>
Company Description	<Describe your company and its product line. Copy the relevant paragraph you earlier wrote in this document.>
Business Strategy	<Describe your company's business strategy relative to your product.>

Parameter	<Your Company Name>
Market Strategy	<Describe your company's market strategy relative to your product.>
Product Strategy	<Describe your company's product strategy, relative to your product.>
Distinctive Strengths	<Describe the core business strengths of your company.>
Distinctive Weaknesses	<Describe the core business weaknesses of your company.>
Company Product	<Describe your company's product.>
Target Market	<Describe the main target market of your product.>
Market Share	<Describe the market share your product has in the main target market.>
Sales Volume	<Describe the sales volume your product has generated in the main target market.>

3. <Competing Company Name>

3.1. Section Objective

This section provides background information on <Enter the competing company name>.

3.2. Company – <Competing Company Name>

<Describe the competing company and its product line. Provide a short paragraph.>

3.3. Product – <Competing Product Name>

<Provide a short, general description of the competing product, its purpose and functionality. Explain how the product fits in to the overall corporate product strategy of the competing company.>

3.4. Target Market Description

<Concisely describe the market at which the competing product is targeted.>

3.5. <Competing Company Name> Information Matrix

Parameter	<Competing Company Name >
Competitor Description	<Describe the competing company and its product line. Copy the relevant paragraph you earlier wrote in this document.>
Business Strategy	<Describe the competing company's business strategy relative to the competing product.>
Markets Strategy	<Describe the competing company's market strategy relative to the competing product.>

Parameter	<Competing Company Name >
Product Strategy	<Describe the competing company's product relative to the competing product.>
Distinctive Strengths	<Describe the core business strengths of the competing company.>
Distinctive Weaknesses	<Describe the core business weaknesses of the competing company.>
Competing Product	<Describe the competing product.>
Target Market	<Describe the main target market of the competing product.>
Market Share	<Describe the market share the competing product has in your main target market.>
Sales Volume	<Describe the sales volume the competing product has generated in your main target market.>
Threat Level	<Describe the perceived threat level the competing company poses to your company, relative to your product.>

<*Example:*

Parameter	*MICROSOFT*
Competitor Description	*Founded in 1975, Microsoft (NASDAQ "MSFT") is the worldwide leader in software, services and solutions that help people and businesses realize their full potential.*
Business Strategy	*Leader in consumer and business software via mergers and acquisitions.*
Market Strategy	*Complete global market dominance.* *Competitive advantage: brand, product proliferation and availability.*
Product Strategy	*Productivity (standards compliant and feature-rich).*
Distinctive Strengths	*Strong brand, multinational, huge budgets, massive manpower, vast experience.*
Distinctive Weaknesses	*Litigation, bureaucratic, unethical competitor (perceived), unreliable (shipping delays), cumbersome processes, leadership failure (internet, wireless).*
Competing Product	*Microsoft Solutions Framework (MSF) is a highly extensible, scalable, fully integrated set of software development processes, principles, and proven practices within Visual Studio Team System, guiding software project teams to deliver enterprise ready solutions.*
Target Market	*Software professionals responsible for process automation and guidance within the software development life cycle (SDLC).*
Market Share	*Not Available.*
Sales Volume	*Not Available.*
Threat Level	*Low.*

>

4. Conclusions

4.1. Section Objective
This section describes the conclusions drawn following the comparative competitor analysis process.

4.2. Conclusions
<List each conclusion separately, explain why that conclusion was reached, and detail any supporting data.
Follow these guidelines:
- Review your company's business, market and product strategies.
- Examine the content you had collected. Summarize your findings and opinions about what the information strategically means to your company.
- Formulate your conclusions in a clear manner in order that executive management can analyze and use them to make decisions.>

5. Action Plan

5.1. Section Objective
This section describes recommended action based on the drawn conclusions.

5.2. Action Plan Items
List of recommended activities:
<Comment: Depending on the specific conditions of your current environment, your action items should help accomplish the following:
- *Provide more value than the competition.*
- *Help build a sustainable competitive advantage.*

In particular to your market strategy, your action items should help accomplish the following:
- *Generating favorable conditions and reasons for customers to bypass your competition and purchase your products.*
- *Help achieve your quantitative marketing objectives, such as increased market area penetration and market share.*
- *Help achieve your qualitative marketing objectives, such as increased customer satisfaction and improved quality perception of products.>*

5.2.1. Action Item # n
Conclusion: <Present the conclusion.>
Recommended Action: <Establish the relevant course of action.>
Goals: <Set attainable goals and metrics to measure the action's effect.>

5.3. Action Plan Tracking Table

Action Item #	Date Started	Date Completed	Comments

Action Item #	Date Started	Date Completed	Comments

6. Supporting Data

6.1. Section Objective

The section provides data in support of claims, assertions, assumptions, and statements made throughout this document.

6.2. Assumptions

<Describe any assumptions made when writing this document.>

6.3. Research Information

<If relevant, describe and list the type and scope of research conducted in the course of writing this document.>

6.4. Product Diagram/Architecture

<If relevant, describe the product's architecture and modules accompanied by a schematic diagram.>

11.2.3 Product Comparison – Template V. 4.0

Company Name: <Enter company name>

Product Name: <Enter product name>

- Date: <Enter date>
- Contact: <Enter your name>
- Department: <Enter department name>
- Location: <Enter location>
- Email: <Enter email address>
- Telephone: <Enter telephone number>

Document Revision History:

Date	Revision	Revised By	Approved By
<Enter date>	<Revision #>	<Enter your name>	<Enter name>

Table of Contents

1. Introduction

1.1. Document Objective

The purpose of this document is to depict a tabular comparison of competing products.

2. The Products

2.1. Section Objective

This section provides background information on the products being compared.

2.2. Product – <Product # X Name>

<Provide a short, general description of the product, its purpose and its functionality.>

2.3. Product – <Product # Y Name>

<Provide a short, general description of the product, its purpose and its functionality.>

3. Product Comparison Table

3.1. Section Objective

This section provides product comparison data in tabular form.

<Comment: Several product comparison table styles are presented. Select the one most appropriate for the given task and audience (internal or external). Please note that capabilities are general categories of ability such as: scalability, security and manageability. You can also use specific product features instead of capabilities.>

3.2. Product Comparison Table – Qualitative Approach

<Comment: This type of table is commonly used to compare products in a rudimentary way. Capabilities for each product are compared and the "winning" product receives a score of 1, while the other receives a 0. Win/loss score is tallied at the bottom of the table. The qualitative approach is mostly used to evaluate features and functionality.>

Capability (or feature)	<Product # X>	Win/Loss Score	<Product # Y>	Win/Loss Score
	<Description.>		<Description.>	
Total				

3.3. Product Comparison Table – Quantitative Approach

<Comment: This type of table is commonly used to finely compare products, especially when there are many capabilities; the products are complex, or very similar. Each capability is assigned a weight designating its relative importance. Scores from 1 to 10 are given each product at the capability level. The total score is tallied at the bottom by summing the results of each weight multiplied by score.>

Capability (or feature)	Weight	<Product # X>	Score	<Product # Y>	Score
		<Description.>		<Description.>	
Total	100%				

3.4. Product Comparison Table – Checklist

<Comment: This type of table is commonly used to compare features as an overview or to verify compliance to standards.>

Capability (or feature)	<Product # X>	<Product # Y>
	√	√

3.5. Product Comparison Table – Descriptive Assessment

<Comment: This type of table is commonly used to compare product capabilities in a simplistic, yet explanatory way. The audience for this type of table is usually the sales force and buyers.>

Capability (or feature)	<Product # X>	<Product # Y>	Why is this capability (or feature) important?
	<Yes/No. Provide details.>	<Yes/No. Provide details.>	

<Example: eCommerce Software Application

Capability (or feature)	App#1	App#2	Why is this capability (or feature) important?
Cross-sell and up-sell	Yes	No	Increased revenue via larger customer order size and greater customer satisfaction, resulting from access to related purchasing choices.
Guided selling	Yes	No	Increased revenue via better customer shopping experience by providing more complete and robust product information across the sales cycle.
Loyalty programs	Yes	No	Increased revenue via repeat purchases using email marketing, discounts, promotions and rewards.

Capability (or feature)	App#1	App#2	Why is this capability (or feature) important?
Backend integration	Yes	No	Reduced costs from appropriate sharing of information with internal systems including procurement, order management, accounting and inventory.
FedEx/UPS integration	Yes	No	Reduced costs and improved accuracy in ordering, shipment handling and invoicing resulting in lower cost of doing business for suppliers and retailers.
External pay processing	Yes	No	Reduced liability, higher reliability with secure interfaces to external credit card payment processors.

>

4. Conclusions

4.1. Section Objective
This section describes the conclusions drawn based on the comparison tables.

4.2. Conclusions
<List each conclusion separately, explain why the conclusion was reached, and detail any supporting data.>

5. Action Plan

5.1. Section Objective
This section describes recommended action based on the drawn conclusions.

5.2. Action Plan Items
List of recommended activities:
<Comment: Reflecting on your product strategy, your action items should help enhance your product so it better fits the needs of the market. Product related action items commonly focus on issues such as: design, customization, innovation, standards, technology and suitability.>

5.2.1. Action Item # n
Conclusion: <Present the conclusion.>
Recommended Action: <Establish the relevant course of action.>
Goals: <Set attainable goals and metrics to measure the action's effect.>

5.3. Action Plan Tracking Table

Action Item #	Date Started	Date Completed	Comments

6. Supporting Data

6.1. Section Objective

The section provides data in support of claims, assertions, assumptions, and statements made throughout this document.

6.2. Assumptions

<Describe any assumptions made when writing this document.>

6.3. Research Information

<If relevant, describe and list the type and scope of research conducted in the course of writing this document.>

6.4. Product Diagram/Architecture

<If relevant, describe the product's architecture and modules accompanied by a schematic diagram.>

11.2.4 Corporate Mission – Template V. 4.0

Company Name: <Enter company name>

Product Name: <Enter product name>

- Date: <Enter date>
- Contact: <Enter your name>
- Department: <Enter department name>
- Location: <Enter location>
- Email: <Enter email address>
- Telephone: <Enter telephone number>

Document Revision History:

Date	Revision	Revised By	Approved By
<Enter date>	<Revision #>	<Enter your name>	<Enter name>

Table of Contents

1. Introduction

1.1. **Document Objective**

This document describes the corporate mission statement. A corporate mission statement defines the company's general business direction and depicts the value customers get.

2. Corporate Mission Statement

2.1. **Section Objective**

This section articulates the corporate mission statement.

2.2. **Corporate Vision Statement**

<Enter the corporate vision statement.>

<Comment: Write a concise vision statement that summarizes the company's purpose, intent, and describes how, in the future, its products and activities shall affect the world. Corporate vision is about what the company does to the world. The corporate vision and mission statements may be found in and copied from the corporate business plan.>

2.3. **Corporate Mission Statement**

"<Enter company name> is a <Enter company description>, whose mission is to provide <Enter target market> with <Enter product name> that/of <Enter statement of value>."

<Comment:

- *Corporate mission is about what the company does for the customer.*
- *Every company wants or claims to deliver value, be profitable, and establish leadership. Try to avoid including these in the corporate mission statement.*
- *Anyone reading the corporate mission statement should be able to clearly articulate the following: the line of business the company is in and its goals relative to the customer.*
- *The corporate mission statement should contain reference to one or more of the following elements: business concept, company philosophy, customer, geographic market, product, public image, and technology. Only use the elements that are relevant to your corporation.*
- *The corporate mission statement can be one paragraph to one page long. A short, clear and concise corporate mission statement is always preferred.*

<Example: "Acme Foods is an environmentally-friendly, global company that is committed to providing its customers with nutritious vegetarian food products of superior quality made from healthy organic ingredients".>

3. Supporting Data

3.1. Section Objective

The section provides data in support of claims, assertions, assumptions, and statements made throughout this document.

3.2. Assumptions

<Describe any assumptions made when writing this document.>

3.3. Research Information

<If relevant, describe and list the type and scope of research conducted in the course of writing this document.>

3.4. Product Diagram/Architecture

<If relevant, describe the product's architecture and modules accompanied by a schematic diagram.>

11.2.5 Product Positioning – Template V. 4.0

Company Name: <Enter company name>

Product Name: <Enter product name>

- Date: <Enter date>
- Contact: <Enter your name>
- Department: <Enter department name>
- Location: <Enter location>
- Email: <Enter email address>
- Telephone: <Enter telephone number>

Document Revision History:

Date	Revision	Revised By	Approved By
<Enter date>	<Revision #>	<Enter your name>	<Enter name>

Table of Contents

1. Introduction

1.1. **Document Objective**

This document describes, to intra-organizational audiences, the actual and desired way in which customers perceive a product when compared to its competition. Product positioning described in this document is the foundation to many product marketing efforts and marketing communication collateral.

<Comment: The common definition for product positioning is "the place a product occupies in the customers' mind relative to competing products". Product positioning is the process that establishes the customers' perception of the product, which is the goal of this process.>

2. Overview

2.1. **Section Objective**

This section aims to provide a better understanding of the forces, trends and situational environment that affect the positioning process and statement.

2.2. **Market Description**

<Define and describe the target market; especially its key characteristics, which the product is targeted towards.>

2.3. **Target Customer**

<Define and describe the general customer profile the solution is targeted towards.>

<Comment: The Customer is the entity that takes (financial) responsibility for the product. The Buyer is the entity that decides to obtain the product (solution). The User is the entity that interacts with the product.>

2.4. **Target Buyers Description**

<Define and describe the buyers, the entities that decide to obtain the product.>

2.4.1. **BDM (Business Decision Maker) Buyers**

<List, define and describe the BDM buyers. Also relate to their level of knowledge and buying authority.>

2.4.2. **TDM (Technical Decision Maker) Buyers**

<List, define and describe the TDM buyers. Also relate to their level of knowledge and buying authority.>

2.5. **Target Users**

<Define, list and describe the targeted users. Also relate to their level of knowledge and influence on the buying decision.>

2.6. **Market Problem**

<Define and describe the market problem for which the product aims to solve.>

2.7. <u>Product Description</u>
<Define and describe the product which aims to solve the aforementioned market problem.>

2.8. <u>Solving the Problem</u>
<Describe how the product solves the market problem.>

2.9. <u>Product's Problem Solving Features</u>
<Define, list and describe the top product features that directly address and solve main facets of the market problem.>

Market Problem Facet	Solution	Feature

2.10. <u>Competitors and Competing Products</u>
<Define, list and describe the competitors and their products that are in direct competition to your product; attempting to solve the same specific market problem.>

3. Product Positioning

3.1. <u>Section Objective</u>
This section deals with developing a product positioning statement, which is used as the basis for developing clear and focused marketing messages that communicate the product's unique psychological placement and value proposition to multiple audiences.

3.2. <u>Current Perception</u>
<If applicable, describe the present disposition and perception the target market may hold towards your company and products.>

3.3. <u>Value Proposition</u>
<Describe the product's "resultant value proposition" and "relative value proposition".>
<Comment:
- *"Resultant Value Proposition" is an implicit promise a product holds for customers to deliver a fixed combination of gains in time, cost and status.*
- *"Relative Value Proposition" is an implicit promise a product holds for customers to deliver a desired ratio of benefits and costs[customer].*
- *"Total Cost of Ownership" (TCO) is the aggregate expenses incurred by the customer from buying and using the product (essentially costs[customer]).*
- *Common relative value propositions, which are based on the ratio between features and "Total Cost of Ownership" (TCO), include:*
  o *Much more features for more TCO.*

  o *More features for the same TCO.*
  o *More features for less TCO.*
  o *Same features for less TCO.*
  o *Less features for much less TCO.>*

3.4. Unique Selling Proposition
<Describe the product's Unique Selling Proposition.>
<Comment: The Unique Selling Proposition is a key value differentiator which sets the product apart from other competing products.>

3.5. Core Two Sentence Positioning Statement
"For the <Enter target customer> who <Enter statement of need or opportunity>, the <Enter product name or category> provides <Enter statement of key benefit>. Unlike <Enter primary competitive alternative>, the <Enter statement of primary differentiation>".
<Comment: You may be able to identify several key or core positioning statements relative to the product itself and its target audiences. You may also be able to articulate internal and external positioning statements relative to your company.>

3.6. Competition's Positioning
<Define, list and describe how the competitors position their products that are in direct competition to your product; attempting to solve the same specific market problem.>

4. Supporting Data

4.1. Section Objective
The section provides data in support of claims, assertions, assumptions, and statements made throughout this document.

4.2. Assumptions
<Describe any assumptions made when writing this document.>

4.3. Research Information
<If relevant, describe and list the type and scope of research conducted in the course of writing this document.>

4.4. Product Diagram/Architecture
<If relevant, describe the product's architecture and modules accompanied by a schematic diagram.>

11.2.6 Sales Axioms – Template V. 4.0

Company Name: <Enter company name>

Product Name: <Enter product name>

- Date: <Enter date>
- Contact: <Enter your name>
- Department: <Enter department name>
- Location: <Enter location>
- Email: <Enter email address>
- Telephone: <Enter telephone number>

Document Revision History:

Date	Revision	Revised By	Approved By
<Enter date>	<Revision #>	<Enter your name>	<Enter name>

Table of Contents

1. Introduction

1.1. <u>Document Objective</u>

Sales axioms help to create an internal common understanding and serve to identify and explain the very fundamental concepts that the product is built upon.

1.2. <u>Sales Axioms Use</u>

Sales axioms are to be used and reflected upon whenever communicating the product to anyone, particularly customers in target markets. The sales axioms frame the category to which the product belongs. The combination of sales axioms also represents **value** to customers.

1.3. <u>Sales Axiom Structure</u>

Each sales axiom is a one-word term that is followed by a concise definition and bullet points that provide any supporting data.

2. Product's Sales Axioms

2.1. <u>Section Objective</u>

This section lists the product's sales axioms.

<Comment: To illustrate the concept of sales axioms, a brief example of a sales axioms listing for a new mid-size family/passenger car ("Automobile") is provided below.>

2.2. <u>Sales Axioms</u>

<List the product's sales axioms.>

<Example:

2.2.1. ***Reliability*** *– How long before breakdowns. The Automobile provides outstanding mechanical and instrument reliability. [Result: Peace of mind.]*

    2.2.1.1. *The Automobile is one of the most reliable vehicles in its class as indicated in reliability ratings by The JD Power Consumer Center for the last five years. This score given by JD Power is based on problems reported with the engine, transmission, steering, suspension, and braking systems after two years of ownership (Proof).*

    2.2.1.2. *With common periodical preventive maintenance, the Automobile can continue functioning with many original parts up to 300,000 miles (Fact).*

2.2.2. ***Efficiency (fuel)*** *– The ratio between the driving range and a unit amount of input fuel (miles per gallon – MPG). The Automobile offers excellent fuel economy. [Result: Reduced operating expenses (gasoline).]*

    2.2.2.1. *With a gas mileage rating of 32 MPG in the city and 40 MPG on the highway for the 5-speed model and 30 MPG in the city and 38 MPG on the highway for the automatic, the Automobile produces, by far, the best gas mileage for a car in its class (Fact).*

2.2.3. **Serviceability** – *Ease of performing periodical preventive maintenance and recovery/repair services. The Automobile is designed for easy maintenance by the owner and authorized mechanics. [Result: Reduced maintenance expenses (labor and parts).]*

    2.2.3.1. *The Automobile has been designed to provide improved access to the vehicle's mechanical components for easier maintenance and repair (Proof).*

    2.2.3.2. *The Automobile's structure places mechanical components far from vulnerable areas affected by collisions. Most frequently damaged components are fastened by screws, instead of welds, which allows for easier, faster, and less costly repair/replacement (Proof).>*

2.3. Non-Sales Axioms

In the interest of clarity, this section lists sales axioms which are NOT applicable to the product.

<List any expected sales axioms NOT associated with the product.>

<Example: "The Automobile was designed as a 'reliable', 'fuel efficient', and 'serviceable' product, but it was NOT built with the following elements as its key/core sales axioms: comfort, performance (speed, acceleration), luxury, safety, road handling, and quietness".>

2.4. Sales Axioms Message

The sales axioms can be distilled into one message which embodies the very fundamental concepts that the product is built upon.

<Describe the product's sales axioms message.>

<Comment: This message may be presented to internal audiences, such as Sales and MarCom, to help them better understand the value (and positioning) of the product.>

<Example: "The Automobile is a vehicle synonymous with 'reliability', 'fuel efficiency', and 'ease of maintenance'. Accordingly, the Automobile is a reassuring purchase that offers an excellent resale value and a high return on investment that is spread over a long service life".>

3. Supporting Data

3.1. Section Objective

The section provides data in support of claims, assertions, assumptions, and statements made throughout this document.

3.2. Assumptions

<Describe any assumptions made when writing this document. Be specific about the assumptions that if changed will alter the direction of the product and resulting this document.>

3.3. **Research Information**

<If relevant, describe and list the type and scope of research conducted in the course of writing this document.>

3.4. **Product Diagram/Architecture**

<If relevant, describe the product's architecture and modules accompanied by a schematic diagram.>

11.2.7 Problem/ Solution/Feature/Benefit – Template V. 4.0

Company Name: <Enter company name>

Product Name: <Enter product name>

- Date: <Enter date>
- Contact: <Enter your name>
- Department: <Enter department name>
- Location: <Enter location>
- Email: <Enter email address>
- Telephone: <Enter telephone number>

Document Revision History:

Date	Revision	Revised By	Approved By
<Enter date>	<Revision #>	<Enter your name>	<Enter name>

Table of Contents

1. Introduction

1.1. Document Objective

The purpose of this document is to describe the ability of <Enter product name> to address the **overall** customer problem by merit (benefits) of its feature scope and capabilities.

2. PSFB Matrix

2.1. Section Objective

The following matrix lists facets of the market problem. Displayed are product features which address and solve facets of the market problem and what overall benefits the customer realizes from solving each facet of the market problem.

2.2. PSFB Matrix

<Comment: To illustrate the concept of PSFB elements, an example pertaining to a passenger vehicle is provided.>

Problem	Solution	Feature	Benefit
<Describe the market problem facet the customer is facing.>	<Describe the general solution category that was applied, in order to solve the problem.>	<On a conceptual or modular level, describe the component(s) built into the product which provides the solution.>	<Describe the benefit the customer has realized from the feature being able to solve the market problem facet.>
<Example #1: Passengers are injured in front-end vehicle collisions.>	*< Example #1: Placing shock absorbing barriers which buffer the shock generated by a collision and protects passengers from the effects of impact.>*	*< Example #1:* • *Internal, passenger compartment mounted driver and passenger air bags.* • *Vehicle equipped with large, fortified, elastic, collision bumper.>*	*< Example #1:* • *Peace of mind.* • *Injury level minimization.>*
< Example #2: While in the vehicle, passengers are still affected by exterior climate conditions.>	*< Example #2: Provide a passenger compartment, temperature modifying, heating and cooling system.>*	*< Example #2: Vehicle equipped with an air-conditioning system that allows passengers to regulate temperature within the passenger compartment.>*	*< Example #2: Controlled comfort levels at different external weather conditions, produce a more relaxed driving experience.>*

3. Supporting Data

3.1. Section Objective
The section provides data in support of claims, assertions, assumptions, and statements made throughout this document.

3.2. Assumptions
<Describe any assumptions made when writing this document.>

3.3. Research Information
<If relevant, describe and list the type and scope of research conducted in the course of writing this document.>

3.4. Product Diagram/Architecture
<If relevant, describe the product's architecture and modules accompanied by a schematic diagram.>

11.2.8 Unique Selling Proposition – Template V. 4.0

Company Name: <Enter company name>

Product Name: <Enter product name>

- Date: <Enter date>
- Contact: <Enter your name>
- Department: <Enter department name>
- Location: <Enter location>
- Email: <Enter email address>
- Telephone: <Enter telephone number>

Document Revision History:

Date	Revision	Revised By	Approved By
<Enter date>	<Revision #>	<Enter your name>	<Enter name>

Table of Contents

1. Introduction

1.1. **Document Objective**

This document defines the Unique Selling Proposition (USP) for <Enter product name>. A USP is the key "statement" that describes the distinct and compelling value of the product, which sets the product apart from other competing products.

<Comment: Relative to the product, the USP embodies value to customers, a competitive differentiator, and target market appeal. The proposition must be one that the competition either can not or does not offer. A USP may also be generated for a brand, product line or company. This template deals with developing a USP for a product.>

1.2. **USP Use**

The USP is used as a tool in developing marketing messages. Messages conveying a USP help build product identity and create a distinction between the product and its competitors.

<Comment: The Unique Selling Proposition (USP) is not a slogan or a branding phrase. It is a real and factual statement about the product with an outward focus. Marketing communications media vehicles and all marketing programs MUST reflect and convey the USP when communicating the product to anyone, particularly to prospective customers.>

2. Unique Selling Proposition (USP)

2.1. **Section Objective**

This section describes the product's Unique Selling Proposition (USP).

2.2. **Unique Selling Proposition (USP)**

<Describe the product's Unique Selling Proposition (USP). The USP can be one word or several paragraphs long. Keeping the USP simple and brief makes it easier to comprehend and more effective.>

<Comment:
- *The three Unique Selling Proposition (USP) elements are:*
  - *Value to customers – The **one** statement that describes the unique value of the product.*
  - *Competitive differentiator – The **one** statement that makes the product different than any other competing products.*
  - *Target market appeal – The **one** reason customers will buy the product even though it may seem to be no different from any other similar products.>*
- *The following may constitute a product's Unique Selling Proposition: particular product attributes, quality, customer service, guarantee, serving a specific market segment, distribution, patriotism, sentimental appeal, rarity, locality, tradition, synergy, fashion, patents, trademarks, convenience, variety, and packaging.*
- *The following are examples of Unique Selling Propositions:*

      o *Advil's USP for its cold medication is fast relief.*
      o *Apple's USP for its computers is user-friendliness.*
      o *Rolls-Royce's USP for its vehicles is luxury.*

2.3. Challenge/Defend the USP
The following are rationales in support of the chosen USP:
- Communicable – <The USP should be easy to communicate. State how the USP will be communicated. Specify if the USP is more communicable in a particular way, such as visually or audibly.>
- Data supported – <List any facts and data that acknowledge the USP is valid and true.>
- Differentiator – <List any facts and data that acknowledge the USP does differentiate the product from its competitors.>
- Easily identified – <Describe how the three USP elements are clearly reflected in the USP.>
- Easily understood – <Verify and explain why the USP is comprehendible and clear to the target customer. The USP should be immediately apparent to the customer.>
- Measurable – <Verify and explain if the USP is measurable/quantifiable or not. For example, time and weight are measurable USPs.>
- Solution oriented – <State how the USP demonstrates that buying the product will solve a problem or satisfy a need.>

3. Supporting Data

3.1. Section Objective
The section provides data in support of claims, assertions, assumptions, and statements made throughout this document.

3.2. Assumptions
<Describe any assumptions made when writing this document. Be specific about the assumptions that if changed will alter the direction of the product and resulting this document.>

3.3. Research Information
<If relevant, describe and list the type and scope of research conducted in the course of writing this document.>

3.4. Product Diagram/Architecture
<If relevant, describe the product's architecture and modules accompanied by a schematic diagram.>

11.2.9 Market Plan – Template V. 4.0

Insert Company

Logo Here

Company Name: <Enter company name>
Product Name: <Enter product name>

- Date: <Enter date>
- Contact: <Enter your name>
- Department: <Enter department name>
- Location: <Enter location>
- Email: <Enter email address>
- Telephone: <Enter telephone number>

Document Revision History:

date	revision	revised by	approved by
<Enter date>	<Revision #>	<Enter your name>	<Enter name>

Table of Contents

1. Introduction

1.1. <u>Document Objective</u>

This document describes the long-term goals, and messages delivered to the target market, relative to the <Enter product name> product.

<Comment: Throughout the document, keep your writing short, clear and concise. This document is the first in a series of three documents that constitute the company's marketing effort:

- o *"Market Plan" – description of the long-term goals, and messages delivered to the target market, relative to a particular company or product (AKA "Strategic Marketing Plan"). Strategic document.*
- o *"Marketing Plan" – description of the selection and application of marketing mixes in the target market. Tactical document.*
- o *"Marketing Program" – short-term marketplace effort designed to obtain a specific goal with respect to a particular product. Operational document.>*

1.2. <u>Executive Summary</u>

<Enter the executive summary.>

<Comment: This section is to be completed once the market plan is complete. Focus on the key elements of the plan and do not exceed two pages.>

2. Structure and Resources

2.1. <u>Section Objective</u>

This section identifies the team leader, key individuals, roles, and resources necessary to formulate a successful market plan.

2.2. <u>Market Plan Team</u>

Team members include representatives from the following areas:

- Product Marketing – <Enter names>
- Product Planning – <Enter names>
- Marketing Communications – <Enter names>
- Engineering – <Enter names>
- Sales Management – <Enter names>
- Executive Management – <Enter names>

<Comment: Add or remove team members as relevant to your needs.>

3. Market Problem and Opportunity

3.1. <u>Section Objective</u>

This section describes the market problem and resulting market opportunity.

3.2. **Market Problem**
<Identify and justify the specific market problem. Explain any other interlinking market problems.>

<Comment: The market problem is a "consumer" or "product" or "technology" problem in the target market. The market problem is essentially a situation (difficulty) that exists in the target market and requires change.

- *Consumer Problem – A marketplace situation in which consumer needs remain unsatisfied (B2C). The solution to a consumer problem is a whole product.*
- *Product Problem – An industry situation in which product requirements' are unmet (B2B). The solution to a product problem is a product component.*
- *Technology Problem – Challenges in applied science. The solution to a technology problem is scientific research.*

3.3. **Market Opportunity**
<Provide a statement detailing the specific market opportunity. Size and substantiate the market opportunity as much as possible. Document the assumptions and facts that validate and justify the market opportunity. Explain any other interlinking market opportunities.>

<Comment: The market opportunity is a lucrative, lasting and sizable market problem. Market Opportunity = Market Problem + Volume + Duration + Earning Potential.>

4. Market Overview

4.1. **Section Objective**
This section describes the market and customer profile the proposed product is targeted towards.

4.2. **Overall Market Overview**
4.2.1. **Overall Market Definition**
<Define the overall market at which the proposed product is targeted.>
<Comment: The Overall Market is all customers who share a need that could be satisfied by the product.>
4.2.2. **Overall Market Description**
<Describe the overall market at which the proposed product is targeted and list the key characteristics of the overall market. Comment on market size, market growth, and any technological, regulatory, cultural, supply conditions, economic, and political trends.>

4.3. **Market/Customer Segmentation**
<Define and describe the most applicable way to segment the market, using criteria such as geographical location, industry, size, or technology.>
<Comment: Market Segmentation is the division of the overall market for a product, into groups of common characteristics. The following table describes various common market/customer segmentation criteria.

Segmentation	B2C Markets	B2B Markets

Segmentation	B2C Markets	B2B Markets
What are the characteristics of the customer?	Age, sex, race Income Family size Life cycle stage Location Lifestyle	Vertical industry Geographical location Size of company Technology Profitability Style/culture of management
How will the customer purchase/use the product?	Size/ frequency of purchase Issues with brand loyalty Purpose of use Purchasing behavior Importance of purchase Source of purchase	Application of product Importance of purchase Volume of purchases Frequency of purchase Purchasing procedure Distribution channel
What are the users' specific needs, and preferences?	Similarity to existing purchases Price elasticity Brand preferences Desired features Service requirements	Performance requirements Assistance from suppliers Brand preferences Desired features Service requirements

Source: Piers Robinson, Marketing for Entrepreneurs, 2004.

The recommended segmentation criteria and hierarchy is: geographic, demographic, and technologic. A different segmentation criteria and hierarchy can be selected and employed in the following "Market/Customer Segments" section to match the composition of any specific overall market.>

4.4. Market/Customer Segments
4.4.1. Target Market (Geographic)
4.4.1.1. <Enter the actual geographic location(s) that will constitute the target market. These can be countries, continents, or any other designated region.>

<Example: North-America, Germany and France.>

4.4.2. Target Market (Demographic)
4.4.2.1. <Enter the actual demographic description of the customer segment(s).

<Example: Automotive manufacturers with over 10,000 employees.>

4.4.3. Target Market (Technologic)
4.4.3.1. <Enter the actual technological characterization of the customer segment(s).>

<Example: Using Linux servers running Apache.>

4.5. Target Market(s) Description
<Enter a statement, based on the results of the market/customer segmentation process, which describes the target market(s).>

<Comment: This essentially defines the Target Market(s), the group or groups of customers selected by a firm to sell to.>

<Example: The target market is automotive manufacturers with over 10,000 employees which employ Linux servers running Apache, and are located in North-America, Germany and France.>

4.6. Target Market(s) Rationale
<Describe why the particular target market(s) were selected and explain the rationale supporting why these target market(s) should be pursued.>

4.7. Customer Overview
4.7.1. Customer Definition
<Define the customer at which the product is targeted.>
4.7.2. Customer Description
<Describe the customer profile at which the product is targeted and list the key characteristics of the customer.>

4.8. Market/Product Segmentation
<Describe and explain which market/product segmentation approach is likely to be most realistic and/or successful. Relevant segmentation approaches are: single segment, selective specialization, product specialization, market specialization, or full market coverage. Reflect on the applicability of presenting product groups and product families as the main offering.>

4.9. Competition
<Describe the competitive landscape and key competitors. Provide a brief overview.>

5. Long-Term Goals

5.1. Section Objective
This section defines and describes the long-term goals that the market plan should generate.

5.2. Long-Term Marketing Goals
<Define and describe the long-term marketing goals that the market plan will attempt to achieve. Detail the goals in **qualitative** marketing terms such as image, awareness and recognition. Do not use any monetary or quantitative marketing terms.>

<Comment: This section outlines the long-term marketing goals which are the desired outcome and what will be accomplished by communicating the marketing messages to the target market within a specified time frame. Long-term marketing goals include: building an identity, exhibiting commitment to customers, achieving a designate level of customer satisfaction, attaining a measured rate of customer awareness, building a favorable image, reaching high recall and recognition factors in the target market; but not market share, profit, revenue volume or sales velocity. All long-term marketing goals must be measurable and time constrained,

and can be sequenced along a time line. Examples of long-term marketing goals are:
- *75% awareness to product in market segment within two years.*
- *50% favorable image in overall market after one year.>*

6. PMTK Value-Marketing Model

6.1. Section Objective

This section describes an implementation of the "*PMTK Value-Marketing Model*", a work model to define and document the product's and company's value and quality factors.

<Comment: Defining and documenting the company's value and quality factors is done only for synchronization and reference purposes as this market plan does not handle corporate branding.>

6.2. Promise of Quality

6.2.1. Promise of Corporate Quality

<Define the company's "*Promise of Corporate Quality*" factor; which is the reward customers get from establishing a relationship with the company. "*Corporate Quality*" is a state where the company delivers a relationship more rewarding than the customers expected.>

6.2.2. Promise of Product Quality

<Define the company's "*Promise of Product Quality*" factor; which is the specific benefits perceived as quality that the customers get by owning and using the product. "*Product Quality*" is a state where the product delivers more benefits than the customers expected.>

6.3. Company Core Competency

<Describe the "*Company Core Competency*".>

<Comment: The "Company Core Competency" is a company's unique ability to deliver value, while differentiating itself from the competition.>

6.4. Value Proposition

6.4.1. Resultant Value Proposition

<Describe the product's "*Resultant Value Proposition*".>

<Comment: The "Resultant Value Proposition" is an implicit promise a product holds for customers to deliver a fixed combination of gains in time, cost, and status. This proposition reflects the product's main and relevant benefit, in absolute terms, to the customer and is what primarily is needed of the product.>

6.4.2. Relative Value Proposition

<Describe the product's "*Relative Value Proposition*".>

<Comment: The "Relative Value Proposition" is an implicit promise a product holds for customers to deliver a desired ratio of benefits and costs[customer]. It is a notion that the customers use to differentiate products of seemingly similar value, although their respective absolute

benefits and costs may be different. "Total Cost of Ownership" (TCO) is the aggregate expenses incurred by the customer from buying and using the product (essentially costs[customer]). Common relative value propositions, which are based on the ratio between benefits (features) and costs (TCO), include:

- *o Much more features for more TCO.*
- *o More features for the same TCO.*
- *o More features for less TCO.*
- *o Same features for less TCO.*
- *o Less features for much less TCO.>*

6.5. Unique Selling Proposition

<Describe the product's "Unique Selling Proposition" (USP).>
<Comment: The "Unique Selling Proposition" is a key value differentiator, which sets the product apart from other competing products.>

6.6. "PMTK Value-Marketing Model" Summary List

6.6.1. *"Promise of Corporate Quality"*: <Enter text>.
6.6.2. *"Promise of Product Quality"*: <Enter text>.
6.6.3. *"Company Core Competency"*: <Enter text>.
6.6.4. *"Resultant Value Proposition"*: <Enter text>.
6.6.5. *"Relative Value Proposition"*: <Enter text>.
6.6.6. *"Unique Selling Proposition"*: <Enter text>.

<Comment: The above is a list of your company's and product's value and quality factors. The summary list is a recap of the previous sections and is meant to provide a complete description of all the value and quality factors which help build "Superior Perceived Value".>

<Example:

- *"Promise of Corporate Quality": fair pricing.*
- *"Promise of Product Quality": functionality.*
- *"Company Core Competency": distribution.*
- *"Resultant Value Proposition": increased productivity.*
- *"Relative Value Proposition": more for same.*
- *"Unique Selling Proposition": usability (better UI).>*

7. PMTK Marketing Messages Model

7.1. Section Objective

This section describes an implementation of the *"PMTK Marketing Messages Model"*, a work model to used create marketing messages that are used to guide product marketing activities.

<Comment: "Product Marketing" is outbound activities aimed at generating product awareness, differentiation and demand. Product differentiation is achieved via "Positioning Messages". Product demand is achieved via "Value

Messages". Product awareness is a by-product of having "Positioning Messages" and "Value Messages" being conveyed to the target market.>

7.2. PMTK Product Positioning Messages Model
7.2.1. Product Positioning Statement
<Enter the product positioning statement. See the *"PMTK Product Positioning"* template.>
7.2.2. Key Product Positioning Marketing Messages
7.2.2.1. Message #P1 – <Enter text>.
  7.2.2.1.1. Data Point #P1D1 – <Enter text>.
  7.2.2.1.2. Data Point #P1D2 – <Enter text>.
  7.2.2.1.3. Data Point #P1D3 – <Enter text>.
7.2.2.2. Message #P2 – <Enter text>.
  7.2.2.2.1. Data Point #P2D1 – <Enter text>.
  7.2.2.2.2. Data Point #P2D2 – <Enter text>.
  7.2.2.2.3. Data Point #P2D3 – <Enter text>.
7.2.2.3. Message #P3 – <Enter text>.
  7.2.2.3.1. Data Point #P3D1 – <Enter text>.
  7.2.2.3.2. Data Point #P3D2 – <Enter text>.
  7.2.2.3.3. Data Point #P3D3 – <Enter text>.
  <Comment: Required are two to three key marketing messages that reinforce the product positioning statement, and two to three "Data Points" that validate each key marketing message. It is highly recommend not exceeding three positioning marketing messages. The "Product Positioning Messages" must reflect a product feature/capability and the derived benefit, relative to the market problem. Each data point must be based on measurable, objective, factual, and provable information. Each message must be supported with data points the customer can actually verify.>

7.3. PMTK Product Value Messages Model
7.3.1. Product Quality, Value, USP
7.3.1.1. *"Promise of Product Quality"*: <Enter text>.
7.3.1.2. *"Resultant Value Proposition"*: <Enter text>.
7.3.1.3. *"Relative Value Proposition"*: <Enter text>.
7.3.1.4. *"Unique Selling Proposition"*: <Enter text>.
<Comment: Copy the product's quality, value, and USP factors which were entered into the "PMTK Value-Marketing Model" summary list (a previous section in this document).>
7.3.2. Key Product Value Marketing Messages
7.3.2.1. Message #V1 – <Enter text>.
  7.3.2.1.1. Data Point #V1D1 – <Enter text>.
  7.3.2.1.2. Data Point #V1D2 – <Enter text>.
  7.3.2.1.3. Data Point #V1D3 – <Enter text>.
7.3.2.2. Message #V2 – <Enter text>.
  7.3.2.2.1. Data Point #V2D1 – <Enter text>.

                7.3.2.2.2. Data Point #V2D2 – <Enter text>.
                7.3.2.2.3. Data Point #V2D3 – <Enter text>.
        7.3.2.3. Message #V3 – <Enter text>.
                7.3.2.3.1. Data Point #V3D1 – <Enter text>.
                7.3.2.3.2. Data Point #V3D2 – <Enter text>.
                7.3.2.3.3. Data Point #V3D3 – <Enter text>.

<Comment: Required are two to three key marketing messages that convey the product's quality, value, and USP, and two to three "Data Points" that validate each key marketing message. It is highly recommend not exceeding three value marketing messages. The "Product Value Messages" must reflect a perceived monetary or material or psycho-social worth, which the customers shall gain from owning and using the product. Each data point must be based on measurable, objective, factual, and provable information. Each message must be supported with data points the customer can actually verify.>

7.4. **PMTK Marketing Messages Plan**
7.4.1. **Marketing Messages**
        7.4.1.1. Message #<Positioning Message ID> – <Copy and enter here the selected positioning message which will be communicated>.
        7.4.1.2. Message #<Positioning Message ID> – <Copy and enter here the selected positioning message which will be communicated>.
        7.4.1.3. Message #<Value Message ID> – <Copy and enter here the selected value message which will be communicated>.
        7.4.1.4. Message #<Value Message ID> – <Copy and enter here the selected value message which will be communicated>.

<Comment: This is an aggregate list of all the marketing messages that will be communicated to the target market. This list is comprised of selected positioning messages and value messages, two of each. It is highly recommended not exceeding a total of four marketing messages.>

7.4.2. **Media Selection**
        7.4.2.1. <Enter media selection options.>

<Comment: Select the media options that shall be used to communicate the marketing messages. Options include: public relations, advertising, sales, electronic marketing, direct marketing, and telemarketing. The key selection factors include: reach, frequency, and impact.>

<Example: Print advertising and telemarketing.>

7.4.3. **Messaging Schedule**
        7.4.3.1. <Enter the selected messaging schedule.>

<Comment: Select the messaging schedule mode or combination of. Options include: continuous, intervals, and blink.>

<Example: Continuous/60day, Intervals (on/12days-off/7days).>

7.4.4. Messages Sequencing
    7.4.4.1. Order: <Enter the order of presenting the marketing messages to the target market>.

        <Example: Order: P2, V1, V2, P1.>

    7.4.4.2. Pattern: <Enter the pattern of presenting the marketing messages to the target market>.

        <Comment: Determine the order and pattern which will be used to introduce the marketing messages to the target market.>

        <Example: Pattern: 2*P2, 1*V1, 1*V2, 1*P. (This pattern means that message #P2 will be communicated twice and then the other messages will be communicated once each. The cycle restarts once the last message in the sequence was communicated).>

7.4.5. Proof Support
    7.4.5.1. <Enter the manner of presenting the data points, which accompany the marketing messages, to the target market.>

        <Comment: Determine the data point inclusion and rotation intervals.>

        <Example: Rotate data point every third marketing message exposure.>

8. Supporting Data

8.1. Section Objective
The section provides data in support of claims, assertions, assumptions, and statements made throughout this document.

8.2. Assumptions
<Describe any assumptions made when writing this document.>

8.3. Research Information
<If relevant, describe and list the type and scope of research conducted in the course of writing this document.>

8.4. Product Diagram/Architecture
<If relevant, describe the product's architecture and modules accompanied by a schematic diagram.>

11.2.10 Company Profile – Template V. 4.0

Company Name: <Enter company name>

Product Name: <Enter product name>

- Date: <Enter date>
- Contact: <Enter your name>
- Department: <Enter department name>
- Location: <Enter location>
- Email: <Enter email address>
- Telephone: <Enter telephone number>

Document Revision History:

Date	Revision	Revised By	Approved By
<Enter date>	<Revision #>	<Enter your name>	<Enter name>

Table of Contents

1. Introduction

1.1. **Document Objective**

This document is focused on creating a company profile document that provides public audiences with a detailed yet basic description of a company. The information contained in a company profile introduces a company to the reader.

<Comment: The primary purpose of a company profile, also known as company bio, company fact sheet or company backgrounder, is to provide the general public with overview information regarding a company. The company profile can also be used to attract potential customers, investors and job applicants. When preparing a company profile, great care should be taken not to overload or overbear the reader with superfluous data. A more comprehensive company profile may be needed to accompany the company's business plan when attempting to attract financial investors.>

2. Company Profile Authoring

2.1. **Section Objective**

This section describes the principals that guide the preparation of a company profile.

2.2. **Company Profile Objectives**

- Demonstrate the company's ability to effectively meet its customers' needs.
- Educate audience to company, its business operations and the value it delivers.
- Help establish credibility with audience (mainly customers and investors).
- Provide anyone with information to assess the company's general merit.

2.3. **Company Profile Distribution Venues**

- Printed Format
  - o To accompany RFP responses.
  - o To attach (or selected parts of the profile) to strategic press releases.
  - o To accompany a company presentation.
  - o As part of a press or media kit.
  - o To provide to investors and lenders.
- Electronic Format
  - o For corporate website.
  - o To support sales quotes.
  - o To send to applicants and customers.

2.4. **Company Profile Guidelines**

- Average number of pages in a company profile is one to two pages.
- Average word count of a company profile is 200-450 words.
- Avoid meaningless superlatives and phrases as: top-class, top-of-the-line, best-of-breed, or cutting-edge.
- Avoid technical jargon and make the company profile meaningful to any reader.

- Include as many as possible, and only, verifiable facts and numbers.
- Proofread the company profile very carefully for grammatical and typographical errors.
- Print on slightly heavier than normal quality paper. Only use a laser printer, not ink-jet, or preferably employ a professional printing service.

2.5. Acceptance and Publication

- Before creating a company profile, secure endorsement regarding the content of the proposed company profile from the following organizational departments: executive management, public relations, corporate marketing, and legal.
- After creating a company profile and before publicly posting or publishing the company profile, secure acceptance and approval to the company profile release candidate from those same organizational departments that endorsed it.
- The content of the company profile can greatly contribute in the preparation of the PMTK Company Presentation (PowerPoint format) and should be leveraged for that purpose.

3. Company Profile

3.1. Section Objective

This section describes the structure and format of a professional outbound company profile. A company profile is prepared by seamlessly weaving pertinent data about the company into a flowing, narrative form.

3.2. Company Profile Template

<Comment: See template in the following pages.>

Corporate Overview

<This section provides a synopsis of the company. Succinctly describe the company using the following content elements: short company description, main line of business, revenue (optional), target market segments or industries and geographical areas of operation, headquarters and any major branch offices, date founded, number of employees, most notable key historical facts, parent company, and subsidiaries, if any. Subject to the specific company being addressed, some of these content elements may not be applicable or necessary. Note in this paragraph the type of organization: public enterprise, private company, or organization sponsored (assisted by government); and the type of business: manufacturer, retailer, authorized agent, or consulting company.>

Mission and Vision Statements

<This section allows readers to better understand the nature and personality of the company. Succinctly describe the company's underlying core principals using the following content elements: corporate mission statement, corporate vision statement, business philosophy, organizational philosophy, and corporate distinctive competency.>

Markets / Industries Served

<This section describes the main markets and industries (vertical industries in particular), that the company serves. Succinctly describe the company's target markets using the following content elements: market description, market share, market trends, major competitors, and key customers.>

Products, Services, and Solutions

<This section describes the company's main products and services. Succinctly describe the company's offering using the following content elements: main product lines, key products and services, patents, notable achievements, brand equity, and the products' general USP (Unique Selling Proposition). Identify any mass markets or niche markets to which products are sold, and any unique or special technologies that are used or served.>

Financial Information

<This section provides an assessment of the current overall financial condition of the company. Succinctly describe the company's financial state and indicators using the following content elements: average annual income, recent annual income, recent profits, annual income growth rate, and any other notable financial statistics. If relevant, include information on: stock exchange where traded and ticker symbol. Also include web links to current stock price, stock chart, market cap, and SEC 10-K.>

Partnerships / Alliances / Affiliations / Joint-Ventures

<This section lists the various relations the company has with other entities, companies and industry players that help improve its competitive position. Succinctly provide the following content elements: partnerships, alliances, affiliations, joint-ventures, mergers, and acquisitions.>

Company History / Chronology

<This section lists facts that present the company's historical progression through time. Succinctly provide the following content elements: historical milestones, mergers and acquisitions, major contracts, date of incorporation, notable achievements, and major public recognitions. Observe any notable growth and expansion indicators. When appropriate, provide web links to news reports, press releases, and success stories.>

Worldwide Locations / Presence

<This section expands on the company's global reach and operations. Succinctly describe the company's worldwide deployment using the following content elements: headquarters location, subsidiaries, major worldwide offices, and regional offices.>

Community Relations

<This section outlines the company's community relations program and activities. Succinctly describe the company's contribution to society using the following content elements: charitable funds, grants, donations, corporate volunteer projects, matching gift programs, and food drives. Observe any notable contributions or achievements.>

Executive Officers

<This section provides pertinent information on the company's management team (this information is often more relevant to investors than customers). Succinctly describe the company's leadership using the following content elements: names and titles of executive officers accompanied by brief biographical information. If relevant, include photographs, salary information, and include links to relevant online information sources.>

Forward Looking Statements

<This section depicts the company's estimates, expectations and future plans. Succinctly describe the company's plans regarding the following issues: new products and services, new offices and facilities, planned mergers, or acquisitions.>

Contact Information

<This section provides all necessary means for the reading audience to reach the company. Provide the following contact information as data bullet points or in any other applicable visual format such as text box: company address, link to online map to company address, phone and fax, email address, and website. Place company logo here.>

11.2.11 Product Backgrounder – Template V. 4.0

Company Name: <Enter company name>
Product Name: <Enter product name>

- Date: <Enter date>
- Contact: <Enter your name>
- Department: <Enter department name>
- Location: <Enter location>
- Email: <Enter email address>
- Telephone: <Enter telephone number>

Document Revision History:

Date	Revision	Revised By	Approved By
<Enter date>	<Revision #>	<Enter your name>	<Enter name>

Table of Contents

1. Introduction

1.1. Document Objective

This document is a product backgrounder template. The product backgrounder provides product overview information at a glance.

2. Product Backgrounder

2.1. Section Objective

This section describes the components of a product backgrounder document.

2.2. Product Backgrounder Template

<Product Name> – Product Backgrounder		
Product Description	<Enter text.>	
Market Needs and Challenges	<Enter text.>	
Target Market	<Enter text.>	
Key Features	<Enter text.>	
Key Benefits	<Enter text.>	
Value Proposition	<Enter text.>	
Competitive Advantages	<Enter text.>	
Technology Summary	<Enter text.>	
Product Category	<Enter text.>	
Distribution	<Enter text.>	
Price	<Enter text.>	
Corporate Background	<Enter text.>	
Contact Information	<Enter text.>	<Enter corporate logo.>
Disclaimer and Copyright Notice	<Enter text.>	

<Example:

iSpam-Apprehender 3.6 – Product Backgrounder	
Product Description	iSpam-Apprehender 3.6 is a server based spam filtering software application that protects any SMTP mail server from spam.
Market Needs and Challenges	Spam (unsolicited email messages) is a conduit for inappropriate or malicious content, which in most companies accounts for a yearly average of $2,000 worth of lost productivity per employee.
Target Market	Companies employing in-house SMTP mail servers.
Key Features	• Automated spam prevention system, reducing administrative overhead • Scans email at the mail server, preventing spam reaching employees • Real-time detection and identification of suspected emails
Key Benefits	• Removes threat to employee productivity and network health • Increases up-time of computer and network infrastructure
Value Proposition	• Resultant value proposition – increased employee productivity • Relative value proposition – more features for the same TCO
Competitive Advantages	The only cross-platform, software only, server based spam filtering software currently available for Intel processor computers.
Technology Summary	32-bit application designed to work with Exchange Server, Notes, I-Mail and most SMTP mail servers.
Product Category	Internet Security
Distribution	Electronic download only from www.iSpam-Apprehender.com
Price	$199.99 MSRP
Corporate Background	iSpam-Apprehender Corporation was founded in 2001 by a partnership of computer professionals, combining their resources to provide a powerful response to the growing technological threats on the internet. For more information, please visit www.iSpam-Apprehender .com
Contact Information	John Smith Senior Product Specialist Tel: 999-999-9999 john@.iSpam-Apprehender .com
Disclaimer and Copyright Notice	Statements in this document involve risks and uncertainties, including the risks associated with the effects of changing economic conditions, trends in the development of the Internet as a commercial medium, market acceptance risks, technological development risks, seasonality and other risk factors.

>

11.2.12 Collateral Matrix – Guidelines V. 4.0

Company Name: <Enter company name>
Product Name: <Enter product name>

- Date: <Enter date>
- Contact: <Enter your name>
- Department: <Enter department name>
- Location: <Enter location>
- E-mail: <Enter email address>
- Telephone: <Enter telephone number>

Document Revision History:

Date	Revision	Revised By	Approved By
<Enter date>	<Revision #>	<Enter your name>	<Enter name>

Table of Contents

1. Introduction

1.1. Document Objective

This document describes the various marketing communications collateral that may be produced in support of marketing the product/company.

2. The Collateral Matrix

2.1. Section Objective

This section describes the marketing communications collateral matrix.

2.2. Marketing Communications Collateral Matrix Glossary

- **Collateral**: Name of the collateral document.
- **Audience**: Intended audience of the collateral document.
- **Key MarCom Objectives**: Directives of what the collateral document aims to achieve and is measured by.
- **Key Messages**: The argument, idea or information the collateral document aims to convey to the intended audience.
- **Format**: The commonly accepted print format in North-America.

2.3. Marketing Communications Collateral Matrix

See below.

Collateral	Audience	Key MarCom Objectives	Key Messages	Format	Owner	Deadline
Case studies	• Journals and newspapers • Prospects • Sales channel	Communicate success in stages: • Complete story • Post implementation benefits • Why beta client selected the product	• Distinctive competence • Key messages to be honed as work is initiated on each piece • USP (unique selling proposition)	Casual collateral on company letterhead until product 75% complete, then four color glossy version		
Company executive biographies	• Journals and newspapers • Prospects • Sales channel	• Establish company credibility • Impress audience with skill set and level of executive experience • Inform audience about the company	• Distinctive competence • Present key executives and provide biographical information which supports business strategy	Front and back on company letterhead		
Company presentation (PowerPoint) (PMTK)	• Analysts • Industry experts • Journalists • Prospects • Sales channel	• Establish company as successful entity with a purpose (vision, mission, leadership, and value.) • Establish company credibility • Inform audience about the company	• Company background • Corporate mission statement • Distinctive competence • Key products and services	PowerPoint and printed handouts		
Company presentation folder	• Journals and newspapers • Prospects • Sales channel	• Establish company as successful entity with a purpose (vision, mission, leadership, and value.) • Establish company credibility • Inform audience about the company	• Distinctive competence • Graphical articulation of new company identity and brand	Four color pocket presentation folder		
Company profile (PMTK)	• Journals and newspapers • Prospects • Sales channel	• Establish company as successful entity with a purpose (vision, mission, leadership, and value.) • Establish company credibility • Inform audience about the company	• Company background • Corporate mission statement • Distinctive competence • Key products and services	Front and back on company letterhead		
Company reference client list	• Journals and newspapers • Prospects • Sales channel	• Establish company credibility	• Company is successful because solves market problems in target markets	Front and back on company letterhead		

Collateral	Audience	Key MarCom Objectives	Key Messages	Format	Owner	Deadline
Interactive demo: • CD-ROM version • Web version	• Journals and newspapers • Prospects • Sales channel • Web surfers	• Clarify any areas of confusion about product For both versions of demo: • Generate interest in learning more • Present product key features and benefits	• Distinctive competence • Key messages to be honed as work is initiated on each piece • USP (unique selling proposition)	• CD-ROM • Website		
Non-technical white paper	• Business decision makers (BDM)	• Generate strong interest in implementing this solution	• Distinctive competence • Product value and ROI • USP (unique selling proposition)	Company letterhead		
• Presentations for press tour • Presentations to introduce product to sales channel	• Journals and newspapers • Sales channel	• Inform and excite journals and newspapers about the product, resulting in press willingness to do a product review or write an article about the product • Inform and excite sales channel about the product and potential sales it can generate for them	• Distinctive competence • Key messages to be honed as work is initiated on each piece • USP (unique selling proposition)	PowerPoint and printed handouts		
Press releases: • Sales channel relationship • Product launch announcement	• Journals and newspapers • Sales channel	• Alert sales channel to product • Clarify relationship • Create media hype around product launch	• Distinctive competence • Key messages to be honed as work is initiated on each piece • USP (unique selling proposition)	Company letterhead		
Product backgrounder (PMTK)	• Analysts • Industry experts • Journalists • Prospects • Sales channel	• Inform of key features and benefits • Overview of market, product and company	• Distinctive competence • Product value and ROI • USP (unique selling proposition)	Company letterhead		

Collateral	Audience	Key MarCom Objectives	Key Messages	Format	Owner	Deadline
Product brochure	• Business decision makers (BDM) • Journals and newspapers • Prospects • Sales channel	• Create product awareness • Create understanding about market gap filled by product • Establish credibility • Satisfy questions on basic features and benefits from business and technical decision makers	• Basic specifications and technical requirements • Company information • Key features and benefits • Market problem solved • Positioning statement • USP (unique selling proposition)	Brochure – four color, double-sided, printed in four colors on gloss paper and folded		
Product datasheet	• Engineers • Technical decision makers (TDM)	• Demonstrate product's overall technical compatibility with customer technical needs and technical environment	• Advanced specifications and technical requirements • Product architecture	Brochure – four color		
Product presentation (PowerPoint) (PMTK)	• Analysts • Industry experts • Journalists • Prospects • Sales channel	• Create product awareness • Create understanding about market gap filled by product • Establish credibility • Satisfy questions on basic features and benefits from business and technical decision makers	• Basic specifications and technical requirements • Company information • Key features and benefits • Market problem solved • Positioning statement • USP (unique selling proposition)	PowerPoint and printed handouts		
Reviewer's guide	• Analysts • Industry experts • Journalists	• Create clear understanding about how product works • Demonstrate key features and benefits • Provide hands-on experience with the product (subject to need)	• Key points of differentiation from competing products • Product features and benefits • Product overview • USP (unique selling proposition)	Spiral bound on company letterhead with cover		

Collateral	Audience	Key MarCom Objectives	Key Messages	Format	Owner	Deadline
Sales channel recruitment tools: • Proposal template • Qualifier form	• Product sales representatives • Prospective sales channels	Tell a consistent product story to prospective sales channels: • Answer all potential questions and objections • Determine if sales channel is good fit with the product and has good chances for success • Educate sales channel about the product, potential revenues, market	• Benefits to sales channel • Competitive landscape • Market size and trends • Product summary	• Company letterhead for qualifier form and proposal template • PowerPoint		
Sales channel sales tools: • Competitor Analysis matrix • Direct mail • PowerPoint • Proposal template • Qualifier form • Regional launch seminar • ROI report • ROI survey • Seminar-in-a-box	• Selected sales channels	All tools will provide some flexibility for customization while ensuring consistent product messages are communicated to prospects: • Clearly identify how the product stands above the competition • Direct mail to generate leads for seminars • Maintain consistent way of proposing product to prospects – use what works best in field • Motivate regional sales • Provide sales channel with standardized tools to sponsor their own seminars • Qualify best prospects for the product • ROI report • ROI survey	• Distinctive competence • Key messages to be honed as work is initiated on each piece • USP (unique selling proposition)	• Company letterhead • PowerPoint		

Collateral	Audience	Key MarCom Objectives	Key Messages	Format	Owner	Deadline
Technical white paper with technical illustrations	• Technical decision makers (TDM)	• Answer TDM's technical questions • Create clear understanding and appreciation for the technical level of sophistication the product has, and for its capabilities • Generate strong interest in implementing this solution	• Benefit of the technology behind the product (possibly include a very concise high level technology description if the technology is dramatically new) • USP (unique selling proposition)	Company letterhead		
Web-based educational tools (subject matter test)	• Journals and newspapers • Prospects • Sales channel • Web surfers	• Educate prospects about their level of knowledge regarding the product, leading them to the conclusion that they need to consider the product as a solution	Test to help prospects determine: • How they compare with their peers • Their readiness for the product	Web based education tool using multiple choice questions and instant feedback		

11.2.13 Press Release Questionnaire – Template V. 4.0

Company Name: <Enter company name>
Product Name: <Enter product name>

- Date: <Enter date>
- Contact: <Enter your name>
- Department: <Enter department name>
- Location: <Enter location>
- Email: <Enter email address>
- Telephone: <Enter telephone number>

Document Revision History:

Date	Revision	Revised By	Approved By
<Enter date>	<Revision #>	<Enter your name>	<Enter name>

Table of Contents

1. Introduction

1.1. **Document Objective**

This document details a list of questions that, when answered, allow product management to provide targeted information that enables marketing communications to write effective press releases.

2. The Press Release Questionnaire

2.1. **Section Objective**

This section describes the press release questionnaire.

2.2. **Press Release Questionnaire**

2.2.1. What is the main point that you want readers to understand from this press release? <Enter text.>

<Comment: This is often the Unique Selling Proposition (USP) for a product or the Distinctive Competency for a company. See the "PMTK Unique Selling Proposition" template.>

2.2.2. What are the three key messages that you want to communicate with this press release (for example: product, competitive, market, industry)? <Enter text.>

2.2.3. What are the supporting data points for the above three key messages? <Enter text.>

2.2.4. Is this a press release about a product release -? (Yes ☐ / No ☐)
   • Product's formal name (primary listing): <Enter text.>
   • Product's trademark: <Enter text.>
   • Product's informal name (subsequent listings): <Enter text.>
   • Product's manufacturer's suggested retail price (MSRP): <Enter text.>
   • Product's general availability date: <Enter text.>

2.2.5. What is the product's value proposition?
   <Describe the product's "resultant value proposition" and "relative value proposition".>

2.2.6. What are the product's three key benefits?
   <Describe the product's three key benefits and how they apply to customers and partners.>

2.2.7. What are the product's three key features?
   <Describe the product's three key features, relative to the key benefits.>

2.2.8. Will someone be quoted in this press release? (Yes ☐ / No ☐)
   • Who will be quoted from the company? <Enter name and title.>
   • What principal message will be communicated through this quotation? <Enter text.>
   • What third parties (e.g. customers, partners) can be quoted in this release? <Enter name, title, company, affiliation, and message.>
   •
   •

11.2.14 Lead Generation – Template V. 4.0

Company Name: <Enter company name>
Product Name: <Enter product name>

- Date: <Enter date>
- Contact: <Enter your name>
- Department: <Enter department name>
- Location: <Enter location>
- Email: <Enter email address>
- Telephone: <Enter telephone number>

Document Revision History:

Date	Revision	Revised By	Approved By
<Enter date>	<Revision #>	<Enter your name>	<Enter name>

Table of Contents

1. Introduction

1.1. <u>Document Objective</u>

This document describes a sales lead generation program. Leads are entities with a potential of becoming paying customers. Lead generation programs employ a combination of marketing tools that aim to discover and qualify prospective customers.

2. Sales Generation Overview

2.1. <u>Section Objective</u>

This section provides an explanation of the lead generation phase within the customer attainment process.

2.2. <u>Customer Attainment Process</u>

Generating leads is one component of an overall customer attainment process that is comprised of four inter-linked stages:

- List
- Lead
- Prospect
- Customer

<Comment: In the first stage a "bulk list" was generated. Obtaining the "bulk list" is part of another process. The "bulk list" is culled by applying qualifiers to create a "targeted list" of entities (individuals or companies) that have a potential of becoming customers. The "targeted list" is therefore comprised of qualified Leads. A qualified Lead can be defined according to various criteria such as: industry, type of company, position, or their market problem. Through marketing efforts, Leads are converted into Prospects. A Prospect is an entity from the targeted list of Leads that the company has made contact via various efforts. As the process moves into the "Lead" phase, the initial step must be to define the strategic objectives of the "Lead Generation Program".>

3. Lead Generation Program

3.1. <u>Section Objective</u>

This section describes the elements that make an effective lead generation program. An effective lead generation plan will result in a new list of quality leads that have the greatest potential to convert to revenue generating customers.

3.2. <u>Lead Generation Program</u>

The Lead generation program is made of the following elements:

3.2.1. <u>Strategy Formulation</u>

3.2.1.1. **Market Problem**

<Describe the market problem customers are trying to solve.>

3.2.1.2. Program Objectives
<Clearly state the lead generation program's objectives.>

3.2.1.3. Target List
<Define the target audience and verify it is within the "targeted list".>

3.2.1.4. Medial Channels
<Choose and list the media channels (web, mail, phone, or events) that will be employed.>

3.2.2. <u>Action Plan</u>

3.2.2.1. Media Per Channel
<Select and list media tools for each media channel (direct mail piece, advertisement, or brochure).>

3.2.2.2. Media Tools Alignment
<Build for each media tool the lead generation offer and/or enticement.>

3.2.2.3. Media Tools CFA
<Determine the appropriate "Call For Action" (CFA) for each media tool. Factor into the selected media tools the appropriate CFA.>

3.2.2.4. Lead Handling
<Create, review and approve an internal process for handling and distributing incoming leads.>

3.2.2.5. Program Metrics
<Select and list overall program metrics and criteria, such as lost deals, closed deals, and revenue.>

3.2.2.6. Company Preparedness
<Create the call scripts and training plan relevant to telemarketers, salespeople, and account managers.>

3.2.2.7. Timeline
<Create the program's schedule of events or tasks.>

3.2.3. <u>Pilot Program</u>

3.2.3.1. Pilot
<Select and list the test audience and success criteria. Execute a small scale pilot and make corrections.>

3.2.3.2. Project Scope
<Ascertain and note the scope, duration, resources, and budget needed for the full lead generation program.>

3.2.3.3. Reschedule
<Make adjustments to the lead generation program timeline.>

3.2.4. <u>Preparation Phase</u>

3.2.4.1. Lead Qualification
<Describe the lead qualification process. List the interview questions and criteria that will be used to qualify all incoming leads.>

3.2.4.2. Lead Distribution

<Describe the lead distribution process. Inform and explain this process to the company's sales force.>

3.2.4.3. Analysis

<Describe the metrics and the analysis process that will be used to gauge the program's merit.>

3.2.5. Program Launch

3.2.5.1. Lead Qualification

<Launch the program. Write all incoming leads in a separate appendix to this document called "Incoming Leads".>

3.2.5.2. Lead Distribution

<Allocate the incoming leads to the sales force. Write the details of incoming leads allocation in a separate appendix to this document called "Leads Allocation".>

3.2.5.3. Results and Conclusions

<If relevant, declare the campaign has ended. Write the conclusions and results of the program in a separate appendix to this document called "Results and Conclusions".>

4. Supporting Data

4.1. Section Objective

The section provides data in support of claims, assertions, assumptions, and statements made throughout this document.

4.2. Assumptions

<Describe any assumptions made when writing this document.>

4.3. Research Information

<If relevant, describe and list the type and scope of research conducted in the course of writing this document.>

4.4. Product Diagram/Architecture

<If relevant, describe the product's architecture and modules accompanied by a schematic diagram.>

11.3 PROCESS EFFICIENCY

11.3.1 Meeting Rules – Guidelines V. 4.0

Company Name: <Enter company name>
Product Name: <Enter product name>

- Date: <Enter date>
- Contact: <Enter your name>
- Department: <Enter department name>
- Location: <Enter location>
- Email: <Enter email address>
- Telephone: <Enter telephone number>

Document Revision History:

Date	Revision	Revised By	Approved By
<Enter date>	<Revision #>	<Enter your name>	<Enter name>

Table of Contents

1. Introduction

1.1. Document Objective

This document describes the rules and general guidelines for conducting effective corporate meetings.

2. Meeting Rules and Guidelines

2.1. Section Objective

This section describes the rules and general guidelines, categorized and defined as action items.

2.2. Corporate Meeting Process

Step	Description
1.	**Communicate Meeting Scope**
	Create a meeting invitation email message with all the following information:
	• Clearly define the meeting's goal or purpose in one sentence
	• Define the meeting's level of importance and criticalness
	• Create a meeting agenda with clear, well-defined topics and a timeline
	• Describe the meeting's desired outcome and deliverables (decisions, action items and consensus)
	• Assess and allow sufficient time to cover and resolve all topics
	• Designate required and optional attendees
	• Determine appropriate date, time and location
	• Request attendee confirmation
	Distribute all above information via email to attendees, as soon as possible.
2.	**Determine Meeting Logistics**
	Prior to the meeting, designate and seek commitment from individuals who will perform the following functions during the meeting:
	• Meeting leader – to manage the meeting and its flow
	• Note taker – to create a textual summary of the meeting
	• Time keeper – to ensure topics are addressed in a timely manner
3.	**Conduct the Meeting**
	At the outset of every meeting declare that punctuality is crucial. Meetings start and end on-time!
	Declare the mode of communication chosen for the particular meeting:
	• Discussion – freely speak when desired
	• Classroom – speak after permission granted. Use hand raising to signal
	• Lecture – no interruptions
	Request all cell-phones, laptops and other distractions are disabled or removed.
4.	**Post Meeting Task**
	Send via email the meeting's textual summary to attendees and relevant parties.

11.3.2 Management by Objectives (MBO) – Guidelines V. 4.0

Company Name: <Enter company name>
Product Name: <Enter product name>

- Date: <Enter date>
- Contact: <Enter your name>
- Department: <Enter department name>
- Location: <Enter location>
- E-mail: <Enter email address>
- Telephone: <Enter telephone number>

Document Revision History:

Date	Revision	Revised By	Approved By
<Enter date>	<Revision #>	<Enter your name>	<Enter name>

Table of Contents

1. Introduction

1.1. **Document Objective**

This document outlines the process of creating a personal MBO (Management by Objectives) plan. MBO is a systematic approach for instilling flow and structure in one's work by setting clear, achievable, measurable and challenging goals. MBO is ultimately an intelligent form of self-management.

1.2. **MBO Use**

Personal MBO plans set common expectations, clarity, and define individual and teamwork contributions in the context of what the organization needs. The MBO approach is most effective if all people working together on the same project, both intra-departmental and inter-departmental team members, have MBO plans.

2. MBO (Management by Objectives) Plan Guidelines

2.1. **Section Objective**

This section outlines the basic guidelines for creating MBO plans. The key to a successful and effective MBO plan is that all elements of the plan are mutually agreed upon between relevant parties and never imposed.

2.2. **MBO Parameters**

- **Timeline increment** – Determine the timeline increment applicable for the individual (to complete the objectives), subject to the person's hierarchical level within the organization. Timeframes are a specified amount of time comprised of several timeline increments.

  Managers commonly use months as time increments and three months as the timeframe, Directors use yearly quarters as time increments and three to four yearly quarters as the timeframe, and Vice Presidents and CEOs use years as time increments, and one to three years as the timeframe.
- **Strategic objectives** – Determine the strategic objectives sought within the chosen timeframe. Strategic objectives can be viewed as long-term objectives. Prioritize the strategic objectives.
- **Tactical objectives** – Support for attaining strategic objectives is created when tactical objectives are met. For each strategic objective, create its supporting tactical objectives. Tactical objectives can be viewed as short-term objectives. Prioritize the tactical objectives related to each strategic objective.
- **Action items** – Action items are drawn from tactical objectives. Determine the realistic, achievable and measurable actions to be accomplished in the timeframe.

2.3. **MBO Plan Principals**

- **Cascading dependency** – When building a MBO plan, each hierarchical level within the organization should reflect on the MBO plan that belongs to the level above it. For example, the managers' and directors' strategic objectives should provide some foundational support for the VP's strategic objectives.

- **Rolling plan** – MBO plans are systematically extended with a timeline increment at the end of the first time increment. For example, a manager whose timeframe is set at three months will add to the plan at the end of the first month, an additional month with MBO information. This allows the manager to always have an MBO plan with a forward-looking three month timeframe.
- **Teamwork** – Each team member should be aware of the other members' MBO plans. Therefore, the team should meet every month and each member presents his/her MBO plan to the entire team.
- **Plan review** – At the end of every timeline increment, each person reviews his/her MBO plan with his/her manager. The purpose of these sessions is to review the past set of objectives and determine why certain action items and objectives were or are not being met. Then modify the plan accordingly, ensure the plan is realistic, and approve the added timeline increment.
- **Component relations** – The relationship between MBO components is one-to-many throughout the internal structure of an MBO plan, when viewed top-down. A strategic objective can have several tactical objectives supporting it, and a tactical objective can have many action items assigned to it.

2.4. **MBO Considerations**

- MBO is a process-oriented and team-oriented work planning instrument.
- MBO is an effective personal planning, control, and development instrument.
- Strategic objectives are very few and focus on the long-term. No more than four strategic objectives are recommended at any hierarchical level.
- Tactical objectives can be numerous and focus on the short-term.
- Strategic and tactical objectives loosely span the timeline. Action items are associated with a particular time increment.

<Comment: Although occasionally used as such, an MBO plan is not an effective performance evaluation or reward tool, nor was it meant to be.>

2.5. **MBO Record Example**

The following example demonstrates MBO record structure and how each MBO at different hierarchical levels supports the MBO objectives of the level above it. In the interest of simplicity only one tactical objective is presented, although several tactical objectives can be introduced in support of any single strategic objective. Likewise for the action items.

Product VP	Year 1
Strategic Objective	Establish leadership in an emerging market segment
Tactical Objective	Initiate a business case to evaluate the market opportunity
Action Item	Secure executive management approval to the initiative
Product Director	**Quarter 1**
Strategic Objective	Plan and implement the product management process
Tactical Objective	Assign a product management team to the project
Action Item	Seek approval to initial staff, budget, and schedule
Product Manager	**Month 1**
Strategic Objective	Articulate market problems and needs
Tactical Objective	Create a Market Requirements Document (MRD)
Action Item	Interview selected customers in the market segment

3. The MBO (Management by Objectives) Plan

3.1. Section Objective
This section describes the MBO (Management by Objectives) plan structure and layout.

3.2. The MBO (Management by Objectives) Plan Template

Objectives	Time Increment	Time Increment + 1	Time Increment + 2
Strategic Business Objectives			
Supporting Tactical Objectives			

Action Items	Time Increment	Time Increment + 1	Time Increment + 2
Strategic Objective # N Action Items			
Strategic Objective # N+1 Action Items			
Strategic Objective # N+2 Action Items			
Miscellaneous			

<Comment: Miscellaneous action items are activities which are loosely linked to the "Strategic Business Objectives" and to the "Supporting Tactical Objectives". The miscellaneous action items constitute the "activity trap" and every effort should be made to minimize their number.>

3.3. Sample MBO Plan for a Product Marketing Manager

Objectives	October, 2010	November, 2010	December, 2010
Strategic Business Objectives	1. **Product Launch** – Ensure a successful product launch (*from a marketing and MarCom perspective*), and confirm messaging integrity in market launch materials 2. **Market Planning** – Enhance overall quality of marketing department's decisions and planning 3. **Domain Expertise** – Reduce dependency on internal/external product/market experts		
Supporting Tactical Objectives	1. Complete positioning and value documents. Create product launch plan and provide input to MarCom 2. Create a competitive tracking and analysis process for gathering and analyzing market information 3. Establish comprehensive knowledge of the product (*including competition*) and market problems		
Action Items	October, 2010	November, 2010	December, 2010
Strategic Objective # 1 Action Items – Product Launch	1. Validate customer use scenarios 2. Complete and sign-off value documents 3. Complete product positioning statements 4. Complete launch plan draft	1. Present all messaging, value, identity to MarCom and Marketing team members with an explanation on purpose/use 2. Choose marketing collateral items and media vehicles for launch	1. Complete launch plan 2. Present possible co-marketing, and co-branding programs 3. Evangelize product to select prospects, partners and analysts
Strategic Objective # 2 Action Items – Market Planning	1. Retain market research firm 2. Gather input from firm	1. Draft data collection and analysis process	1. Present draft of tracking and analysis process. Gain approval 2. Begin process implementation
Strategic Objective # 3 Action Items – Domain Expertise	1. Undergo product training with Product Manager 2. Exploratory visit to key customer	1. Undergo product training with Product Manager 2. Attend industry conference 3. Exploratory visit to key customer	1. Provide list of topics for articles and whitepapers 2. Write short article on product
Miscellaneous	None	Help MarCom find external advertising agency	None

11.3.3 Decision Making – Guidelines V. 4.0

Company Name: <Enter company name>

Product Name: <Enter product name>

- Date: <Enter date>
- Contact: <Enter your name>
- Department: <Enter department name>
- Location: <Enter location>
- Email: <Enter email address>
- Telephone: <Enter telephone number>

Document Revision History:

Date	Revision	Revised By	Approved By
<Enter date>	<Revision #>	<Enter your name>	<Enter name>

Table of Contents

1. Introduction

1.1. Document Objective

This document describes guidelines and a methodology that drives an effective decision making process within a project for the purpose of bringing closure to all outstanding issues.

2. Overview

2.1. Section Objective

This section describes the need for an effective decision making process.

2.2. The Need for Closure

All project issues must achieve closure and the only way to do so is by making decisions, which means reaching a binding conclusion or passing judgment.

Rarely one finds a solution which is optimal, efficient and acceptable to all parties and almost always the decision making process is based on maximizing an objective subject to several constraints. Once one accepts these notions, it is much easier to make a decision, otherwise the lack of decisions and the existence of procrastination can result in project delay or stagnation.

3. Basic Workplace Psychology

3.1. Section Objective

This section describes the human aspects and perspectives of decision making.

3.2. Workplace Psychology

3.2.1. *"Mediocre decisions are BETTER than a perpetual state of indecisiveness"*. Accept and remember this. There are obvious costs to adopting such an approach, but it is possibly the only realistic means to achieving finality and a chance at product success.

3.2.2. Getting results is the first necessary step on the road to success, so always focus yourself on securing decisions and not just collecting views and opinions.

3.2.3. Try to educate yourself and others to be:
- Decisive in the face of indecision
- Clear in the face of ambiguity
- Concise in the face of the verbose

    3.2.3.1. The key to driving any process or project to completion is done first by you being *decisive, clear* and *concise*. Promote the same in others by reiterating constantly the above mentioned. Act and apply it consistently until it comes natural to you and acceptable to others.

3.2.4. Once a major decision has been made, regardless of who made it, document the decision, launch a sign-off (if applicable), and propagate the agreed upon and approved decision to all relevant parties internal and/or external to the company.

3.3. The Key Axioms
- Decisions mobilize a project
- Decisions are the building blocks to making a product materialize
- Decisions must be made, and in a timely manner

4. Decision Making Guidelines

4.1. Section Objective
This section describes the four primary guidelines that drive decision making.

4.2. Guideline Number One
"Decisions are made by ONE person with others supporting the decision making process".
This means that if you raise an issue that needs resolution, make sure to specify the one (only one!) individual you feel should make that decision. Whether done in the context of a meeting or in an email message, make sure that everyone is aware of who is being singled out as the one and only decision maker. It need not always be the same person or the highest ranking, but for each decision there should only one person in this assigned role.

4.3. Guideline Number Two
"Discussions are a tool that support the decision making process".
This means that if you raise an issue that needs resolution, make sure you conspicuously specify the individuals that are requested to comment or provide information for the decision maker in support of the process. Whether done in the context of a meeting or in an email message, make sure that all are aware of their role as contributors which also mean that they actually do have to contribute. Consensus is important and nice to have, but not critical. Your focus should always be on attaining a sound decision, not mutual agreement.

4.4. Guideline Number Three
"Decisions must be made and in a timely manner".
Make this obvious and request a decision be made within a reasonable timeframe. Do not impose or dictate deadlines, but be firm.

4.5. Guideline Number Four
"Decisions must become public knowledge, once made".
Propagate and inform all parties concerned that a decision has been reached. Do not assume people will hear or learn about the decision somehow or understand how it was made and why. Initiate a sign-off process to secure a commitment from everybody regarding the decision.

5. Implementing the Guidelines

5.1. <u>Section Objective</u>

This section describes the application of the effective decision making guidelines via email.

5.2. <u>Using Email for Effective Decision Making</u>

- The message is addressed to (To:) only one person (the decision maker).
- The message is copied (Cc:) to all those who should comment and provide input in support of the decision making.
- A time limit has been placed for reaching a decision with consequences of indecisiveness described.

Here is a sample email message applying the methodology:

```
-----Original Message-----

From: Gabriel Steinhardt
Sent: Tuesday, March 16, 20xx 1:35 PM
To: Software Architect
Cc: Development Team; Lead Developer
Subject: Programming language choice

Hi,
What programming language do you recommend we use to develop future
versions of our products?

Notes:
    * Decision maker: software architect
    * Decision support: development team; lead developer
    * Decision due date: Friday, April 16, 20xx
    * If no decision: continue using ANSI C
    * All on Cc: line: please provide your comments and opinion.


Thanks,
--Gabriel

-----End Message-----
```

11.3.4 Deliverable Sign-Off – Guidelines V. 4.0

Company Name: <Enter company name>
Product Name: <Enter product name>

- Date: <Enter date>
- Contact: <Enter your name>
- Department: <Enter department name>
- Location: <Enter location>
- Email: <Enter email address>
- Telephone: <Enter telephone number>

Document Revision History:

Date	Revision	Revised By	Approved By
<Enter date>	<Revision #>	<Enter your name>	<Enter name>

Table of Contents

1. Introduction

1.1. Document Objective

This document describes the process of initiating a deliverable sign-off. A sign-off is a means of securing acceptance and commitment to a project phase or deliverable.

2. Overview

2.1. Section Objective

This section describes the scope and use guidelines for a deliverable sign-off.

2.2. Deliverable Sign-Off Goal

The main goal of a deliverable sign-off is to remove any ambiguity on whether or not deliverables (such as documents or decisions) have been officially approved for release, and to bring closure to specific project stages. Closure of one stage of a project is commonly the signal to begin the subsequent stage.

2.3. Deliverable Sign-Off Use Guidelines

- Deliverable sign-offs are used when there is a need to secure the acceptance of a certain important deliverable and handoff.
- Deliverable sign-offs make it harder for individuals to reverse their decisions or re-open them for additional discussion.
- Do not overuse deliverable sign-off documents. Use discretion and apply a sign-off ONLY to important deliverables.

3. Initiating a Sign-Off

3.1. Section Objective

This section describes the structure of a deliverable sign-off message via email.
<Comment: Deliverable sign-off is commonly initiated via email, although there are other methods including paper documents. This section describes how to initiate a deliverable sign-off using Microsoft Outlook.>

3.2. Sign-Off Email Message Structure

- Subject line of the email message must refer to what deliverable for which the addressees are being asked to sign-off.
- Body of the message will contain the following:
  - Reference to the project and product
  - Purpose of the specific sign-off email being sent
  - Names and teams of the individuals signing-off
  - Actions being requested of the individuals who are signing-off
  - Description of the deliverable or decision being signed-off, including a listing of what has been reviewed (optional)

- o Statement concerning how further changes might be handled once the sign-off has been signed
- o Statement of what will be done and considered if individuals do not respond in the allotted time period
- o An advisory statement as to the implications of re-opening the topic, after it has been approved
- Each message will display voting buttons (used in MS-Outlook) which can be viewed at the top headers of message.
- Every addressee will respond to the message using the voting buttons no later than a specific date.
- All voting responses will be tallied and propagated in a second message sent by the sign-off initiator, indicating that the addressees and teams have signed-off.

3.3. <u>Example of a Sign-Off Request Email Message</u>

```
-----Original Message-----

From: Gabriel Steinhardt
Sent: Monday, September 15, 20xx 4:04 PM
To: Person1, Person2, Person3
Subject: SIGN OFF: Marketing plan - Product ABC - Project XYZ
Importance: High

* Product: ABC
* Project: XYZ
* Sign-off deliverable: marketing plan
* Sign-off roles: person1 for the marketing team, person2 for the
  development team, person3 for the executive team.
* Reviewers: sign-off deliverable had been reviewed by person1, person2,
  and person3.
* Changes: following successful completion of this sign-off, changes to
  the sign-off deliverable can be done only at a VP level. Any
  amendments or changes whatsoever will be officially propagated to all
  addressees of this email message.
* Response resolution: sign-off deliverable will be considered approved
  only by a unanimous vote of all required voters.
* Implications:
  * Approval of the sign-off deliverable means that all approving parties
    have reviewed and approved the final version of the sign-off
    deliverable which includes all previously discussed changes,
    additions, deletions or corrections.
  * By approving the sign-off deliverable the teams have consented to
    proceed to the next stages in the project.
  * Any further changes to the structure, objectives, or content of the
    sign-off deliverable, will likely result in a delay in the final
    delivery date and could result in a variety of additional costs to
    the company.

Please cast your vote using the Approve/Reject voting buttons which can
be viewed at the top headers of this message and reply no later than
Thursday, September 25, 20xx.

Thanks,
--Gabriel

-----End Message-----
```

3.4. <u>Example of a Sign-Off Completion Email Message</u>

-----Original Message-----

From: Gabriel Steinhardt
Sent: Monday, September 15, 20xx 4:04 PM
To: Audience
Cc: Person1, Person2, Person3
Subject: Unanimous Approval: SIGN OFF: Marketing plan - Product ABC - Project XYZ
Importance: High

* Project: XYZ
* Product: ABC
* Sign-off deliverable: marketing plan

The sign-off deliverable has been unanimously approved by all reviewers.

Attached to this message are the original sign-off request email message and the reviewers' approval responses.
No further action is needed.

Thanks,
--Gabriel

-----End Message-----

11.3.5 Generic Document – Template V. 4.0

Company Name: <Enter company name>

Product Name: <Enter product name>

- Date: <Enter date>
- Contact: <Enter your name>
- Department: <Enter department name>
- Location: <Enter location>
- Email: <Enter email address>
- Telephone: <Enter telephone number>

Document Revision History:

Date	Revision	Revised By	Approved By
<Enter date>	<Revision #>	<Enter your name>	<Enter name>

Table of Contents

1. INTRODUCTION

   1.1.   DOCUMENT OBJECTIVE

2. OVERVIEW

   2.1.   SECTION OBJECTIVE

3. TOPIC

   3.1.   SECTION OBJECTIVE
   3.2.   SUBTOPIC
   3.3.   SUBTOPIC

4.   SUPPORTING DATA

   4.1.   SECTION OBJECTIVE
   4.2.   ASSUMPTIONS
   4.3.   RESEARCH INFORMATION
   4.4.   PRODUCT DIAGRAM/ARCHITECTURE

1. Introduction

1.1. **Document Objective**

This document describes <Enter text.>

2. Overview

2.1. **Section Objective**

This section describes <Enter text.>

3. Topic

3.1. **Section Objective**

This section describes <Enter text.>

3.2. **Subtopic**

<Enter text.>

3.2.1. Subtopic

<Enter text.>

3.2.1.1. Subtopic

<Enter text.>

3.3. **Subtopic**

<Enter text.>

- Subtopic

<Enter text.>

  o Subtopic

<Enter text.>

4. Supporting Data

4.1. **Section Objective**

The section provides data in support of claims, assertions, assumptions, and statements made throughout this document.

4.2. **Assumptions**

<Describe any assumptions made when writing this document.>

4.3. **Research Information**

<If relevant, describe and list the type and scope of research conducted in the course of writing this document.>

4.4. **Product Diagram/Architecture**

<If relevant, describe the product's architecture and modules accompanied by a schematic diagram.>

11.3.6 Bundle Book – Guidelines V. 4.0

- ⊟ 📁 Bundle_Book_Structure
  - ⊟ 📁 Marketing_Communications
    - 📁 Advertisements
    - 📁 Articles
    - 📁 Data_Sheets
    - 📁 Press_Releases
    - 📁 White_Papers
  - ⊟ 📁 Miscellaneous
    - 📁 Documentation
    - 📁 Legal
  - ⊟ 📁 Product_Marketing
    - 📁 Competitive_Analysis
    - 📁 Corporate_Mission
    - 📁 GoTo_Market_Strategy
    - 📁 Launch_Plan
    - 📁 Market_Data
    - 📁 Marketing_Plans
    - 📁 Messaging
    - 📁 Positioning
    - 📁 Product_Comparison
    - 📁 Value_Documents
    - 📁 Vision
- ⊟ 📁 Product_Planning
  - 📁 Customers
  - 📁 Functional_Specification
  - 📁 Market_Data
  - 📁 Market_Requirements
  - 📁 Partners
  - 📁 Product_Features
  - 📁 Product_Status
  - 📁 Roadmap
  - 📁 Use_Cases
  - 📁 Win_Loss_Analysis
- ⊟ 📁 Project_Management
  - 📁 Processes
  - 📁 TimeLine

<Comment: A bundle book is a central repository of documents related to a particular product. The ZIP file accompanying this document contains an empty folder structure (directory tree) used to create a network shared bundle book. Copy the unzipped folder structure to a network server and allow file sharing in read-only mode. This will allow other users to copy the folder structure or copy documents from the folder structure.

The bundle book file name convention is:
"Folder Name"_"Product Name"_"Author Initials"_"Revision Number".ext
For example:
Launch_Plan_SLC450_GS_07.doc

This name convention enables easy identification and sorting of the file's location, purpose, product, owner, and revision.>

11.3.7 Gap Analysis – Template V. 4.0

Company Name: <Enter company name>
Product Name: <Enter product name>

- Date: <Enter date>
- Contact: <Enter your name>
- Department: <Enter department name>
- Location: <Enter location>
- Email: <Enter email address>
- Telephone: <Enter telephone number>

Document Revision History:

Date	Revision	Revised By	Approved By
<Enter date>	<Revision #>	<Enter your name>	<Enter name>

Table of Contents

1. Introduction

1.1. **Document Objective**

This document describes the process of performing a gap analysis on product management activities.

<Comment: Perform a gap analysis every month. Assess improvement every yearly quarter. Always note critical gaps that need particular attention.>

2. Gap Analysis Process

2.1. **Section Objective**

Gap analysis is a procedure for assessing how well product management tasks are being performed. Gap analysis identifies areas of improvement, priorities and task ownership.

2.2. **Gap Analysis Glossary**

- **Importance**: The importance of the activity to the company.
  (H=high, L=low).
- **Assessment**: How well is the activity being performed.
  (H=high, L=low, ND=not done).
- **Current/Proposed Owner**: The role or person or corporate function associated with the activity.
  (PP=product planning, SE=sales engineering, PM=product marketing, MC=marketing communications, D=development, EX=executive management).
- **Hours/Week**: The total number of hours per week that should be allocated or are actually being devoted to the activity.

2.3. **Gap Analysis Worksheet**

<Complete and fill in the worksheet below using the glossary definitions. Proposed ownership changes come last.>

2.3.1. Product Planning

PMTK Phase	PMTK Task	Task Description	Importance	Assessment	Current Owner	Proposed Owner	Hrs/Wk
Planning *Describe market problems and needs.*	Market Requirements	Documenting functionality sought to address the market problem.					
	Use Cases	Ways various users put the product to use and under which scenarios.					

PMTK Phase	PMTK Task	Task Description	Importance	Assessment	Current Owner	Proposed Owner	Hrs/Wk
Definition *Define solutions to market problems.*	Features Matrix	Managing actual product characteristics.					
	Product Roadmap	Plan or vision that describes a product's evolution.					
Development *Build solutions that solve market problems.*	Pricing Model	Building a product pricing model.					
	Product Evangelism	Performing actions that promote and distribute information for a company.					
Maintenance *Sales channels support and product revisions.*	Win/Loss Analysis	Process whose output helps improve products and develop better sales functions.					
	Customer Visit	Planning customer visits with the intent of better understanding their needs.					

2.3.2. Product Marketing

PMTK Phase	PMTK Task	Task Description	Importance	Assessment	Current Owner	Proposed Owner	Hrs/Wk
Evaluation *Examine opportunities to serve the market.*	Business Case	Examination of a potential market opportunity on a product level.					
	Competitor Analysis	Analysis of competing companies, partially via their products.					
	Product Comparison	Tabular comparison of competing products.					
Strategy *Formulate the*	Corporate Mission	General business direction and company purpose.					

PMTK Phase	PMTK Task	Task Description	Importance	Assessment	Current Owner	Proposed Owner	Hrs/Wk
market approach.	Product Positioning	Clear and focused messages that communicate the product's value proposition to multiple audiences.					
	Value Documents	Sales Axioms – Fundamental concepts the product is built upon.					
		PSFB – Outlining a product's ability to address the overall customer problem by merit of its feature scope and capabilities.					
		USP – Key value differentiator which sets the product apart from other competing products.					
	Market Plan	Description of the long-term goals, and messages delivered to the target market, relative to a particular product.					
Readiness *Prepare market tactics and MarCom activities.*	Company Profile	Overview description of a company.					
	Product Backgrounder	Product/service overview information at a glance.					
	Collateral Matrix	List of various marketing communications collateral items.					
	Press Releases	Eliciting targeted information for creating meaningful press releases.					
	Launch Plan	Introducing new products to the market.					
Execution *Deliver value and build*	Company Presentation	Broad overview of a company for internal and external audiences.					

PMTK Phase	PMTK Task	Task Description	Importance	Assessment	Current Owner	Proposed Owner	Hrs/Wk
competitive advantage.	Product Presentation	Broad overview of a product for internal and external audiences.					
	Lead Generation	Process to discover and qualify prospective customers.					
	Marketing Review	Comprehensive inspection of the market and the company's preparedness for it.					

2.3.3. Process Efficiency

PMTK Phase	PMTK Task	Task Description	Importance	Assessment	Current Owner	Proposed Owner	Hrs/Wk
People	Meeting Rules	Rules and general guidelines for conducting productive corporate meetings.					
	Management By Objectives	Intelligent form of self-management.					
Decisions	Decision Making	Driving an effective process of decision making within a project.					
	Deliverable Sign-Off	Tool for securing acceptance and commitment to deliverables.					
Deliverables	Generic Templates	General Microsoft Word and PowerPoint templates.					
	Bundle Book	Central repository of documents related to a particular product.					

PMTK Phase	PMTK Task	Task Description	Importance	Assessment	Current Owner	Proposed Owner	Hrs/Wk
Learning	Gap Analysis	Procedure for assessing how well product management tasks are being performed.					
	Performance Review	Product management merit and performance measurement process and tool.					

2.4. Gap Analysis Review
<Comment: Perform the steps below after completing the worksheet.>

2.4.1. Gap Correction Plan
<Define and describe a plan to address the gaps in the performance of activities.>

<Comment: Scan the worksheet for the most severe gaps and identify areas where you are underachieving or overachieving based on importance.>

2.4.2. Task Ownership Plan
<Define and describe a plan to address problems in task ownership. Assess employee skills and introduce a plan to improve them. Go through the worksheet and assign proposed ownership changes.>

<Comment: Review the current team structure. Do you have the right owners for each activity? How might you assign or combine activities differently in light of existing skill sets? What additional skills are required in the product planning group to fulfill all activities?>

2.4.3. Task Efficiency Plan
<Define and describe a plan to address the gaps in staffing.>

<Comment: Use the hours/week column to determine where team members are currently spending their time. Determine how much time should be spent on the various activities, and divide the total number of hours by 40 to determine how many people are needed to do the job.>

2.5. Gap Analysis Conclusions
<Provide a summary of conclusions derived from performing this gap analysis.>

3. Supporting Data

3.1. Section Objective

The section provides data in support of claims, assertions, assumptions, and statements made throughout this document.

3.2. Assumptions

<Describe any assumptions made when writing this document.>

3.3. Research Information

<If relevant, describe and list the type and scope of research conducted in the course of writing this document.>

3.4. Product Diagram/Architecture

<If relevant, describe the product's architecture and modules accompanied by a schematic diagram.>

11.3.8 Performance Review – Template V. 4.0

Company Name: <Enter company name>

Product Name: <Enter product name>

- Date: <Enter date>
- Contact: <Enter your name>
- Department: <Enter department name>
- Location: <Enter location>
- Email: <Enter email address>
- Telephone: <Enter telephone number>

Document Revision History:

Date	Revision	Revised By	Approved By
<Enter date>	<Revision #>	<Enter your name>	<Enter name>

Table of Contents

1. Introduction

1.1. **Document Objective**

This document introduces a product management merit and performance measurement process called the "PMTK Performance Review". The goal of this process, and the related tool – the "PMTK Performance Matrix", is to improve product management functions through the measurement and monitoring of non-financial performance indicators in product management.

<Comment: The issue of Key Performance Indicators (KPI), relative specifically to product management and the "PMTK Action Model", is handled in PMTK in the form of assessment and measurement templates. The "PMTK Gap Analysis" template does assessment on product management activities, but does so in qualitative form. More in tune with the quantitative concept of KPI is the "PMTK Performance Review" template which measures non-financial performance indicators in product management. With the "PMTK Performance Review" template you can generate FOMs (Figure Of Merit) which are numbers that indicate levels of performance and allow you to baseline improvement and/or perform ongoing measurement of performance. In addition to generating FOMs, the "PMTK Performance Review" template also indicates via directional and practical indicators, the particular flaw in product management the company is at fault with and guides which actions (or documents) need to be taken (or revisited) in order to improve performance.>

2. Performance Measurement

2.1. **Section Objective**

This section positions the critical topic of measuring performance in product management as a key learning and feedback component in the PMTK methodology. Performance measurement in PMTK is aimed at supporting the effective management, improvement and execution of product planning and product marketing activities (both disciplines being part of product management).

2.2. **Performance Measurement Goals**

Measuring the efficiency and effectiveness of product planning and product marketing tasks contributes to the attainment of the following company goals and objectives:

- Demonstrate improvements in processes
- Identify ways to best-practice implementation
- Improve interdepartmental cooperation
- Integrate operational measures and strategic objectives
- Proactively generate growth in revenues
- Respond to events and take corrective action

2.3. <u>PMTK Performance Review</u>

The "PMTK Performance Review" is an ongoing process in which product management performance is measured at quarterly intervals, using the "PMTK Performance Matrix". Additional performance measurements are taken over the course of time and compared to each other to see if there is improvement or regression, especially if attempts for improvement have been made after the last measurement point. The scoring is done by defining a performance bar, which acts as a baseline, and then subjectively measuring and assigning a score to each PMTK task.

2.4. <u>PMTK Performance Measurement</u>

This section presents the "PMTK Performance Matrix" which is a scoring table of product management tasks. Performing the "PMTK Performance Review", is about utilizing the "PMTK Performance Matrix" and the resulting output to help identify areas of needed change or improvement in product management activities being measured.

<Comment: The "PMTK Performance Matrix" allows measuring merit changes in task performance, processes, product management disciplines and related competencies.>

2.5. <u>PMTK Performance Matrix</u>

Competency	Average Score	Merit	Measurement
Market Opportunity	<0.00>		
Customer Understanding	<0.00>		
Product Support	<0.00>		
Process Efficiency	<0.00>		

PMTK Performance Index	Merit	Measurement
<0.00>		

Performance Bar	3.00

<Comment: Use the "PMTK Performance Matrix" MS-Excel spreadsheet to calculate the averages and performance index. Follow the instructions contained within the spreadsheet.>

3. Conclusions and Recommendations

3.1. <u>Section Objective</u>

This section provides conclusions and recommendations reached after conducting the "PMTK Performance Review" and completing the "PMTK Performance Matrix".

3.2. <u>Conclusions</u>
<Identify and describe any conclusions reached after conducting the "PMTK Performance Review" and completing the "PMTK Performance Matrix".>

3.3. <u>Recommendations</u>
<Make specific recommendations on the company's choice and use of strategies, tactics and performance parameters.>

4. Supporting Data

4.1. <u>Section Objective</u>
The section provides data in support of claims, assertions, assumptions, and statements made throughout this document.

4.2. <u>Assumptions</u>
<Describe any assumptions made when writing this document.>

4.3. <u>Research Information</u>
<If relevant, describe and list the type and scope of research conducted in the course of writing this document.>

4.4. <u>Product Diagram/Architecture</u>
<If relevant, describe the product's architecture and modules accompanied by a schematic diagram.>

11.4 PERSONNEL MANAGEMENT

11.4.1 Curriculum Vitae – Template V. 4.0

Company Name: <Enter company name>

Product Name: <Enter product name>

- Date: <Enter date>
- Contact: <Enter your name>
- Department: <Enter department name>
- Location: <Enter location>
- Email: <Enter email address>
- Telephone: <Enter telephone number>

Document Revision History:

Date	Revision	Revised By	Approved By
<Enter date>	<Revision #>	<Enter your name>	<Enter name>

Table of Contents

1. Introduction

1.1. **Document Objective**
This document provides a framework for preparing a product management oriented curriculum vitae.

<Comment: The curriculum vitae, (a.k.a. curriculum vita, CV, résumé) is a document that lists an individual's professional history, skills sets and specific key contributions that convey the individual's current and future value potential to an organization. It is recommended that the curriculum vitae be prepared after preparing a PMTK Professional Development Plan.>

2. Curriculum Vitae Authoring

2.1. **Section Objective**
This section describes the principals that guide the preparation of a product management oriented curriculum vitae.

<Comment: The curriculum vitae is not only about what you did. It is also about what you can do, your potential contribution and the value you can provide a company when you are entrusted with a particular role. What you did should provide as much indication as possible of what you can do and your potential contribution. The CV probably should have both – what you have accomplished and how you accomplished it – demonstrates what you can do in the future and the value of that future contribution (based on the value of past contributions)>.

2.2. **Scope of Skills**
Those in the field of product management must possess a multitude of skills with a cumulative emphasis on strategic thinking and numeric analysis. Responsibilities may vary from company to company, but the core job function encompasses formulating market requirements and contributing to the search for the most productive way to build long-term value for a product.

<Comment: Hiring managers, when looking for qualified product managers, carefully consider and query candidates on the four business competency components. Subsequently, product managers' curricula vitae should reflect their capability levels in the four business competency components.>

2.3. **Business Competency Components**
- Domain Expertise
  Specific industry experience and technological know-how.
  - Industry experience.
  - Workplace accomplishments.
  - Appropriate blend of education, training, and credentials.
- Functional Expertise
  Knowledge in processes, tools and techniques to plan/market products.
  - Writing quality market requirements.
  - Ability to execute specific product management tasks.

      o Understanding of relevant terminology and definitions.

      o Knowledge of product management processes and procedures.

      o Familiarity with product definition and management team structures.

- Soft Skills
  Non-technical skills, mostly communicative (written, verbal and presentation), used in business.
  - o Thought leadership.
  - o Communication skills.
- Strategic Aptitude
  Long-term planning and decision making abilities that help achieve corporate objectives.
  - o Professional development.
  - o Executing a product definition process.
  - o Product and market strategy formulation.

2.4. CV Preparation Guidelines

- Include and use product management terminology as appropriate.
- Be more strategic than tactical and more managerial than technical.
- Be clear about the particular products you managed and their performance.

3. Product Management CV

3.1. Section Objective

This section describes the structure and format of a professional product management oriented curriculum vitae.

3.2. Product Management CV Template

<Comment: See template and example in the following pages.>

Objective

<Succinctly describe your personal professional vision that embodies the role and responsibilities you are professionally seeking.>

Career Summary

- <Enter text.>
- <Enter text.>
- <Enter text.>

<Comment: In the first bullet point describe your education and your own unique selling proposition (USP). Using no more than three bullet points, in descending order of tenure or importance, describe the highlights of your career in the form of accumulated experience and skills gained. This section must be as factual as possible and reflective of the competencies you have acquired over time via your accomplishments. Alternatively, you can merge the data points into a short paragraph of no more than two sentences.>

Professional Experience

COMPANY (company description), City, State, Country
Workplace Title, Begin Date-End Date

- <Enter text.>

<Comment: Using no more than three bullet points, in descending order of tenure or importance, succinctly describe your workplace accomplishments, notable contributions, or personal professional gain. The reader must be able to clearly infer that these can translate to future workplace contribution and job performance. In this section do not list your job description, rather note what you were responsible for.>

Education

INSTITUTION, School, City, State, Country
Degree, Graduation Date

- <Enter text.>

<Comment: Using no more than two bullet points, in descending order of tenure or importance, succinctly describe your workplace accomplishments, notable contributions, or awards. The Education section can precede the Professional Experience section if your employment history is too short.>

- Certifications: <Enter text.>
- Training: <Enter text.>

Additional Information

- Languages: <Enter text.>
- Technical Skills: <Enter text.>

Objective
A product marketing leadership position in network security, with an emphasis on market strategy formulation, process improvement and product portfolio management.

Career Summary
- Marketing MBA specializing in high-tech product marketing of security products.
- Senior level team leader with six years experience in product portfolio management.
- Four security (firewall, NIST) products brought to market with all objectives achieved.

Professional Experience
OCTAGON (information security software developer), Boston, MA, USA
Director of Product Marketing, 2001-Date
- Developed and executed market strategy for e-secure product line. Promoted sales from $1.4Million to $19Million in three years.
- Launched the e-secure firewall product globally in 2004 and established market leadership (37%) in terms of unites sold.

CUBICLE (information security systems integrator), New-York, NY, USA
Senior product Marketing Manager, 2000-2001
- Created and executed the e-safe marketing plan, increasing market share by 86%.
- Launched two NIST products in North America and managed sustaining marketing efforts. Products achieved all awareness and market share objectives in 2001.
- Performed a business case for the e-gate portal security application.

Education
DARTMUTH, Tuck Business School, Hanover, NH, USA
MBA, Information Systems and Marketing, 2000
- Finalist, Amos Tuck business venture competition.
- Research assistant, marketing strategies course.

GEORGIA TECH, College of Management, Atlanta, GA, USA
BA, Business and Marketing, 1998
- Graduated cum laude.

- Certifications: CCNA(2001), CISSP(2004).
- Training: Blackblot SPM, BMP.

Additional Information
- Clearances: DOD(2000), NSA(2001).
- Languages: Fluent in English and Spanish.
- Technical Skills: TCP/IP, HTTP, Firewall, Intrusion Detection, VPN.

11.4.2 Professional Development Plan – Template V. 4.0

Company Name: <Enter company name>

Product Name: <Enter product name>

- Date: <Enter date>
- Contact: <Enter your name>
- Department: <Enter department name>
- Location: <Enter location>
- Email: <Enter email address>
- Telephone: <Enter telephone number>

Document Revision History:

Date	Revision	Revised By	Approved By
<Enter date>	<Revision #>	<Enter your name>	<Enter name>

Table of Contents

1. Introduction

1.1. **Document Objective**

This document introduces a professional development plan template for product management professionals. The goal of this document is to help individuals develop the skills they need for their current or future roles. The long-term objective is to produce constant, structured and escalating professional competencies which translate to better job performance at the workplace.

<Comment: The three types of competencies required by product management professionals are: business competence (set of professional skills and knowledge that relate directly to performing product management), social competence (set of human interaction skills which relate directly to communicating and managing relationships with others in a professional environment's social structure), and personal competence (set of individual personality traits which enable individuals to manage themselves independently and capably). This template is only focused on evaluating and building business competence. It is highly recommended that the preparation of the PMTK Professional Development Plan be performed in collaboration with an experienced product management and/or human resources professional.>

2. Growth Environment

2.1. **Section Objective**

This section facilitates a better understanding of the business environment in which one aims to grow professionally and in their career.

<Comment: By better understanding their entire business environment, individuals can ensure that the professional choices they make correlate with the dynamics and potential of this environment.>

2.2. **Market Overview**

<Describe in very general terms the markets in which your industry operates. List the main target market's key characteristics and comment on market size, market growth, and any technological, regulatory, cultural, supply conditions, economic and political trends.>

2.3. **Industry Overview**

<Describe in general terms the industry to which your company belongs. Note in particular contentions, competitive rivalries and existing partnerships, which take place among the industry players.>

<Comment: Industry is the group of companies which produce and sell a particular type of product.>

2.4. **Company Overview**

<Describe in general terms your company. Note the company's internal work environment and culture, policies and processes.>

2.5. Company Organization
<Describe your company's organizational structure and reporting hierarchy. Expand on role clarity, promotions policies, internal relationships and management style.>

3. Professional Development

3.1. Section Objective
This section positions planned professional development as a critical element in an individual's own professional growth.

<Comment: Preparing a professional development plan (focused on business competencies) is an individual task in which the output is used solely for the benefit of the designated individual. The plan enables individuals to set professional goals and manage the best way to achieve them. You must reflect upon your own personal and life goals to ensure that the professional choices you make are correlated with your values and beliefs.>

3.2. Professional Vision
<Describe where you want to be in five years from a professional competence and career perspectives. Outline your progressive professional competence and career growth goals.>

<Comment: Your professional vision should realistically reflect your career aspirations and embody your life goals. Focus diligently on areas that are important to you and your career.>

3.3. Professional Vision Motivators
<Describe your professional motivation which explains why you wish to attain your specific professional vision.>

<Comment: Common professional motivators are: respect, recognition, wealth, contribution to society, influence, power, self-fulfillment, self-realization and potential manifestation.>

3.4. Professional Vision Attainment
<Describe what shall be the criteria which would indicate you had attained, in part or in full, your professional vision.>

<Comment: The criteria must be objective and realistic as possible.>

3.5. Mentor Assignment
<If applicable, note the actual name of the person(s) who will serve as your mentor(s)>.

<Comment: Mentors are individuals who via a range of diverse support activities help others achieve their goals. Mentors counsel, guide, support, challenge and assist the individual. Mentors do not instruct or govern the individual's actions. Having a solid and reliable mentor(s) is highly recommended.>

3.6. **Mentor Guidance**
<Describe the type of support you would like your mentor(s) to provide you with. Explain how your mentor can help you accomplish your own professional vision.>

4. Personal Introspection

4.1. **Section Objective**
This section facilitates an individual's better understanding of one's self as the basis to initiating a professional improvement process.

4.2. **Aversion Zones**
<Describe your aversion zones; the professional occupational activities and areas of low interest to you that you dislike and least enjoy doing.>

4.3. **Comfort Zones**
<Describe your comfort zones; professional occupational activities and areas of high interest which you like and most enjoy doing.>

4.4. **Professional SWOT Analysis**
<Fill the table below. Full candor and self-awareness are of utmost importance. Also judge yourself in retrospect via past feedback and input others had provided you with.>

Strengths	Weaknesses
<Describe the things you do best and personal traits that assist you at excelling. Segment your answer to two groups: 1. Strengths and traits which are natural to you. 2. Strengths and traits that were acquired diligently.>	<Describe the things you should try to improve upon and the personal traits that hinder you. Segment your answer into two groups: 1. Weaknesses and traits intrinsic to you, which would require too much effort to change with little to be gained or improved by changing them. 2. Weaknesses and traits intrinsic to you, which much can be gained or improved by changing them.>
Opportunities	**Threats**
<Describe all internal and external factors and possible events which can offer you a chance at attaining your professional vision.>	<Describe all internal and external factors and possible events which could jeopardize your chance at attaining your professional vision. Do not include your own weaknesses as a threat.>

4.5. **Myers Briggs Personality Type**
<Take the Myers Briggs personality test and summarize the result.>
<Comment: Taking the Myers Briggs personality test is optional yet highly recommended. The Myers Briggs model and personality test identify your personality preferences and can provide great insight to your strengths and

weaknesses, allowing you better judgment in your career decisions. For more information, please visit www.myersbriggs.org .>

5. Skills Assessment

5.1. Section Objective

This section assesses the mix of business, technical and soft skills which product management professionals need.

<Comment: This plan does not address the development of personal competencies (diligence, discipline, honesty, responsibility and dedication), social competencies (leadership, team management, conflict management and negotiation), or core soft skills (listening, presentation, etiquette and writing).>

5.2. Scope of Skills

Those in the field of product management must possess a multitude of skills with a cumulative emphasis on strategic thinking and numeric analysis. Responsibilities may vary from company to company, but the core job function encompasses formulating market requirements and contributing to the search for the most productive way to build long-term value for a product.

5.3. Business Competency Components

1. Domain Expertise – specific industry experience and technological know-how.
2. Functional Expertise – knowledge in processes, tools and techniques to plan/market products.
3. Soft Skills – non-technical skills, mostly communicative (written, verbal and presentation), used in business.
4. Strategic Aptitude – long-term planning and decision making abilities that help achieve corporate objectives.

<Comment: Hiring managers, when looking for qualified product managers, carefully consider and query candidates on the four business competency components. Subsequently, product managers' curricula vita should reflect their capability levels in the four business competency components.>

5.4. Competency Table Glossary

- **Importance**: The importance of the activity to attaining the professional vision. (High, Low).
- **Assessment**: How well is the activity being performed. (High, Low, Not Done).
- **Current Proficiency**: Present level of skillfulness or knowledge. (None, Basic, Skilled, Advanced).
- **Target Proficiency**: Desired level of skillfulness or knowledge. (None, Basic, Skilled, Advanced).
- **Developmental Actions**: Specific actions to be taken so the target proficiency is attained.

<Comment: Common developmental actions include various forms of education, training, and gained experience. Be very explicit and specific when describing the developmental actions sections.>

- **Success Criteria**: Measurable standard that indicates the target proficiency is attained.
- **Time Frame**: Time period in which the target proficiency is to be attained.
- **Proof**: Description of the evidence that the success criteria were met.

5.5. Competency Domains Table

<Fill the table below using the aforementioned glossary.>

Competency Domain	Impor-tance	Assess-ment	Current Proficiency	Target Proficiency	Developmental Actions	Success Criteria	Time Frame	Proof
1. Domain Expertise								
1.1. Industry experience								
* Company								
* Competitors								
* Customers								
* Market								
* Regulation								
* Technology								
1.2. Workplace accomplishments								
* Employee awards								
* Patents issued								
* Products delivered or launched								
* Promotions								
1.3. Appropriate blend of education, training, and credentials								
* Academic education								
* Certifications								
* Diplomas and credentials								
* Internal and on-the-job training								
* Professional training								

Competency Domain	Impor-tance	Assess-ment	Current Proficiency	Target Proficiency	Developmental Actions	Success Criteria	Time Frame	Proof
2. Functional Expertise								
2.1. Writing quality market requirements								
* Creating MRDs								
* Performing VOC process								
* Using requirements management software								
2.2. Ability to execute specific product management tasks								
* Product marketing								
* Product planning								
2.3. Understanding of relevant terminology and definitions								
* Product marketing								
* Product planning								
2.4. Knowledge of product management processes and procedures								
* Product marketing								
* Product planning								
2.5. Familiarity with product definition and management team structures								

Competency Domain	Impor-tance	Assess-ment	Current Proficiency	Target Proficiency	Developmental Actions	Success Criteria	Time Frame	Proof
* Product definition team model								
* Product management team model								
3. Soft Skills								
3.1. Thought leadership								
* Commitment to quality								
* Creativity and innovation								
* Leadership and initiative								
* Market orientation								
* Process improvement								
3.2. Communication skills								
* Conflict management								
* Presentation and public addressing								
* Product demonstration								
* Teamwork and leadership								
* Time management								
* Writing and authoring								
4. Strategic Aptitude								
4.1. Professional development								
* Decision making								

Competency Domain	Impor-tance	Assess-ment	Current Proficiency	Target Proficiency	Developmental Actions	Success Criteria	Time Frame	Proof
* Domain expertise growth								
* Greater responsibilities								
* P&L accountability								
* Progressive career roles								
* Strategic planning and organization								
* Team management								
4.2. Executing a product definition process								
* Product definition team management								
* Product frames model								
4.3. Product and market strategy formulation								
* Business case								
* Marketing plan								

6. Action Plan

6.1. <u>Section Objective</u>
This section categorizes and prioritizes the "developmental actions" (that build competencies) into actionable and sequentially executed subset plans.
<Comment: Each subset plan must be reviewed on a regular basis to ensure the developmental actions are still relevant and being executed properly.>

6.2. <u>Short-Term Action Plan</u>
<List and prioritize the "developmental actions" that you will execute during the first year of your five-year professional action plan.>

6.3. <u>Medium-Term Action Plan</u>
<List and prioritize the "developmental actions" that you will execute during the second and third year of your five-year professional action plan.>

6.4. <u>Long-Term Action Plan</u>
<List and prioritize the "developmental actions" that you will execute during the fourth and fifth year of your five-year professional action plan.>

7. Summary Report

7.1. <u>Section Objective</u>
This section is summary of the preceding sections, thus depicting an overview of the professional development plan.
<Comment: This section constitutes an executive summary of the professional development plan; allowing an effective means to communicate it to relevant parties.>

7.2. <u>Summary Review</u>
- Professional Objective – <Enter text.>
- Professional Vision – <Enter text.>
- Years of Experience – <Enter text.>
- Education and Credentials – <Enter text.>
- Notable Achievements – <Enter text.>
- Strengths – <Enter text.>
- Weaknesses – <Enter text.>
- Top Skills – <Enter text.>
- Desired Skills – <Enter text.>
- Short-Term Action Plan – <Enter text.>

8. Conclusions and Recommendations

8.1. **Section Objective**

This section provides conclusions and recommendations reached after preparing the professional development plan.

8.2. **Conclusions**

<Identify and describe any conclusions reached after conducting the professional development plan.>

8.3. **Recommendations**

<Describe any relevant recommendations.>

9. Supporting Data

9.1. **Section Objective**

The section provides data in support of claims, assertions, assumptions, and statements made throughout this document.

9.2. **Assumptions**

<Describe any assumptions made when writing this document.>

9.3. **Research Information**

<If relevant, describe and list the type and scope of research conducted in the course of writing this document.>

11.4.3 PMTK Role Descriptions – Guidelines V. 4.0

Company Name: <Enter company name>
Product Name: <Enter product name>

- Date: <Enter date>
- Contact: <Enter your name>
- Department: <Enter department name>
- Location: <Enter location>
- Email: <Enter email address>
- Telephone: <Enter telephone number>

Document Revision History:

Date	Revision	Revised By	Approved By
<Enter date>	<Revision #>	<Enter your name>	<Enter name>

Table of Contents

1. Introduction

1.1. Document Objective

This document provides an outline of roles in product management that conform to the PMTK methodology, as described in the *"Blackblot Product Management Team Model"* and *"Blackblot Product Definition Team Model"*. The role descriptions in this document are presented in a manner that provides easy integration with the *"PMTK Job Description Template"*, which can be published and used for recruiting individuals for open positions in the company.

<Comment: A "Job" is a workplace labor position, which is labeled with a work title and assigned to a particular person, that represents a collection of diverse duties, tasks and obligations. A job description is in essence a documented statement of the terms and conditions of an employment opportunity.

A "Role" is an occupational activity with a focused set of tasks and a clear and definitive goal, which demands a specific level of expertise in order to be successfully accomplished. A role description is in essence a documented statement of the functionality that is to be performed.

One or more roles are commonly combined to create a job and thus the owner of a job can be assigned several roles. For example, the designation "Product Manager" is a generic job title and a loosely defined collective term that is used to describe a combination of roles. Accordingly, a job description is an aggregate of the prescribed employment conditions and the assigned role descriptions.

To create a job description, please see the "PMTK Job Description Template". For more information regarding the Blackblot team models and related roles, please see the "Blackblot Product Management Team" and "Blackblot Product Definition Team" chapters in this book.>

1.2. Types of Expertise

The discipline of product management consists of several roles that require specific types of expertise. The following nomenclature is used to describe the types of expertise required for each product management role, as defined by the PMTK methodology.

"Domain Expertise" is knowledge in the technical and business aspects of the product, industry, market, and technology. *"Functional Expertise"* is the ability to use tools and execute techniques, processes and tasks that create winning products. Each *'expertise type'* (domain or functional) may have a specific *'expertise focus'* (market, industry, product, or process). For example, a person can have domain expertise in the software industry (*'expertise type'*) and be a market expert (*'expertise focus'*).

1.3. **Education and Mindset**
In most cases, the person assuming a product management related role will have at the least an undergraduate degree level of education in a specific or related field to the product or market, or will have an equivalent number of years of work related experience. The following nomenclature is used to describe the educational requirements required for each product management role as defined by the PMTK methodology.

- Undergraduate Degree – BS/BA degree in any subject.
- Graduate Degree – MS/MA/MBA degree in any subject.
- Technical Undergraduate Degree – BSC degree in a particular field of science such as mathematics, physics, computer science, or engineering.
- Technical Graduate Degree – MSC degree in a particular field of science such as mathematics, physics, computer science, or engineering.

It should also be noted that different roles usually favor different mindsets; with "*Mindset*" being a mental attitude that determines how people interpret and respond to situations.

2. Product Planner Role Description

2.1. **Section Objective**
This section describes the "*Product Planner*" role. The "*Product Planner*" has domain expertise in a particular market. "*Product Planning*" is a discipline that is focused on executing an ongoing process of identifying and articulating market requirements that define a product's feature set.

2.2. **Role Overview**
"*Product Planner*" is a strategic role that is owned by a **market expert** who articulates the market problem and needs. The "*Product Planner*" researches the market, identifies the market opportunity, and articulates user and buyer needs in the form of market requirement statements.

The primary deliverable of the "*Product Planner*" is the "*Market Requirements Document*" (MRD), which reflects a complete, accurate, and true understanding of the market and its needs. Other supporting documents that might be prepared include product use cases, product roadmaps, and pricing models.

The prime goal of the "*Product Planner*" role is to create satisfied product buyers and users. This satisfaction level means contentment with the product's ability to solve business or consumer problems (in a market) and meet their needs.

The "*Product Planner*" must be able to communicate well with both external and internal organizations. External to the company, the "*Product Planner*" communicates and works with customers to determine their problems and identify market requirements. Internally, the "*Product Planner*" communicates and works with organizational functions such as Engineering, Product Marketing, and Sales.

The *"Product Planner"* also acts as a communication interface between the product management team and the product definition team.

2.3. **Role Skill Set**

The following set of skills, listed in alphabetical order, is essential to the *"Product Planner"* role:

- Authoring Skills – Able to articulate and document the customers' market problem in a manner that encapsulates knowledge and represents a true understanding of the market and its needs.
- Interpersonal Skills – Able to build strong rapport and relationships with customers as to gain in-depth understanding of customers' problems and needs.
- Interview Skills – Able to interview customers in order to comprehensively understand their market problem.
- Language Skills – Able to communicate, in written and verbal form, with diverse audiences, internal and external to the company, in a clear and comprehendible manner.
- Methodological Skills – Able to structure and craft market requirements using a formal and structured methodology.
- Process Skills – Able to implement and/or follow the product planning process component of the product delivery process.
- Research Skills – Able to perform market research, market analysis, and competitive intelligence studies.

2.4. **Role Overview Table**

The *"Role Overview Table"* provides the role's general profile and a list of its key characteristics.

Attributes/Role	*"Product Planner"*
Alias	Product Manager.
Expertise Type	Domain expertise.
Expertise Focus	Market expert.
Essential Function	Identify and articulate market requirements.
Professional Goal	Satisfied product buyers and users.
Primary Deliverables	Market Requirements Document (MRD).
Support Deliverables	Roadmap, Pricing Model.
Internal Interfaces	Engineering, Product Marketing, Sales.
External Interfaces	Customers.
Education	Undergraduate degree (specific or diverse subjects).
Mindset	Formalized, deterministic.
Skill Set	*<Comment: See the skills listed in the "Role Skill Set" section.>*

<Comment: The "Role Overview Table" is by no means an unwavering recommendation or a precise depiction of neither the role nor the qualities the person assuming the role should possess, or must have in order to succeed at this role.>

3. Product Marketer Role Description

3.1. Section Objective

This section describes the "*Product Marketer*" role. The "*Product Marketer*" has functional expertise in the discipline of product marketing. "*Product Marketing*" is a discipline that is focused on outbound activities aimed at generating product awareness, differentiation, and demand.

3.2. Role Overview

"*Product Marketer*" is a strategic role that is owned by a **marketing expert** who analyzes product oriented market opportunities, formulates plans that evaluate those market opportunities, and then creates plans that guide the subsequent marketing efforts.

From a deliverables perspective, the "*Product Marketer*" drives the making of the product business case, and following approval writes the market plan. Other supporting documents that might be prepared include product positioning, competitor analysis, and value documents. The "*Product Marketer*" also assists and guides with the formulation of a product launch plan, provides content and selection to marketing collateral, and provides content to product press releases.

The "*Product Marketer*" is focused on enhancing the company's competency in using marketing tools and executing techniques, processes and tasks that aim to generate awareness, differentiation and demand for the product.

The prime goal of the "*Product Marketer*" role is to have a satisfied sales force. The market environment, as created by the actions of the "*Product Marketer*", leads to a very favorable situation where the market buys the product as opposed to the salespeople actively selling the product. Accordingly, the marketing actions initiated by the "*Product Marketer*" contribute to shorter sales cycles and higher sales revenue over a period of time.

The "*Product Marketer*" must be able to communicate well with both external and internal organizations. External to the company, the "*Product Marketer*" communicates and works with various vendors that provide the company with marketing tools and services. Internally, the "*Product Marketer*" communicates and works with organizational functions such as Sales, MarCom, and Corporate Marketing.

3.3. Role Skill Set

The following set of skills, listed in alphabetical order, is essential to the "*Product Marketer*" role:

- Abstraction Skills – Able to comprehend and summarize conceptual ideas and notions that apply to the different stages of the product's marketing lifecycle.
- Analytical Skills – Able to perform a risk-adjusted, cost-benefit analysis, and evaluation of market opportunities.
- Marketing Skills – Able to select and apply the right marketing tools to given market scenarios, and execute marketing techniques, processes, and tasks.

- <u>Planning Skills</u> – Able to develop and implement a product marketing process that generates awareness, differentiation, and demand for the product.
- <u>Psycho-Social Skills</u> – Able to understand, factor-in and consider the market's relevant emotions, beliefs, and behaviors; in the selection of marketing actions.

3.4. Role Overview Table

The *"Role Overview Table"* provides the role's general profile and a list of its key characteristics.

Attributes/Role	*"Product Marketer"*
Alias	Product Marketing Manager.
Expertise Type	Functional expertise.
Expertise Focus	Marketing expert.
Essential Function	Evaluate market opportunities and plan/guide marketing efforts.
Professional Goal	Satisfied sales force.
Primary Deliverables	Business Case, Market Plan.
Support Deliverables	Value Documents, Positioning Statements.
Internal Interfaces	Sales, MarCom, Corporate Marketing.
External Interfaces	Vendors of marketing tools and services.
Education	Graduate degree (BA, but often an MBA degree).
Mindset	Conceptual, probabilistic.
Skill Set	*<Comment: See the skills listed in the "Role Skill Set" section.>*

<Comment: The "Role Overview Table" is by no means an unwavering recommendation or a precise depiction of neither the role nor the qualities the person assuming the role should possess, or must have, in order to succeed at this role.>

4. Product Architect Role Description

4.1. Section Objective

This section describes the *"Product Architect"* role. The *"Product Architect"* has domain expertise in a particular technology or product type, from an engineering perspective. *"Product Architecturing"* is a discipline that is focused on the formation, structure and design of a product.

4.2. Role Overview

"Product Architect" is a tactical role that is owned by a **product expert** who creates a high-level design for the product. The *"Product Architect"* understands the market opportunity, interprets market requirements, and is well-versed in technology and development processes. The *"Product Architect's"* main task is to devise a functional solution to the market problem according to the market requirements that are outlined in the *"Market Requirements Document"* (MRD).

The primary deliverable of the *"Product Architect"* is the *"Product Requirements Document"* (PRD), which is a high-level description of the functional solution, its intended use, and the set of features it provides that address the market problem and satisfy needs. Through the PRD, the *"Product Architect"* articulates the product's architectural vision and structure, and specifies the product's components and interfaces which create the features that the market requirements prescribe. The *"Product Architect"* contributes to other supporting documents including the product's feature matrix, roadmap, and technical specification documents.

The prime goal of the *"Product Architect"* role is to have satisfied product developers. This means that the product's design and its architecture are compatible with the company's current internal development processes and technologies. Consequently, the product's design and its architecture conform to the development team's competencies, schedule, and technical quality demands.

The *"Product Architect"* must be able to communicate well with both external and internal organizations. External to the company, the *"Product Architect"* communicates and works with contract development firms, technology partners and customers. Internally, the *"Product Architect"* communicates and works with organizational functions such as Engineering, Product Marketing, and Product Planning. The *"Product Architect"* also acts as a communication interface between the product planning team and the engineering team.

4.3. Role Skill Set
The following set of skills, listed in alphabetical order, is essential to the *"Product Architect"* role:
- Business Skills – Able to comprehend the business context and market problem that drive the building of a product.
- Conceptualization Skills – Able to create product architecture, and evaluate and foresee the applicability of diverse architectural designs relative to the product.
- Engineering Skills – Able to advocate and relate to different product development methods and modeling techniques.
- Leadership Skills – Able to rally and gain backing from internal stakeholders in order to build organizational support for the proposed architecture.
- Mentoring Skills – Able to counsel teams and individuals to wholly understand and effectively implement the proposed architecture.
- Technology Skills – Able to understand in-depth, analyze and select current and emerging technologies that are pertinent to the product and company.
- Visionary Skills – Able to create and articulate architectural and technical visions for the product.

4.4. Role Overview Table
The *"Role Overview Table"* provides the role's general profile and a list of its key characteristics.

Attributes/Role	*"Product Architect"*
Alias	Requirements Engineer, Requirements Manager, Solution Architect, Business Analyst, Systems Analyst

Attributes/Role	"*Product Architect*"
Expertise Type	Domain expertise
Expertise Focus	Product expert
Essential Function	Devise a functional solution
Professional Goal	Satisfied product developers
Primary Deliverables	Product Requirements Document (PRD)
Support Deliverables	Product Feature Matrix, Roadmap (contributory role)
Internal Interfaces	Engineering, Product Marketing, Product Planning
External Interfaces	Contract development firms, technology partners, customers
Education	Technical undergraduate degree (specific or diverse subjects)
mindset	Technical, formalized, deterministic
Skill Set	*<Comment: See the skills listed in the "Role Skill Set" section.>*

<Comment: The "Role Overview Table" is by no means an unwavering recommendation or a precise depiction of neither the role nor the qualities the person assuming the role should possess, or must have, in order to succeed at this role.>

5. Sales Engineer Role Description

5.1. Section Objective

This section describes the "*Sales Engineer*" role. The "*Sales Engineer*" has domain expertise in a particular technology or product type, from a sales perspective. "*Sales Engineering*" is a discipline that is focused on a consultative style of interaction with customers to help them realize the value and functionality of a product.

5.2. Role Overview

"*Sales Engineer*" is a tactical role that is owned by an **advocacy expert** who is primarily responsible for outbound product-centric activities, such as pre-sale support and product demonstrations. The "*Sales Engineer*", relying on his/her technical skills, helps customers understand how the product delivers the necessary value and functionality that address the customers' business or consumer problem. Another objective of the "*Sales Engineer*" is to provide critical input or feedback to the "*Product Planner*" regarding customer needs and problems. All this is accomplished via frequent on-site customer visits and public engagements at conferences and conventions.

The "*Sales Engineer*" understands the business context and the market problem relative to the product, is well-versed in the product's internals and feature set, and is a consummate communicator.

From a deliverables perspective, the "*Sales Engineer*" drives the making of the company and product presentations, product demo scripts, and product review guides. Other supporting documents that might be prepared include win/loss analysis questionnaires and reports, and marketing collateral.

The prime goal of the *"Sales Engineer"* role is to ensure that customers have adequate knowledge of the value that a product holds and an understanding of its functionality.

The *"Sales Engineer"* must be able to communicate well with both external and internal organizations. External to the company, the *"Sales Engineer"* communicates and works with customers, reviewers, analysts, and journalists. Internally, the *"Sales Engineer"* communicates and works with organizational functions such as Engineering, Product Marketing and Product Planning.

<Comment: Sales engineers often operate under titles such as product evangelist, technical evangelist, technical sales support, pre-sale engineer, outbound product manager, or technical product manager; yet regardless of the title, they all perform a relatively similar set of tasks.>

5.3. Role Skill Set

The following set of skills, listed in alphabetical order, is essential to the *"Sales Engineer"* role:

- Business Skills – Able to comprehend the business context and market problem that drive the building of a product.
- Interpersonal Skills – Able to build strong rapport and relationships with customers as to gain in-depth understanding of customers' problems and needs.
- Interview Skills – Able to interview customers in order to comprehensively understand their market problem.
- Language Skills – Able to communicate, in written and verbal form, with diverse audiences, internal and external to the company, in a clear and comprehendible manner.
- Technology Skills – Able to understand the technologies incorporated in the product or used in its assembly or manufacturing.

5.4. Role Overview Table

The *"Role Overview Table"* provides the role's general profile and a list of its key characteristics.

Attributes/Role	*"Sales Engineer"*
Alias	Product Evangelist, Technical Evangelist, Technical Sales Support, Pre-Sale Engineer, Outbound Product Manager, Technical Product Manager.
Expertise Type	Domain expertise.
Expertise Focus	Advocacy expert.
Essential Function	Outbound product-centric activities; i.e., pre-sale support and product demonstrations.
Professional Goal	Customer knowledge of product value and functionality.
Primary Deliverables	Company and product presentations, product demo scripts, product review guides.
Support Deliverables	Win/loss analysis questionnaires/ reports, marketing collateral.
Internal Interfaces	Engineering, Product Marketing, Product Planning.

Attributes/Role	*"Sales Engineer"*
External Interfaces	Customers, reviewers, analysts, journalists.
Education	Technical undergraduate degree (specific or diverse subjects).
mindset	Technical, formalized, deterministic.
Skill Set	*<Comment: See the skills listed in the "Role Skill Set" section.>*

<Comment: The "Role Overview Table" is by no means an unwavering recommendation or a precise depiction of neither the role nor the qualities the person assuming the role should possess, or must have, in order to succeed at this role.>

6. MarCom Manager Role Description

6.1. Section Objective

This section describes the *"MarCom Manager"* role. The *"MarCom Manager"* has functional expertise in the discipline of marketing communications. *"Marketing Communications"* (MarCom) is a discipline that is focused on the application of a mix of media vehicles that support marketing objectives.

6.2. Role Overview

"MarCom Manager" is a tactical role that is owned by a **media expert** who is primarily responsible for creating interest and memorable presence through the conception and copywriting of all collateral material, advertising, direct response mail, web, and other types of communications media.

The *"MarCom Manager"*, relying on language, creative and artistic skills, is primarily engaged in art direction of the company's collateral documents and media deliverables. Other responsibilities include media placement and scheduling, campaign management and measurement, budgeting and budget tracking, and advertising management (conception, pricing, placement, and scheduling).

The prime goal of the *"MarCom Manager"* role is to ensure a consistent image and positioning in the target market, according to messages and directives provided by the *"Product Marketer"*.

The *"MarCom Manager"* must be able to communicate well with both external and internal organizations. External to the company, the *"MarCom Manager"* communicates and works with advertisement agencies, creative/design bureaus and production houses. Internally, the *"MarCom Manager"* communicates and works with organizational functions such as Sales, Product Marketing and Corporate Marketing.

6.3. Role Skill Set

The following set of skills, listed in alphabetical order, is essential to the *"MarCom Manager"* role:

- Budgeting Skills – Able to prepare and track a spending plan that will be used to fund the planned media activities.

- Creative Skills – Able to devise new forms of creative expression in the way of symbols, ideas and notions; in an original, novel, or unconventional way.
- Cultural Skills – Able to perceive and realize the manner in which to adapt and create content that is compatible with the target market's local customs, nuances, norms, and behaviors.
- Language Skills – Able to communicate, in both written and verbal form, with diverse audiences, internal and external to the company, in a clear and comprehendible manner.
- Negotiation Skills – Able to partake a leadership role in a process of searching for an agreement that satisfies all parties which have competing interests.
- Project Management Skills – Able to perform the overall planning and coordination of tasks, scheduling, and resource assignments aimed at producing a deliverable.

6.4. Role Overview Table
The "*Role Overview Table*" provides the role's general profile and a list of its key characteristics.

Attributes/Role	"*MarCom Manager*"
Alias	Market Communications Manager.
Expertise Type	Functional expertise.
Expertise Focus	Media expert.
Essential Function	Conception and copywriting of all collateral material.
Professional Goal	Consistent image and positioning in the target market.
Primary Deliverables	Art direction of collateral and media deliverables.
Support Deliverables	Media placement and scheduling, campaign management and measurement, budgeting, budget tracking, advertising management.
Internal Interfaces	Sales, Product Marketing, Corporate Marketing.
External Interfaces	Advertisement agencies, creative/design bureaus, production houses.
Education	Undergraduate degree (specific or diverse subjects).
Mindset	Artistic, imaginative, creative.
Skill Set	*<Comment: See the skills listed in the "Role Skill Set" section.>*

<Comment: The "Role Overview Table" is by no means an unwavering recommendation or a precise depiction of neither the role nor the qualities the person assuming the role should possess, or must have, in order to succeed at this role.>

7. Director of Products Role Description

7.1. Section Objective
This section describes the "*Director of Products*" role. The "*Director of Products*" has solid functional expertise in the product planning and product marketing disciplines, acute strategy formulation expertise, and complete understanding of product management tools and processes.

7.2. **Role Overview**

"*Director of Products*" is a highly strategic and encompassing role that is owned by a **strategy and process expert** who leads the product management team by providing overall product vision, product and market strategies, and team leadership.

The "*Director of Products*" is responsible for balancing corporate goals with long-term market trends and opportunities, and for directing, establishing, maintaining, and planning the overall policies and strategies for the product management department.

On the strategic level, this role formulates the company's product and market strategies and drives their implementation, while balancing corporate goals with long-term market trends and market opportunities.

On the tactical level, this leadership position provides coaching and mentorship to the product management team members and is responsible for furnishing them with resources, tools, and uniform processes to do their respective jobs. The "*Director of Products*" role creates and manages the overall product management process and oversees its effective execution.

From a deliverables perspective, the "*Director of Products*" directs, supports, and contributes primarily to the making of the product business case, market plan, and market requirements document (MRD). The "*Director of Products*" also guides and assists with the formulation of a product launch plan and the value documents.

The prime goal of the "*Director of Products*" role is to continuously oversee the successful formulation and execution of the product and market strategies and to achieve better consistency in the internal application of the product management discipline.

The "*Director of Products*" must be able to communicate well with both external and internal organizations. External to the company, the "*Director of Products*" communicates and works with customers and partners. Internally, the "*Director of Products*" communicates and works with organizational functions such as Sales, MarCom, Corporate Marketing, and Engineering.

7.3. **Role Skill Set**

The following set of skills, listed in alphabetical order, is essential to the "*Director of Products*" role:
- Analytical Skills – Able to engage in creative problem solving and draw conclusions that orient towards correction and improvement.
- Business Skills – Able to comprehend the business context and market opportunity that drive the building of a product.

- <u>Decision Making Skills</u> – Able to make sound decisions by exercising analysis and resoluteness.
- <u>Interpersonal Skills</u> – Able to build strong rapport and relationships with internal and external organizations.
- <u>Leadership Skills</u> – Able to exercise guidance and influence within the product management team and the company to forge commitment and consensus.
- <u>Mentoring Skills</u> – Able to counsel, assist, and share knowledge and experience with teams and individuals to facilitate improved job performance.
- <u>Process Skills</u> – Able to develop and implement a structured product management process that promotes a more effective execution of product management procedures and operations.

7.4. **Role Overview Table**

The "*Role Overview Table*" provides the role's general profile and a list of its key characteristics.

Attributes/Role	*"Director of Products"*
Alias	Director of Product Management.
Expertise Type	Functional and domain expertise.
Expertise Focus	Strategy and process expert.
Essential Function	Lead the product management team by providing overall product vision, product and market strategies, and team management.
Professional Goal	▪ Continuously guide the successful formulation and execution of the product and market strategies. ▪ Achieve better consistency in the internal application of the product management discipline.
Primary Deliverables	Business Case, Market Plan, Market Requirements Document.
Support Deliverables	Product Launch Plan, Value Documents.
Internal Interfaces	Sales, MarCom, Corporate Marketing, Engineering.
External Interfaces	Customers, Partners.
Education	Graduate degree (BA, but very often an MBA degree).
Mindset	Conceptual, formalized, creative.
Skill Set	<*Comment: See the skills listed in the "Role Skill Set" section.*>

<*Comment: The "Role Overview Table" is by no means an unwavering recommendation or a precise depiction of neither the role nor the qualities the person assuming the role should possess, or must have, in order to succeed at this role.*>

11.4.4 PMTK Job Description – Template V. 4.0

Company Name: <Enter company name>

Product Name: <Enter product name>

- Date: <Enter date>
- Contact: <Enter your name>
- Department: <Enter department name>
- Location: <Enter location>
- Email: <Enter email address>
- Telephone: <Enter telephone number>

Document Revision History:

Date	Revision	Revised By	Approved By
<Enter date>	<Revision #>	<Enter your name>	<Enter name>

Table of Contents

1. Introduction

1.1. Document Objective

This document provides a framework for preparing a job description which is made public and depicts an open position (that needs to be staffed) in a company.

<Comment: A job is a workplace labor position which is labeled with a work title and assigned to a particular person, that represents a collection of diverse duties, tasks and obligations. A job description is in essence a documented statement of the terms and conditions of an employment opportunity.

A role is an occupational activity with a focused set of tasks and a clear and definitive goal which demands a specific level of expertise in order to be successfully accomplished. A role description is in essence a documented statement of the functionality that is to be performed.

One or more roles are commonly combined to create a job and thus the owner of a job can be assigned several roles. For example, the designation "Product Manager" is a generic job title and a loosely defined collective term that is used to describe a combination of roles. Accordingly, a job description is an aggregate of the prescribed employment conditions and the assigned role descriptions.>

2. PMTK Job Description

2.1. Section Objective

This section describes the structure and format of a job description. The job description in this document is structured in a manner that provides easy integration with the roles described in the Blackblot team models.

2.2. PMTK Job Description Authoring Guidelines

- Use plain English to convey essential information about this position using few words as possible. Be extremely focused and concise.
- Avoid making assumptions about the level of knowledge readers may have regarding the company's own terminology and acronyms.
- A job description can be a legally binding document. Pay careful attention to the wording and when relevant, have the company's legal team scrutinize the job description.
- Do not cram just about anything possible into the job description. It does not legally shield the company, and will produce a job description that appeals to a very large audience of unfitting candidates.

2.3. PMTK Job Description Template

<See the job description template below.>

Job Specification

- Job Title — <Enter the formal job title of this position.>
- Job Reference — <Enter the formal job reference number of this position.>
- Job Ranking — <Enter the job level assigned to this position. Job rankings are commonly: entry, junior, senior, level 1, level 2, level 3, etc.>
- Department — <Enter the name of the department and/or business unit to which this position will organizationally belong.>
- Reporting To — <Enter the job title of the position to which this position reports. For example, this could be the *"Director of Product Management"*, CEO, etc.>
- Direct Reports — <Enter the job titles of any positions to be supervised by this position.>
- Timeframe — <Enter the official desired timeframe of work for this position in weekly or monthly hours.>
- Contract Type — <Enter the type of contract this position is attributed with. For example, this could be full-time, part-time, contractor, short-term assignment, etc.>
- Pay Type and Range — <Enter job pay type (salary/hourly) and the relative pay range.>
- Location — <Enter the geographic location where this position situated. Location details include at a minimum the town, state and country.>
- Date — <Enter the formal date of availability for this position.>

<Comment: Subject to relevancy, retain or delete one or more of the above options.>

Company Overview

<Enter company name> is a <Enter company description>.
<Comment: Include the company's mission statement in the company's description.>

Domain/Product

The <Enter job title> is tasked with handling the <Enter description of the market and/or product(s) that constitutes this position's field of operation>.

Summary of Position

<Enter a short paragraph which describes the overall purpose of this position and how it contributes to the objectives of the company.>

Assigned Roles

The roles assigned to the <Enter job title> position are the <Enter list the assigned roles accompanied by their relative weight in percentile terms> roles. See the detailed role descriptions that are appended this job description.

<Comment: The outline of this job description conforms and supports the roles defined in the PMTK methodology. For example, the job position might be called "Product Manager" and the assigned roles are those of a "Product Planner" and "Product Marketer". Also for example, the company might have three "Product Manager" positions of the same title, but each product

manager is actually assigned a different combination of roles taken from the Blackblot team models, such as "Product Planner", "Product Architect", and/or "Product Marketer".

For more information regarding the Blackblot team models and related roles, please see the "PMTK Role Descriptions Guidelines" template, and the "Blackblot Product Management Team" and "Blackblot Product Definition Team" chapters in this book.>

Related Experience
- At least <Enter number of years> year(s) experience in <Enter description of the relevant industry, market and products> related field of business.
- At least <Enter number of years> year(s) experience in <Enter particular activity or roles> or related roles.

Education and Training
- Bachelor's or Master's degree in <Enter profession> or at least <Enter number of years> year(s) experience in a related field of knowledge.
- <Enter training institute and course name> product management training graduate highly desired.
- <Enter certifying institute and certification name> product management certification highly desired.

Citizenship and Immigration
- <Enter nationality> citizenship required.
- Security clearance <Enter security level> required.
- Immigration status with valid credentials.

<Comment: Subject to relevancy, retain or delete one or more of the above options.>

Work Environment
- Overseas travel required.
- Fluency in <Enter languages> highly desired.
- Performance reviews are performed every <Enter review period in months> months.

<Comment: This section may also list any physical demands, need for prolonged overseas travel or any other relevant work environment requirements to perform the role.>

Selection Criteria
<Enter the list of candidate selection criteria in general order of priority.>

<Comment: It is essential a company proactively determines the selection criteria to which candidate skills and competencies can be assessed against. Relative weights reflecting the relative importance of each criterion is at the company's sole discretion. In rare instances this section is a legal requirement but commonly is optional and may be completely omitted from the job description, if desired.>

How to Apply

- Qualified candidates are invited to apply directly to <Enter recruiter name>, recruitment manager, via email <Enter recruiters email address, such as recruiter@company.com> and specify position #<Enter position number> in the subject line.
- Qualified candidates are invited to apply directly via our website at <Enter the company's job URL, such as www.company.com/jobs/ .>

<Comment: Subject to relevancy, retain or delete one or more of the above options.>

Compensation, Incentives and Benefits Package

<Comment: This section lists the base salary, bonuses, stock options, other compensation and benefits such as health (medical/dental/vision) coverage, life insurance, and 401k plans. This section is optional and may be completely omitted from the job description, if desired.>

Additional Information

- All applicants will receive an acknowledgment of their application.
- Only qualified candidates will be contacted.
- Relocation assistance available.
- <Enter company name> is an equal employment opportunity employer and considers all qualified applicants for employment.

<Comment: Subject to relevancy, retain or delete one or more of the above options.>

Appendix – Role Descriptions

- <Enter role #1 description.>
- <Enter role #2 description.>
- <Enter role #n description.>

<Comment: Copy and paste here all the relevant role description sections from the "PMTK Role Descriptions Guidelines" document.>

Review and Approval (Internal Use Only)

- Prepared By — <Enter the name of the person who prepared the job description. This is normally the hiring manager, the person this position reports to. Optionally include the date of completion.>
- Reviewed By — <Enter the name of the person who reviewed the proposed job description. This is normally the recruiting manager from the human resources department. Optionally include the date of review.>
- Legal Approval — <Enter the name of the person at the company's legal department which approved the content of the job description. Optionally include the date of approval.>
- Sanctioned By — <Enter the name of the person who authorized the publishing of the job description and commencing with the recruiting process. This is normally the vice president or general manager of the business unit.>
- Date Posted — <Enter the date when the job description was made public.>
- Date Removed- <Enter the date when the job description was removed from public notice.>
- Hiring Status — <Enter the status of this position: Open/Closed.>

11.4.5 PMTK Interview Process – Guidelines V. 4.0

Company Name: <Enter company name>

Product Name: <Enter product name>

- Date: <Enter date>
- Contact: <Enter your name>
- Department: <Enter department name>
- Location: <Enter location>
- Email: <Enter email address>
- Telephone: <Enter telephone number>

Document Revision History:

Date	Revision	Revised By	Approved By
<Enter date>	<Revision #>	<Enter your name>	<Enter name>

Table of Contents

1. Introduction

1.1. **Document Objective**

This document provides a framework for administering a product management oriented interview process.

1.2. **PMTK Interview Process**

The *"PMTK Interview Process"* is a procedure that evaluates a prospective employee (a.k.a. candidate) for a product management position. An interview is an ongoing exchange of information between company employees (interviewers) and a candidate to determine whether there is a match between the candidate's professional history, skills sets and past workplace contributions in conjunction to the job's description, requirements and needs. The candidate's overall *"fit"* for the job is evaluated by the interviewers on three levels: *"personal fit"*, *"team fit"*, and *"professional fit"*. The impression of a personal and team fit is formed during interpersonal interaction with the team members and is done on an emotional and unscientific level. Establishing professional fit is done in a more structured and rationalistic way through a questioning process, which is the focus of this document.

1.3. **Interview Reciprocity**

From the company's perspective, the objective of the interviewing process is to verify if the candidate can successfully perform the core functions of the job, and create dynamics that help establish a notion if the candidate will fit in with their assigned team on a social level. Yet the interview is a reciprocal exchange during which the candidate is also evaluating the interviewers (the candidate's future team members and peers) and the company. Seemingly unprofessional and poorly carried out interviews can discourage a good candidate from accepting the job if he/she has more than one job offer to consider. Knowing how to interview is an acquired skill, yet lack of interviewing experience and knowledge can be considerably alleviated by performing planned interviews within the context of a structured interview process.

<Comment: The goal of the "PMTK Interview Process" is to make the interviews more organized, efficient and successful by helping to guide the interaction that takes place with a focus on finding a mutual fit between the company and the candidate.>

2. Product Management Interview Context

2.1. **Section Objective**

This section describes the contextual focus of a product management oriented interview process.

2.2. **Scope of Skills**

Those in the field of product management must possess a multitude of skills with a cumulative emphasis on strategic thinking and numeric analysis. Responsibilities may vary from company to company, but the core job function encompasses formulating market requirements and contributing to the search for the most productive way to build long-term value for a product.

<Comment: Hiring managers, when looking for qualified product managers, should carefully consider and query candidates on the four business competency components: domain expertise, functional expertise, soft skills, and strategic aptitude. Therefore, the product management oriented interview process is designed to uncover and assess the candidates' capability levels in these four areas.>

2.3. **Business Competency Components**

This section identifies and discusses the various types of business competency components that the candidate's background and experience should exhibit. These are: domain expertise, functional expertise, soft skills, and strategic aptitude.

- Domain Expertise

  Specific industry experience and technological know-how.
  - o Industry experience.
  - o Workplace accomplishments.
  - o Appropriate blend of education, training, and credentials.
- Functional Expertise

  Knowledge in processes, tools and techniques to plan and market products.
  - o Writing quality market requirements.
  - o Ability to execute specific product management tasks.
  - o Understanding of relevant terminology and definitions.
  - o Knowledge of product management processes and procedures.
  - o Familiarity with product definition and management team structures.
- Soft Skills

  Non-technical skills, mostly communicative (written, verbal and presentation), used in business.
  - o Thought leadership.
  - o Communication skills.
- Strategic Aptitude

  Long-term planning and decision making abilities that help achieve corporate objectives.
  - o Professional development.
  - o Executing a product definition process.
  - o Product and market strategy formulation.

3. Product Management Interview Process Logistics

3.1. Section Objective

This section describes the logistics that guide a product management oriented interview process.

<Comment: There are three classes of interviews used in the overall hiring process: a 'screening interview' (normally conducted over the telephone), an 'appraisal interview' (initial in-person interview), and a series of one or more 'hiring interviews' that follow. The class of interview described and focused upon in this document is a hiring interview. This document does not elaborate on screening or appraisal interviews. There are three types of hiring interviews: 'unstructured interviews' which are based on questions that are not planned, 'semi-structured interviews' that use a combination of interviewer experience and pre-interview question planning, and 'structured interviews' which are based on questions prepared in advance and asked of all job candidates. The "PMTK Interview Process" advocates and relies on 'structured interviews'. This document does not deal with 'unstructured interviews' or 'semi-structured interviews'.>

3.2. Company Recruiter Briefing

The company recruiter meets the candidate on the day of interviewing, before and after the series of actual hiring interviews. These meetings are referred to as the *Initial Recruiter Briefing* and *Final Recruiter Briefing*.

Section	Content	Duration
Initial Recruiter Briefing	o The company recruiter provides the candidate with information about the interview process, its schedule and conditions. o The company recruiter reviews the job description with the candidate and explains its specification and characteristics. *<Comment: See the "PMTK Job Description" template.>* o The candidate signs any required legal documents.	Thirty Minutes.
Final Recruiter Briefing	o The company recruiter summarizes the day's events. o The candidate provides feedback on the interviews. o The company recruiter informs the candidate on future steps.	Fifteen Minutes.

3.3. Hiring Interviews Team

The hiring interviews team is comprised of at least four individuals who are often peers (usually people the candidate will directly work with) and the hiring manager. Each hiring interview team member interviews the candidate on a different business competency component. The last person to interview the candidate should be the actual hiring manager.

The company recruiter is the first and last person that the candidate meets with during the day of the hiring interviews. The company recruiter will meet the candidate for the *Initial Recruiter Briefing*, and then introduce the candidate to the first interviewer. The first interviewer will introduce the candidate to the second interviewer and so on. The last interviewer should bring the candidate back to the company recruiter with whom the candidate will be briefed on the next steps and the timeframe in the hiring process.

<Comment: The hiring manager is the person that makes the final determination of whether to hire the candidate or not, based on his/her own impression and feedback from the other interviewers. The hiring manager is often the most senior ranking member of the team, but not necessarily so.>

3.4. <u>Hiring Interview Session Characteristics</u>

The total amount of time allotted for each hiring interview session is fifty minutes, which allows the candidate a ten minute gap to rest between sessions and transition to the next hiring interview. Each session is aimed at gleaning enough relevant information to support making the correct hiring decision. Each hiring interview session is comprised of three sections: *introduction, core*, and *ending*.

Section	Content	Goal	Duration
Introduction	Casual and cordial exchange on light topics that are not business or job related.	Get acquainted and establish comfortable environment.	Five Minutes.
Core	A discussion prompted by deliberate pre-planned questions that are focused on a particular business competency component.	Verify the candidate has the appropriate level of the business competency component for the job.	Forty Minutes.
Ending	A candidate led Q&A and a recap of the interview session by the interviewer.	Summarize the session and conclude on a positive note.	Five Minutes.

3.5. <u>Interviewer Guidelines</u>

From the interviewer's perspective, the actual interview session is part of three distinct stages: *"before the interview"*, *"during the interview"*, and *"after the interview"*. The instructions for the interviewer per each stage are listed below.

- *Before The Interview*
  - o Read the job description and the candidate's curriculum vitae (a.k.a. résumé).
  - o Turn off all possible office distractions (e.g. phone or email), and post a '*do-not-disturb*' sign outside the room to deter untimely visitors.
  - o Prepare at least five questions that will serve as a platform for the discussion. Internalize the gist of the questions.

    <Comment: Prepare intelligent, insightful, job-centered interview questions that challenge the candidate professionally.>
  - o Acquaint yourself with the legal constraints that govern interviewing and understand which types of questions or comments are considered illegal or inappropriate.

    <Comment: Illegal or inappropriate questions or comments often deal with issues pertaining to race, religion, gender, marital status, disabilities, health, family, ethnicity, and individual privacy. The company's legal and/or human resources department should brief all interviewers on current laws in this matter.>

    o Wear proper clothing attire, mind your appearance, and always be punctual (keep a clock in view while interviewing).
- *During the Interview*
  - o Ask realistic, direct and poignant questions and give the candidate ample time to think and answer.
  - o Remember to probe on the answers and do a "drill-down" to uncover the candidate's knowledge and views on the topic. Listen carefully to the replies.
  - o Be constantly aware not to reveal confidential information or corporate plans.
  - o Remain neutral and polite at all times. Focus on the candidate, not yourself.
  - o Jot notes and comments only after the interview session is complete.
  - o Close the interview in a friendly and constructive manner.
- *After the Interview*
  - o Escort the candidate to the next interviewer.
  - o Send the company recruiter written interview feedback and your hiring recommendation immediately after the interview session.

3.6. **Interview Questions Guidelines**

This section provides suggestions for potential interview questions for each of the business competency areas: domain expertise, functional expertise, soft skills, and strategic aptitude.

- Domain Expertise

Questions in this area focus on the candidate's work history, industry experience and technological know-how. For example:
  - o Describe the positions you held and the challenges you overcame in previous roles.
  - o Describe the industries' dominant players, their success and mistakes.
  - o Describe the advantages and disadvantages of a particular technology, or product.
- Functional Expertise

Questions in this area focus on the candidate's knowledge in processes, tools and techniques to plan and market products. For example:
  - o *Questions on Product Planning*
    - ☐ Describe the structure of an MRD and the methodology for writing quality market requirements.
    - ☐ Describe the process you would follow to create a product's pricing model.
    - ☐ Describe the overall product planning process.
    - ☐ Describe the structure of a product definition team and its roles.
  - o *Questions on Product Marketing*
    - ☐ Describe the structure of a market plan.
    - ☐ Describe the process you would follow to create a product differentiation or demand.
    - ☐ Describe the overall product marketing process.
    - ☐ Describe the role of a product marketer.
- Soft Skills

Questions in this area focus on the candidate's human interaction skills which relate directly to communicating and managing relationships with others in a professional environment's social structure.

<Comment: Please visit www.blackblot.com/career/ for a list of open-ended soft skills and strategic aptitude interview questions.>

- Strategic Aptitude
  Questions in this area focus on the candidate's potential to assume in the future broader leadership roles that demand strategic planning and decision making abilities. The questions center on managing people, executing overall and broad product management processes, and product and market strategy formulation.

  <Comment: Please visit www.blackblot.com/career/ for a list of open-ended soft skills and strategic aptitude interview questions.>

4. Product Management Interview Process

4.1. Section Objective

This section describes the structure and format of a professional product management oriented interview process.

<Comment: Given the importance and cost of labor it is in the best interest of companies to hire the right people. This is of greater importance with regard to roles, as those in product management, that are crucial to a company's success. Accordingly, it is of essence to execute a consistent and structured interviewing process that will help identify the right people for the job.>

4.2. Overall Interview Process Guidelines

The following describes the overall interview process guidelines for interviewing job candidates.

- The hiring interviews process a candidate undergoes begins with an *Initial Recruiter Briefing*, at least four hiring interview sessions, and ends with the *Final Recruiter Briefing*.
- Ideally, the candidate is interviewed by progressively more senior individuals (tenure, seniority or rank) ending with the hiring manager.
- All interviews are personal encounters meant to verify a professional fit, and are not a confirmation or validation process of the candidate's curriculum vitae (a.k.a. résumé).

4.3. Overall Interview Process Stages

The following provides a sample overall interview process, according to stages. The candidate progresses through the stages, and must pass each stage to continue to the next. The overall interview process stages are:

1. The company recruiter initiates a phone screening interview with the candidate.
2. The hiring manager conducts a phone appraisal interview with the candidate.
3. The candidate is invited to the company site for an in-person appraisal interview with the hiring manager.

<Comment: Following this stage the hiring manager will decide if there is good potential for the candidate being a job fit. If so, the candidate will progress to a series of hiring interviews that are scheduled for a later date.>

4. The hiring manager selects a team of interviewers, and assigns each interviewer with a business competency they will cover during the interview session.

   o Interviewer Assignment

   ☐ Interviewer #1 discusses with the candidate their domain expertise.
   ☐ Interviewer #2 discusses with the candidate their functional expertise.
   ☐ Interviewer #3 discusses with the candidate their soft skills.
   ☐ Interviewer #4 discusses with the candidate their strategic aptitude.

   <Comment: Interviewers #1-3 are possible candidate peers and interviewer #4 is the hiring manager.>

5. Each interviewer prepares their interview questions and sends their proposed questions to the hiring manager and the company recruiter to verify legality, validity and coverage.

6. The candidate is invited for a series of hiring interviews at the company site, and begins by meeting the company recruiter for the *Initial Recruiter Briefing*.

7. A series of hiring interviews is performed, at the company site.

8. The candidate meets the company recruiter for the *Final Recruiter Briefing*.

9. All interviewers send written interview feedback immediately after the interview session, via email and using a standard template. The feedback is sent only to the company recruiter and hiring manager.

   <Comment: Stages 6-9 are planned and meant to occur on the same day.>

10. Interview feedback is analyzed jointly by the company recruiter and the hiring manager, with the final hiring decision being made by the hiring manager.

    <Comment: Depending on the company, the company recruiter can veto a decision to hire a candidate. This is a safety measure to reduce the possibility of cronyism, nepotism, or unilateral or bias decision making.>

11. A hiring decision is made and propagated.

4.4. **Feedback Template Email**

After each hiring interview, each interviewer summarizes their experience with the candidate and sends a report back to the hiring manager and the company recruiter. Below is a suggested template for the interviewer to summarize their hiring recommendation and impressions of the candidate.

```
-----Start Message-----
From: Interviewer
Sent: Monday, October 16, 20xx 3:24 PM
To: Hiring Manager, Company Recruiter
Subject: Interview feedback — <Enter position name> — <Enter candidate
name>
Importance: High

* Hiring Decision — I recommend that <Enter candidate name> <Enter 'be
  hired' or 'not be hired' decision> for the position of <Enter job name>.
  <Comment: A recommendation to hire the candidate constitutes a
  declaration that the candidate is a fit for both the job and the team.
  The default should always be not to hire when the interviewer is
  uncertain which decision to make.>
```

```
•  <Enter employment potential for this candidate in other areas of the
   company and explain why.   This section is contingent on a not to
   hire recommendation.>
   <Comment: Only if the recommendation is not to hire the candidate,
   then the interviewer may also indicate if the candidate is a
   potential fit for other jobs or functions in the company.>
*  Decision Rationale — <Enter a concise, clear and unbiased explanation
   why the particular hiring decision was reached.  Be objective.>
*  Decision Support — <Enter information and examples about the candidate
   that justify and support the hiring decision.  Be factual.>
*  Business Competency Questions — <Enter the name of the business
   competency component that was the focus of the interview, and list the
   key business competency component questions that the candidate was asked
   during the interview.>
*  Comments — <Enter any additional comments and conclusions whatsoever.>

Regards,
<Enter interviewer name.>

-----End Message-----
```

4.5. **Candidate Reference Checks**

Candidate reference checks can occur at any time within the overall interview process. This task is usually performed by the company recruiter, and the timing for checks is at their own discretion. Reference checks are commonly done before the hiring interviews or after a decision to hire the candidate was made. Information obtained during the reference checks that were carried out before the hiring interviews, is made available to the interviewers. Reference checks are used to verify various issues about the candidate, including:

• Achievements and accomplishments.
• Educational background.
• Employment background.
• Past titles and positions.
• Salary history.

11.5 PMTK IMPLEMENTATION

11.5.1 PMTK Implementation Plan – Template V. 4.0

Company Name: <Enter company name>
Product Name: <Enter product name>

- Date: <Enter date>
- Contact: <Enter your name>
- Department: <Enter department name>
- Location: <Enter location>
- Email: <Enter email address>
- Telephone: <Enter telephone number>

Document Revision History:

Date	Revision	Revised By	Approved By
<Enter date>	<Revision #>	<Enter your name>	<Enter name>

Table of Contents

1. Introduction

1.1. **Document Objective**

This document introduces a PMTK implementation plan for corporate product management functions. The goal of this plan is to help companies improve their product management processes through effective execution of product management processes and tasks that are based on the Blackblot PMTK methodology. The long-term goal of the PMTK implementation plan is to promote continual improvement via the ongoing identification of areas of relative benefit that the PMTK methodology holds for the company, and reaping those benefits by adapting the relevant parts of the PMTK methodology.

<Comment: Solid understanding of PMTK is a prerequisite to implementing PMTK in any organization. Although not a direct requirement, it is strongly recommended that at least one person who has attended PMTK based training shall manage and lead the execution of the "PMTK Implementation Plan". Assistance from a PMTK expert in the planning and execution of the "PMTK Implementation Plan" is highly recommended.>

2. PMTK Implementation Plan

2.1. **Section Objective**

This section facilitates a better understanding of the underlying principals of a process improvement initiative embodied in the PMTK implementation plan.

<Comment: The objective of this section is to evaluate the company's current product management practice utilizing the PMTK methodology, to identify gaps in roles, responsibilities, processes, procedures, tools, and techniques, and to develop an implementation plan to address the identified gaps and improve the overall product development process. The implementation of this plan does not imply that perfection will be the result. The ultimate goal is to develop a continuous process improvement process that reviews current product management processes at regular intervals to ensure continued success.>

2.2. **PMTK Implementation Principals**

- A conscious and continuous effort to improve the company's product management processes must be made for continued success.
- Commitment from employees and executive management to enact product management process improvement activities must be secured.
- Employees are officially empowered to improve the product management process by being granted the authority, training, and resources.
- Realization must be present that product management process improvement is driven by the adoption of current best practices.
- The company's product management processes are to be compared and evaluated without prejudice to industry best-practices and established product management methodologies.

2.3. __PMTK Implementation Task Table__

<Complete the table below using the task table glossary and pursuant to the embedded instructions. Follow the outlined order of the PMTK implementation tasks and execute them in sequence. Complete each task as they are all interconnected.>

PMTK Implementation Task	Task Objective	Developmental Actions	Time Frame	Task Owner
1. Foundation Stage				
Assessment and Measurement				
1.1. Perform an individual "*PMTK Gap Analysis*".	Assess own product management competency. Identify gaps and draw conclusions.	<Concisely note the conclusions. List and prioritize the action items.>		
1.2. Present team with "*Blackblot Models*" presentation showing what was learned in the training.	Inform and acquaint peers to PMTK methodology. Solicit feedback and identify key areas of improvement.	<Concisely note the conclusions. List and prioritize the action items.>		
1.3. Perform collaborative team "*PMTK Gap Analysis*".	Assess team's competency in performing product management.	<Concisely note the conclusions. List and prioritize the action items.>		
1.4. Perform collaborative team "*PMTK Performance Review*".	Measure the team's performance level in product management.	<Concisely note the conclusions. List and prioritize the action items.>		
General Processes and Structures				
1.5. Compare the overall structure of the internal product management process to the "*PMTK Action Model*".	Verify overall product management process completeness. Establish linkage between current product planning and product marketing activities.	<Concisely note the conclusions. List and prioritize the action items.>		
1.6. Compare the overall flow of the internal product management process stages to the "*PMTK Flow Model*".	Verify proper sequence and execution of product management tasks is being performed in a logical order.	<Concisely note the conclusions. List and prioritize the action items.>		
1.7. Compare the internal roles and responsibilities to those defined in the "*Blackblot Product Management Team Model*".	Verify proper product management team structures.	<Concisely note the conclusions. List and prioritize the action items.>		

PMTK Implementation Task	Task Objective	Developmental Actions	Time Frame	Task Owner
1.8. Compare the internal roles and responsibilities to those defined in the *"Blackblot Product Definition Team Model"*.	Verify proper product definition team structures.	<Concisely note the conclusions. List and prioritize the action items.>		
1.9. Compare the internal roles and responsibilities to those defined in the *"PMTK Task Model"*.	Verify proper allocation of assignments to the relevant individuals.	<Concisely note the conclusions. List and prioritize the action items.>		
1.10. Compare the internal product management documents to PMTK templates.	Verify consistency, completeness and appearance of internal product management documents.	<Concisely note the conclusions. List and prioritize the action items.>		
1.11. Compare the internal general management process and activities to those defined in the "process efficiency" section of the *"PMTK Action Model"*.	Verify general management tasks are performed routinely in an efficient manner.	<Concisely note the conclusions. List and prioritize the action items.>		
Product Planning Processes				
1.12. Compare the internal product planning process to the corresponding process in the *"PMTK Action Model"*.	Verify overall product planning process completeness.	<Concisely note the conclusions. List and prioritize the action items.>		
1.13. Compare the internal product planning and product definition processes to those defined in the *"Blackblot Product Frames Model"*.	Verify there is a foundational and methodological guideline that is governing the internal product planning process.	<Concisely note the conclusions. List and prioritize the action items.>		
1.14. Compare the internal principals for creating market requirements with those defined in the *"Blackblot Procedural Requirements Management Model"*.	Verify there is suitable methodology and formal language that is used for creating market requirements.	<Concisely note the conclusions. List and prioritize the action items.>		

PMTK Implementation Task	Task Objective	Developmental Actions	Time Frame	Task Owner
1.15. Compare the internal product pricing process to the elements in the "*PMTK Pricing Model*".	Verify pricing is diligently performed and that product prices properly reflect market-value.	<Concisely note the conclusions. List and prioritize the action items.>		
Product Marketing Processes				
1.16. Compare the internal product marketing process to the corresponding process in the "*PMTK Action Model*".	Verify overall product marketing process completeness.	<Concisely note the conclusions. List and prioritize the action items.>		
1.17. Compare the company's value statements and documents to the PMTK value documents.	Verify completeness and proper definition of the company's value statements and documents.	<Concisely note the conclusions. List and prioritize the action items.>		
1.18. Perform a "*PMTK Marketing Review*" [optional].	Establish foundational information for use in an entire range of strategies, tactics, and performance parameters.	<Concisely note the conclusions. List and prioritize the action items.>		

2. Commitment Stage

Building Consensus

PMTK Implementation Task	Task Objective	Developmental Actions	Time Frame	Task Owner
2.1. Locate cross-departmental links (individuals to support change).	Find individuals in the company who shall internally support and help implement new product management practices.	<List individuals and their roles.>		
2.2. Convene team and cross-departmental links to discuss current analysis and conclusions.	Determine feasible and realistic action plan in a group setting.	<Categorize and prioritize all previous "developmental actions" into an actionable and sequentially executed action plan.>		
2.3. Set monthly and quarterly objectives reflected as achievable milestones.	Build a measurable list of milestones that shall foster a positive change in product management practices.	<List the monthly and quarterly objectives.>		

PMTK Implementation Task	Task Objective	Developmental Actions	Time Frame	Task Owner
2.4. Build master schedule. Set appointments for monthly and quarterly review sessions, including a quarterly *"PMTK Performance Review"*.	Factor the milestones with the action plan into a reasonable schedule.	<Build master schedule, and have it approved by team and stakeholders.>		
2.5. Seek executive sponsor to proposed changes and schedule.	Locate an individual at the executive management level to help drive change.	<Note name of executive sponsor.>		
3. Execution Stage				
Enacting Change				
3.1. Present executive team with proposed changes and schedule.	Gain executive management agreement and commitment to the proposed changes and schedule.	<Prepare a brief ten-minute, ten-slide presentation of the proposed changes and schedule.>		
3.2. Allocate the effort to make proposed changes and schedule between the team members.	Introduce action items and measurable goals, which drive the proposed changes and schedule, into the team's work plan.	<Create individual and team MBO plans.>		
3.3. Announce and propagate the *"PMTK Implementation Plan"* and launch date.	Make all aware that an internal change in product management processes has begun.	<Issue an announcement informing of the *"PMTK Implementation Plan"* launch date.>		
3.4. Launch the *"PMTK Implementation Plan"*.	Improve product management practices at the company.	<*Comment: Continuously monitor and control plan execution.*>		

2.4. **PMTK Implementation Table Glossary**

• **Developmental Actions**: Specific actions taken so improvement is attained.
• **Time Frame**: Time period in which the developmental actions are taken.
• **Task Owner**: Individual responsible for execution of the developmental actions.

3. Conclusions and Recommendations

3.1. Section Objective
This section provides conclusions and recommendations reached after preparing the professional development plan.

3.2. Conclusions
<Identify and describe any conclusions reached after developing the PMTK implementation plan.>

3.3. Recommendations
<Describe any relevant recommendations.>

4. Supporting Data

4.1. Section Objective
The section provides data in support of claims, assertions, assumptions, and statements made throughout this document.

4.2. Assumptions
<Describe any assumptions made when writing this document.>

4.3. Research Information
<If relevant, describe and list the type and scope of research conducted in the course of writing this document.>

Addendum

Online Reference

Blackblot Content Retention Tools

People learn in different ways, often showing preference to a particular learning mode. Accordingly, the diversity in preferences prescribes a multi-modal learning approach. This approach is based on three recognized modes of knowledge transfer: instructor-led training, computerized content retention tools (CRT), and self-study.

Content retention tools promote post-training content retention and help product management professionals to further deepen their knowledge. These tools challenge individuals with a series of multiple-choice questions, which are based on chapters in this book that support a specific seminar in Blackblot's product management training program. The content retention tool experience is delivered in a test-like format using a professional test engine.

The content retention tools can also be used to achieve additional goals:

- Learning Aid – supplements regular studies through interaction.
- Self Assessment – allows uncovering areas for self improvement.
- Interview Preparation – builds confidence and serves as a refresher.

Available content retention tools are:

CRT Download	Corresponding Book Chapter	Relevant Course(s)	Questions	Registration
CRT WDYC	Who's Driving Your Company?	Strategic Product Management for Planners™ and Strategic Product Management for Marketers™	40	Freeware
CRT PMT	Product Management Team	Strategic Product Management for Planners™ and Strategic Product Management for Marketers™	88	Freeware

(continued)

CRT Download	Corresponding Book Chapter	Relevant Course(s)	Questions	Registration
CRT PDT	Product Definition Team	Strategic Product Management for Planners™	109	Freeware
CRT CMR	Crafting Market Requirements	Strategic Product Management for Planners™	122	Freeware
CRT COM	Concept of Marketing	Strategic Product Management for Marketers™	150	Freeware
CRT VMM	Value-Marketing Model	Strategic Product Management for Marketers™	126	Freeware

For more information, please visit www.blackblot.com/retention/

Blackblot Concept Presentations

Pictures act as messengers that convey information. Extensively used in the corporate world, computer-based visual presentations are among the more important tools used for internal and external knowledge transfer.

Concept presentations help facilitate the dissemination of product management knowledge and information. The presentation files are available in Microsoft PowerPoint format with properly documented slide notes sections. Available presentations are:

- Blackblot Product Management Models – conceptual overview of Blackblot's product management models.
- Blackblot Product Management Training Program – concise overview of the Blackblot product management training program.
- Blackblot BPMP Certification Program – concise overview of the "Blackblot Product Management Professional™" (BPMP) certification program.
- Blackblot Content Licensing Program – concise overview of Blackblot content licensing program.

For more information, please visit www.blackblot.com/presentations/

Additional Services

Blackblot Product Manager's Toolkit™ (Lifetime Subscription)

The "Blackblot Product Manager's Toolkit™" (PMTK) is a set of professional, comprehensive, fully-customizable product planning and product marketing templates that leverage the best practices being used today.

The PMTK Commercial Package is a collection of editable Microsoft Office document formats ("Word".DOC, "Excel".XLS, and "PowerPoint".PPT). The PMTK Commercial Package license grants registered users with lifetime free unlimited updates and upgrades. The PMTK Commercial Package is hosted online at www.blackblot.com/pmtk/ and its files are downloadable.

For more information, please visit www.blackblot.com/toolkit/

Blackblot Product Management Training Program

The Blackblot product management training program is an occupational core and advanced skills training program for high-tech product management professionals. Based on the "Blackblot Product Manager's Toolkit™" (PMTK), Blackblot's comprehensive high-tech product management training program illustrates notable best practices and processes used by top technology companies to create successful market-driven products and services. Available courses are:

- Strategic Product Management for Planners™
- Strategic Product Management for Marketers™
- Market-Value Pricing™
- Interactivity and Communication™

For more information, please visit www.blackblot.com/training/

Blackblot Product Management Professional™ (BPMP) Certification Program

The "Blackblot Product Management Professional™" (BPMP) certification program was developed exclusively by Blackblot to provide product management professionals with a way to differentiate themselves, validate skills, and gain professional acknowledgement; and enable companies to achieve better consistency in the internal application of the product management discipline. Available tests are:

- "Blackblot Product Management Professional™ in Product Management" core certification test
- "Blackblot Product Management Professional™ in Product Planning" advanced certification test
- "Blackblot Product Management Professional™ in Product Marketing" advanced certification test

For more information, please visit www.blackblot.com/certification/

Blackblot Content Licensing

Blackblot provides companies and academic institutions with all the resources needed to build a high-tech product management training business or executive education program.

As part of the licensing agreement, Blackblot partners receive a licensee kit that holds all the required professional content. This includes processes, templates, course presentations, business models, brochures and web content, training logistics, train-the-trainer services and more. Blackblot partners can customize and create their own versions of the content, according to conditions outlined in the licensing agreement.

Getting the right competencies to provide high-tech product management training and consulting is a major professional challenge. The learning curve on the topic of product management is highly demanding, complex and requires true long-term commitment.

Content licensing is available to qualified individuals, companies and academic institutions worldwide that possess proven professional competencies and relevant industry experience to credibly deliver product management training services. The content licensing agreement is based on full reciprocity and profit-sharing. There are no licensing fees whatsoever.

For more information, please visit www.blackblot.com/licensing/

Lightning Source UK Ltd.
Milton Keynes UK
22 February 2011

167944UK00001B/18/P